The New Testament: The Facts and The Fiction

The Gospels and the Book of Acts

Have You Ever Critically Looked at the New Testament? Shouldn't a Christian Know What It States?

Are You Really Living the Christian Life that God the Father Desires of You?

Real Christian Books ™

Initial Release

Copyright 2011 Brian Schaefer
ISBN 978-0-9819418-2-0 Paperback
ISBN 978-0-9819418-3-7 Hardcover

All rights reserved, including translations. This book or any parts there of cannot be reproduced without written permission from the copyright holder.

Manufactured in the United States of America
Distributed by Real Christian Books Publishing, Inc
Author: Brian V Schaefer

Preface

"The just shall live by faith." That simple profound statement found once in the Old Testament and twice in the New Testament is what set the Reformation into action. These are the words that brought about Protestantism. But ask yourself, faith in what?

If we punish our children for doing wrong, we teach them violence. Isn't that what is taught today? That liberal (progressive) philosophy has led to no discipline in the home, at school, or in public. What has happened to mankind in the western world where "kindness" and "rehabilitation" of offenders has replaced punishment for bad conduct? Our society has lost its way. In the first chapter of the Book of Romans you learn that man, if left to his own devises, will fall into moral decay, as we have. Paul calls it a reprobate mind. Which now brings us back to our original question. What do the "just" people of God have faith in?

God will deliver those that obediently live by the life He expects us to live. It is a message that is found throughout the Holy Scriptures. But, what are the Holy Scriptures? In II Timothy Chapter 3, verse 16, Paul tells Timothy that "all scripture is given by inspiration of God, and is profitable for doctrine, for reproof, for correction, for inspiration and for instruction in righteousness." So, Christians try to understand the sometimes conflicting message that they learn as they read their Bibles. But, how can it be conflicting if it is given by inspiration of God?

Can God be conflicting? God is, was, and always will be! That means that He is the same yesterday, today, and tomorrow. He is perfect. Why would He change? Then why does the New Testament and the Old Testament conflict with each other from time to time? The God of the Old Testament demanded obedience, but the God of the New Testament, in many verses, is more about love, at least where modern "warm and fuzzy" Christians are concerned. Why not let Paul explain it to you. In II Timothy Chapter 3, verse 15, just before the scripture I referenced two paragraphs back, Paul explains that the Holy Scriptures are those that Timothy learned as a child. That would make the scriptures that Paul quotes from, from time to time, the Old Testament.

When a Christian holds to the teachings of the New Testament, has he or she scrutinized the letters we call the New Testament? How much of it is real, factual, or even inspired? Of those parts that are factual or inspired, does he or she follow those teachings? Test your knowledge of the New Testament and ask yourself, "Is my Christianity really founded on God's Word?" This is a scary adventure into the truthfulness of the New Testament. The mere fact that most Christians don't question what they are taught in church explains why they are so easily shown to be fools when they try to defend the Bible. The Bible doesn't need to be defended. It stands on it's own if you understand who, when, and why it was written.

The Old Testament is solid. You can't find a teaching in one part that is denied in another area. The New Testament is another story. This is the problem with modern Christianity. It hangs on each verse in the New Testament. The New Testament constantly contradicts itself. Why? The New Testament is authored in three categories, the history books, the letters, and the Book of

Revelation. You will find almost nothing that contradicts the Old Testament in the letters and Revelation. This leaves the history books. They are the softer, gentler books of the Bible that consequently also disagree with what we know to be true of God. When I break the New Testament into fact and fiction it is a pretty easy split. The history books consisting of Matthew, Mark, Luke, John and Acts are where you will find the conflicting messages that I refer to as fiction.

Remember, the Bible was not a single book given to man by God many years back. It is 66 separate books that were put together into a single book by the Roman Catholic Church over 1500 years ago. Since that time it has been refined into what we hold in our hand today. Are you sure that this book is really the inerrant word of God? Test it! It wasn't too long ago that all science and religion held that the world was flat. Then a man came along named Galileo who stated that it was round. He was held as a heretic and a fool. Open your mind and read the words of each of these 66 books and then you decide, "was this author speaking for God, or did he presume the story he was telling." The whole world of Christianity is stating that it is from God. Is it? After all, the church called Galileo a heretic! Do you believe that the world is flat? If you went to church during the time of Galileo they would have told you it was flat! Was the church right or wrong?

So are the only correct facts to be found in the letters and Revelation? No, but they are perfectly aligned with the Old Testament. Many verses are taken out of context in many areas and we will observe these passages in another book. The gospels on the other hand are so obviously incorrect that I am surprised that anyone actually has faith in them at all. I can't say that they are "All" incorrect. You will learn that the gospel of John is a pretty much first-hand witness to the ministry of Jesus Christ and should be cherished in one's daily walk. But then, once you have scrutinized the other three gospels in relationship to John's account, you will see that they are not the "Inerrant Word of God."

They are not as Paul would attest: "given by inspiration of God." No, I believe these books and the Book of Acts are written by men that were trying to do good works with their books, but are definitely in error. Once you can decide between fact and fiction you will learn more of what God wants from your daily walk and then you can lovingly do it for Him!

Table of Contents

Why Do We Call Ourselves Christians	1
The Authenticity of the New Testament	12
The Authors of the History Books	18
The History Books	27
Up to and Including Jesus Christ's Baptism	33
After the Baptism	45
The Calling of Matthew	52
The Feeding of 5000 and Walking on Water	58
The Mountain of Transfiguration	81
The Triumphal Entry	95
Catching Up with John	113
The Stories of Luke	125
Early Events after the Triumphal Entry	141
The Betrayal and Last Supper	153
In the Garden, the Arrest, and the Trial	173
The Crucifixion and Burial	192
In the Grave, the Resurrection, the Assention, and After	201
The Book of the Acts of the Apostles	213
Are the History Books Trustworthy	233

Why Do We Call Ourselves Christians?

Before I hit home the reasons why you should identify yourself as a Christian, let's see what all Christians should believe. From a small glimpse at the New Testament, you will note that the early church was accepted as a sect of Judaism. It wasn't accepted by all traditional Jews, but at the first, the early church members were just Jews that believed that some of the Old Testament scriptures had been fulfilled. The early church believed in the Old Testament, and taught from it. There wasn't a New Testament compiled until hundreds of years later, so when they wanted to teach from scripture about Jesus, they taught out of the scrolls that were in the synagogue. What do you think that they taught?

God had sent His Christ to live among the people. He was the Messiah, He was Jesus Christ. When He was crucified on the cross, it became the payment for our sins, if we accept it. He was our Passover Lamb that now sits on the right hand of God. He is the reason for our joy.

This book should enforce this message. But, it will show why certain texts found in the New Testament are not inspired. Should that fact shake your belief that Jesus came to us from God and died for our sins? No, but it will help you to understand why some texts disagree with other texts.

If someone wrote an account of the Civil War and was factually incorrect, does it mean that the Civil War never happened? No, it just means that the author was sharing bad facts. If you wanted to learn about the Civil War, you would discount the obvious bad authors and go find a factual author on that topic. I will show the same. Some New Testament authors are factual and so I trust them. Some are not, so I discount them. You should too.

Many young Christians, and some more seasoned, mature ones, believe that they don't have to worry about anything as their salvation is secure. Nothing is worth being concerned about because they believe that they are saved because they believe that they are. They have nothing to do, but wait for the rapture, which could come any day. What is this belief based on? How naive! It isn't scriptural. Oh, it may be found by hunting for the odd verse that is taken out of context, but just the parable of the sower of seeds in the four soils teaches that it is the one that bears fruit that is saved, not the other three types of soil. And remember, all four hearers of the word accepted it with great joy.

If you are a 10 year old child and believe that you are a member of the best little league team ever, what is this fact based on? The coach may have trained you. The team may have had some great practices, but until you start playing other teams and winning, you have nothing to base it on. Yet, children still believe.

Same with Christianity. What are you comparing your values to, when you believe that you are really a Christian or in saved status? Don't you believe that God the Father is considering your lifestyle choices? Who is going to be deciding whether you are really saved? Unfortunately, just as a young person may trust his coach in little league, most Christians trust the man in the pulpit who teaches them the catch phrases that they believe will secure their after-life disposition.

Salvation is a <u>free</u> gift from God. But, is it for everyone? I love the following quote attributed to Jesus Christ: Narrow is the path to eternal life and few shall find it, but broad is the path to destruction. Both paths are found in the Bible. These paths are documented in the New and Old Testament. Are you really sure that you are on the correct one? Is your coach really telling you the truth or just pumping you up so that you will come back again?

If you don't have a real good understanding of the Bible and how it became the form that it is today, you have no clue if it is really a true document from God or a false path. After reading this book and spending a little time studying for yourself you will know what is real from God, and what is a false path made by man.

I love it when Christians tell me, " Brian, if it wasn't really entirely from God, why has He allowed it to be preserved for 2000 years? Has it? Take a better look at it. Open the front pages and read what type of Bible you have. If it isn't a Catholic Bible, then it is at best, only several hundred years old, and most are less than 100 years old. Even the Catholic Bible is probably less than 1500 years old. Remember there weren't even Catholics until several hundred years after Jesus Christ died!

The Protestant Bible threw out a lot of the Catholic Bible and the King James Version is on it's 4th revision. Why did the Protestants throw out a lot of the Catholic Bible and why is the King James version on it's 4th revision? For that matter, why are there so many new versions of the Bible? We will cover that more in the coming chapters, but the simple answer is that we have learned that much of what we thought to be true, early on, was found to be incorrect. Does this make the new versions better? Not exactly. That is why you will have to do a lot of studying for yourself. I am still learning, and actually learned a lot about the trustworthiness of the New Testament while I was writing this book. But let's get back to what makes you a Christian.

When you think of what a Christian should be, you are inferring a closeness to the life that Jesus Christ would want you to live, hence the title Christian. Most so-called Christians believe that they are followers of Jesus. If this is to be true, what is it that Christians follow that they believe make them followers of Jesus? Most would say the Bible, but more accurately it would be the New Testament.

I used to believe that everyone that called themselves a Christian at least occasionally read their Bibles. I'm not so sure anymore. After I wrote my first book I enjoyed talking about the Bible with those that disagreed with my viewpoint. Not that it was my viewpoint, it was God's. It came directly from His book. I used to be amused when so-called Christians would tell me that you can "read anything that you want" into the text of the Bible. That just isn't so. It is quite clear, if you read it from front to back.

I guess if you take a verse here, and a verse there, then you could make doctrine that supports just about anything. But that is because you are purposefully taking it out of context. No, those that really disagree with me are usually those that have never read their Bible from front to back. More importantly they haven't read it several times. They are usually Christian sheep that are led around by the minister and a doctrine that is presented to them as they sit in the pew.

If you examine the teachings in the New Testament, what did Jesus teach that He wanted His followers to believe and follow? Does the church that you attend follow those teachings? Are you sure, or is that just so-called Christians spreading a myth or fictional representations from what they want to glean from their choice verses found in the New Testament?

Most so-called Christians have pet verses that they think if they follow, will be all they need, to be a "good" Christian. Some more modern Christians believe that they don't need the Bible at all. They believe that they can get all they need to build their relationship with the Father and Jesus through prayer and the Holy Spirit. The Bible teaches otherwise. I am constantly shocked when I start talking "Bible" to a so-called Christian and they have no understanding of the scriptures. Do Christians ever read their Bibles anymore, or do they just rely on absorbing those pet verses? Just the mere fact that you call yourself a Christian begs the question: Do you really believe what is "really" taught in the New Testament? Do I live my life as it directs? Or, do I do what I want, then state that it is all the Holy Spirit has placed on my heart?

To be a true follower of God you are either "all in" or you are "all out." There is no middle ground. My son questioned me on this statement. I had to elaborate for him, and hence I will elaborate it to you. Do you understand why God gave us the family? It was to understand not only the loving relationship between an earthly father and his son or daughter, but also the respect for the parents' position. That is the relationship that our Heavenly Father desires with us. He is the Father and we are the children of the Father. Does there appear to be any equality with that relationship? No, the Father is in charge and directs us to live a certain way. Does a child have the right to demand equality from the Father? No, of course not. That is the rub for many so-called Christians. You may want to do something that the Father has directed you not to do. He considers it wrong to even continue in the desire.

When I was very young, and I didn't do something my earthly father had instructed me to do, it was called disobeying. What is the difference between then, and now, when I decide to do something that my Heavenly Father has instructed me to do, or not to do? There isn't any difference. As a parent I now understand the stress that I put my earthly father through when I was disobedient. Did he still love me? Of course he did, but he was displeased. If I knowingly kept being disobedient, then it proved that I felt my desire to do what I was doing was equal to or greater in importance to what my father wanted me to do. That places my desires for what I want to do at a level equal to, or above, my father's desires in importance.

So, what is the difference when I snub my nose to my earthly father or to my Heavenly Father? There isn't one. If I do something that I know is disobedient to God and have no remorse, then I really don't care what He thinks. It is placing what I want to do at an equal to or greater than importance to what He has told me to do. That is why you are "all in or you are all out." Either you believe that He is greater than you and you want to lovingly follow all His directions, or you feel that it really doesn't matter to follow Him. He gave us two commandments, love God and love man. To make it plainer, He broke those two commandments into the 10 Commandments.

We all know the 10 Commandments. They can be found in the Books of Exodus, Leviticus and Deuteronomy. They can also be read on the walls of the United States Supreme Court. The first four commandments, of the 10 Commandments being love God, and the last six, love to man. But knowing that man will pollute just about everything, He broke the 10 commandments into 600 plus "thou shalt(s) and thou shalt not(s)," found throughout the first five books of the Bible. We call this the Law.

When you break one of these, found in the Law and the Prophets (Old Testament), and you do not have any remorse for your action, you are stating to God, "I am equal to or greater than you." How can you justify breaking His Law in any other way? This breaking of the Law is called sinning. If you feel it is OK for you to sin, then you may want to put this book down as it will do you no good to read any farther.

Whether the New Testament is completely accurate or totally prefabricated will not matter in your salvation. You have already decided that you are greater than God. But, if you are so unlearned that you feel a Christian doesn't come under the Law, then you haven't read your New Testament. In the New Testament you will read that we are saved by Grace through Faith unto good works. But you are still not instructed to discard the Law.

On the contrary, the guy that tells you of "Grace" is the Apostle Paul. If you want to understand your relationship with the Law and Grace read the Book of Romans. Read it several times. After Paul explains Grace, he then asks the question at the end of Chapter 3. "Do we then make void the Law because of Grace?" And, then he answers it: "No, we embrace it." Why would you embrace the Law? It is because it teaches you the difference between right and wrong. We should lovingly embrace the Law in our lives and when we break it, it should weigh heavy on our hearts!

Where did the word Christian originate? If you call yourself a Christian, do you understand where it originated? Like so many other traditions used in modern Christianity, we take certain words for "gospel," as if they were always used as we use them today. The word Christian is the Greek word "Christianos," and is used a total of three times in the New Testament. That's it, only three times in the entire Bible. If you look at the Greek translation in all three of these scripture passages, it is actually calling them the "Anointed-ians." This is because "the Christ" was to be the Anointed One. So, why do followers of Jesus call themselves Christians?

The author of the Book of Luke documented two of these three scripture passages. Later in this book I will show why the author of Luke is not the most accurate of Bible authors. If they weren't referred to as Christians, what were early church members called? How were they identified? You will see the members of the early church referred to as "the way" or "this way" more often than the word "Christian." The Greek word for "way" was "hodos." Generally, it meant a road or path that took you somewhere. This was appropriate, as following God the Father through the justification we receive by accepting the payment for sin, given to us by His Son Jesus, is a Life Journey. We are following "the way" home to God.

The first problem with Christianity is it's intense focus on Jesus. Where does God the Father fit into Christianity? Jesus never taught us to worship Him, although He is worthy of worship. He tells you to not only worship God the Father, but also to pray directly to Him! Remember the Lord's Prayer? How does Jesus start it? "Our Father, which art in Heaven..."

This brings up the nonsense of a Trinity. Shouldn't your religious "Christian" beliefs at least be based on the New Testament? Where does it state anywhere in the New Testament that Jesus Christ is the same as God the Father? It isn't anywhere in the Bible, let alone the New Testament. He's not God, as in God of the Bible, He is His Son! There is God the Father, His Son Jesus Christ, and the Holy Spirit. But They are not "One" as thought of by most Christians today.

The only verse that expressly tells you that the Father, Son, and Holy Spirit are "One," as Christians speak of the Trinity today, can be found in 1 John Chapter 5, verse 7, "For there are three that bare record in heaven, the Father, the Word, and the Holy Ghost, and these three are One." Without trying to get into this subject too deep, please look for this verse in the only thorough compilation of the Bible, the Westcott and Hort. This verse is not there. The verse is not in any authentic recorded manuscript. It was added by the Roman Catholic Church in the Latin. I will discuss this passage in depth in a future book. This verse is left out of newer more thoroughly documented Bibles for good reason, it wasn't written by the author, or found in any of the earlier Greek documents.

If you would like a complete look at all the New Testament passages that look directly at the Man, Jesus Christ, you may want to look at another of my offerings, *Who is Jesus Christ?* It helps readers to understand who Jesus Christ is, was, and always will be. Is He out of time, like the Father? Let the Old and New Testament help you with a real understanding. But to quickly answer this, read the first few passages in the Book of Revelation.

In them, you will learn that Jesus is telling John that He, Jesus, has been given a revelation from God the Father, that He is now passing on to John. If Jesus Christ was the same as God, why would He have to be given the revelation by the Father? That is because it is a foretelling of events in the future. God the Father knows the future, but Jesus does not. That is because the Father works outside of time and Jesus is working within it, just like us!

All New Testament writers write of Jesus, and yet Christians just won't believe what these authors say of Him. Instead they try to make Him into something that He is not. In the above paragraph I called Jesus a man. Is He a man right now? Don't take my word for it, that is what the Apostle Paul tells you. Do you believe Paul? If you don't believe Paul, you have bigger problems than trying to understand who Jesus Christ is. Paul is the author, prophet, and apostle that gives you more doctrine than any other. Without Paul you really have no Christianity to believe in.

This book, *The New Testament, the Facts and the Fiction* is written to show so-called Christians that what we call Christianity today is not found in the New Testament. The softer gentler Christianity of today is all-inclusive, but "the way" that the New Testament writers were living was <u>exclusive</u>. The two are incompatible. Today's Christianity is not "the way" Christians should live. This book, will give you a quick swipe of the New Testament. It mainly covers the history books, which are the gospels and the Acts of the Apostles. Have you ever read each book in one sitting and asked yourself, what did each author portray?

As each book of the New Testament was a letter, have you asked yourself, could this letter be incorrect? Just because it is in the New Testament, do you think it has to be God-ordained? If it was God-ordained, could it have errors? You will see that most of the gospels and the Book of

Acts are not correct at all. This isn't to say that you have to throw the whole book out just because it is WRONG! Just understand that it was written by men, and for whatever reason, it is truly fallible. Don't believe me, just follow along in these pages and then read your Bible for yourself. It is as plain as the nose on your face.

Does this mean that there is no reason to be a Christian? No, of course not. But you shouldn't be a sheep walking to slaughter either. God the Father is waiting for you to learn of the love from Him and longing for you to learn of Him. Much of this will come when you shed those ridiculous traditions you hold that come from a lot of bad doctrine formed from faulty scripture. After you have read each chapter in this book, you should read the corresponding text found in the New Testament. Your Christianity should be based in fact. The Christian's facts should come from the New Testament, not some guy in a pulpit that is teaching a doctrine other than the one found in the New Testament!

You will see that Christianity is not for everyone. Is that what is taught in your church today? Do you believe that everyone is saved that wants to be saved? Do you want to believe that? Why not listen to the words of Jesus? "Narrow is the path to life and few shall find it, broad is the path to destruction." That is paraphrased from the several accounts that are recorded, but the intent is the same from all of the passages. Most are not saved. Will you be saved?

Don't you believe that you should live your life as the authors that wrote of Jesus Christ have directed you to live? This book will cover a quick overview of what each book is about and what truths can be found. It will also dispel many modern Christian beliefs. We are asked to live a life that is worthy of salvation. Just because someone told you that the way you are living is acceptable to God the Father, does that make it correct? We will use the New Testament to answer this question.

Case in point: Do you believe it is OK for a Christian to throw out the Old Testament Law as if it doesn't apply to Christians, as you may feel Christians are under Grace? That's how most churches teach today. Just because they teach this way, does it make it correct? If through exhaustive study it specifically explains this to be true in the New Testament, then modern Christianity would have a point. The Law wouldn't matter. The only thing that would matter is what the Holy Spirit places in your heart. But, what if it doesn't actually teach this, and in no uncertain terms it teaches that we are to embrace the Law? Would you embrace it? Would you follow it? More importantly, would you live it?

Modern Christianity, and I am talking about any church formed after 100 AD, has polluted what is written in the entire Bible whether it is the Old or New Testament. Do you want proof? Do you believe the Book of Revelation? It is a vision given to the Apostle John by Jesus. Read

Revelation Chapters 2 and 3. You will see that Jesus is declaring that these seven churches have already polluted themselves and the message that they are sharing. Many of them are churches that have been discussed in the New Testament several times, and yet, in less than one generation, they are teaching faulty doctrine. Your goal should be to live the life that you know to be true as delivered by God, not your church.

What was the difference between an ordinary Jew of that day and an early Church member? Nothing, except that the early church member believed that Jesus had come as the Messiah and the common Jew of the day felt that the Messiah hadn't yet come. How different did they live their lives? They didn't. They still went to the synagogue on Sabbath, they still followed the health laws, they were Jews. They still followed the Old Testament. The only difference was the early church member believed that Jesus had come and died as payment for their sins. They are referred to as a sect of Judaism several times throughout the New Testament. Is that the way that Christian life is taught to be followed today?

It was lived that way in the New Testament times, but not that way today. Many churches take a verse here and there and try to make a doctrine by using them totally out of context. Case in point are the food laws. Find me one actual scripture passage where you can find someone "saved" anywhere in the Bible eating Levitically unclean food. I'm not saying any unclean food, just Levitically unclean food. What is the difference? By the time that the events in the New Testament occur, the Jewish leadership were already following additional rules to make food even cleaner. They called these the traditions of the elders.

Levitically unclean foods are things like pork or shell fish. There are many others, but most Christians choose to ignore this commandment of God because we like to eat them, and glean a verse here and there to support this act. God even states that they are an abomination. Find me any mention of a "saved" person having a pork chop. You can't. It's not there. There is no actual statement anywhere in the Bible that can support God changing His mind. How could He? Then He wouldn't be the same yesterday, today, and tomorrow.

Read Malachi Chapter 3, verse 6. There are many other verses similar throughout the Bible. "For I am the Lord, I change not." How could God change? He is perfect. If He changed He would be imperfect. Unfortunately, without an understanding of the entire Bible, modern unschooled Christians somehow believe that God has become different in the New Testament. That would mean that they are worshiping a polluted idea of who God really is. God can't change.

How about breaking the Sabbath? Is breaking the Law of God in the New Testament? That is the fiction that has been brought into Christianity. We are taught that the New Testament gives us license to throw out the Old Testament. But that is just bad doctrine. It is self serving to those who claim it. Unfortunately it isn't found anywhere in the New Testament. It is a rouse to increase membership. It is just a man made belief, or as Jesus would have called it, a tradition of man. If you aren't following the teaching found in the Bible, why do you call yourself a Christian?

I challenge you to thoroughly read the New Testament many times and then ask yourself, does my church really follow God's desire in my life? You will have to say no. But, when you do reach that point in your life, what will you do with it? Let's get acquainted with the New Testament and the authors.

It is believed that there were only eight authors that wrote the New Testament. Why it is believed and not known is because it is commonly believed that the author of the Book of Luke also wrote the Book of The Acts of the Apostles, and Paul might have written the Book of Hebrews. Neither letter was signed. Although the authorship of The Acts of the Apostles is pretty certain, it is a poor case to say that Paul wrote the Book of Hebrews. Either way, there were very few authors that wrote what we call the New Testament.

Of these authors we have three groupings of letters. There are the first five books of the New Testament that are the history letters, four of which we call the gospels along with the Book of the Acts of the Apostles. These tell of what we believe we know of Jesus Christ's life and the early church. These books and their authenticity is the focus of this book.

The purposeful letters follow the history letters. Each of these letters has a self-contained message. As these letters were in manuscript form, don't you think that the author was expecting you (the reader) to read it completely in one sitting? Of course he did, just as you would expect someone to read a letter from you. He wasn't expecting you to take one sentence out of the middle of the letter (a verse) and then say, "I understand what he was saying." No, he would have expected you to read the entire letter as written and then ponder on the profound thoughts that he may or may not have told you.

Take the Book of Philemon by Paul. What is the profound message in this book? I would hazard to say that most people would not know what was in this short one-page book of the New Testament. That is because there really isn't anything to it. It is a letter from Paul to a man named Philemon, asking him to forgive a servant named Onesimus who had run off and somehow come to serve Paul. Paul brought Philemon to Jesus Christ, and so he is reminding Philemon that he is in debt to Paul for this. As such, he is asking Philemon to forgive Onesimus in exchange for the great gift Paul has already given to him.

For the average Christian, there isn't anything to base Christian doctrine on in the Book of Philemon, except maybe forgiveness. As forgiveness is taught throughout the Bible, it doesn't make this a teachable moment. It's more of a barter, than a teaching lesson in forgiveness. But, if you are a slave that ran away from your master, and if your master is a Christian, it may be a good book to reference if you are caught and brought back. Sorry, I can't help but throw in a little humor from time to time.

Face it, Paul was asking a favor from a man that had every right at that time in history to trash a servant, and Paul was asking him for mercy. This short description of the Book of Philemon is how each chapter of the history books will be covered. If there was a more important message, then it will be expanded to ensure you understand the message. This way, you can really compare your present values to the New Testament.

Other than the history letters or documents, and the purposeful written letters, we have the last book in the Bible. It is the Book of Revelation. It is the only all prophetic book in the New Testament. There are other prophetic visions that are mentioned in the New Testament, but this book is one complete prophecy. So, there you have it: five history letters, 21 purposeful letters of direction or information, and one prophetic letter.

All the history letters will be covered at the same time so that you can see the real message on the pages, although most times the pages are in disagreement. Lastly, we will sum up what the history letters have taught you about their inerrancy.

As I won't be taking the verses that I like and discounting those I don't, you will see that the Bible is not the inerrant word of God. If the Bible was inerrant, it would agree with itself always, but it doesn't. This is why when we read each book together, you will see that there are errors. The New Testament is believed by most Christians to be written by Spirit-filled men. I believe and will show that the New Testament was written by men, and able to error. Many of these errors are mistranslations, but some things that are written in the New Testament are just plain wrong. The author of the Book of Luke is the most error prone witness. This is why you will need a couple of extra resources besides your Bible.

Get a really good concordance. I use the Strong's latest revision. A concordance will help you understand the translation better. If you come to a passage like "the first day of the week" (presumably Sunday) you can look up each Greek word to see how the translators got to that translation. It is kind of like a dictionary. You can see for each Greek or Hebrew word, all the English words that have been translated from them.

I also would recommend an interlinear scripture analyzer. This is a complete compilation in the Greek and Hebrew tongue. The difference between these two resources is that the concordance is a single word reference, but the Interlinear Scripture Analyzer is a constant stream of Greek words as we believe they were written by the original Bible authors.

You can find them hardbound, but there is a very good one on the web that is "free" (www.scripture4all.org). This is an awesome resource. It will give you the original Greek and Hebrew words in their native symbols and in the English words that they symbolize (ie. Alpha and Omega). It then gives you the translated words to each of the original words (ie. Alpha =First alphabetical letter; and Omega = last alphabetical letter), followed by the translated passage. The above interlinear scripture analyzer is in the Westcott and Hort Greek compilation.

For a better understanding of the compilations, read my book called *Are You A Christian Or Are You Just Playing One?* It will explain why I read the King James, but cross it with a Westcott and Hort compilation. It's not like I am trying to sell books. It is distributed for almost the cost of production, and at the time of this book's release it is free to read and download at our publishing website: www.realchristianbooks.com.

The Authenticity of the New Testament

One day while I was in the middle of writing this book, my wife and I began to argue about the meaning of the word "star," used somewhere in the Book of Revelation. She had been reading and took it literally. I believed that it couldn't be an actual star (celestial body) as we know them today. The argument came full circle with a question that had been asked of me many times. "If you don't believe what is plainly said here, what do you believe, and where do you stop doubting?" It was a deeply profound question. This had troubled me just a few days before. I was talking with a very mature friend, that was young in Christianity. He told me that I scared him, when I starting talking about the obvious errors in the Bible.

What can you trust, if you look as critically as I do at the scriptures? The friend had actually told me that he couldn't see the love in my heart, as I was always trying to spoil what He wanted to believe to be true. It had troubled me, and I struggled with myself. Now, a couple of days later my wife was asking me the very same thing.

How could I reconcile the fact that I believed in God the Father and Jesus Christ His Son, and yet I didn't believe all that I read in the Bible. Another thought came into my head. It was from another Christian who had asked in the past: "why is it still here after all these years?" If the Bible is misleading as it is printed today, why would God allow it?

My God is huge. My God has no limits. These were profound thoughts that I had to answer. And then it came to me. What is the real history of the Bible? Paul made the statement to Timothy in II Timothy Chapter 3, verses 15-18: "And that thou from a child hast known the Holy Scriptures, which are able to make thee wise unto salvation through faith in Jesus Christ. All scripture is given by inspiration of God, and profitable for doctrine, for reproof, for correction, for instruction in righteousness: That the man of God may be perfect, thoroughly furnished unto all good works."

This one quote is used more than any other to justify the scripture that is found in the New Testament, to include the gospels. So, how then was this the answer to my problem? It in itself is a history lesson. Was Paul talking about the New Testament? No.

He is not referring to the New Testament when he is using the word "scripture." At the time of Paul's death there was no New Testament, but there were scriptures. I'm not hammering on the scriptures, I am hammering on the epistles, or the early letters. The scriptures were and are the

Old Testament. When Paul made that statement to Timothy, the Old Testament was and had been disseminated throughout the world.

Have you ever thought about the Old Testament? Where did it come from, and how do we know that it is a sure document? The writings that we call the Old Testament were considered sacred to the Jewish people. They were the instrument that led the nation. They were protected by the state. Just as we have a Constitution of the United States of America, they had their Law and the Prophets.

But it wasn't just found in one place, by the time that Paul wrote to Timothy, these scriptures had been distributed throughout the entire known world. They were found in every synagogue. They could be compared if there was an error found. It would be like looking at the World Book encyclopedia. Even though they were hand scribed, if one copy read one way and another read differently, they could be compared to another and the error corrected.

Since that time they have been well documented and shown to be flawless. When the Dead Sea scrolls were found, they were a copy of the Old Testament. It is the same Old Testament as you have in your Bible today. So, Paul has told you that this document is "given by inspiration of God, and profitable for doctrine, for reproof, for correction, for instruction in righteousness: That the man of God may be perfect, thoroughly furnished unto all good works."

But lets take it a step further. About the time I concluded writing this book I was questioned by someone that I worked with whether she could or should trust the Old Testament. I had to think just a little and then it was plain to answer. You can test the Bible and the Books in it with prophesy.

The Old Testament authors delivered a lot of prophetic events that were, at the time, in the future. Then years later, as they prophesied, it came true. Only the ability to see in the future can provide this power. Mankind does not have this power, only God the Father. If a prophet claimed to have a vision, then they and you can test the vision. Most people will agree that Moses was a prophet and he is profoundly remembered even in Egypt today.

If you go back and reference all the times Jesus Christ quoted from the scriptures you will see that He affirms Moses as a prophet and quotes from Deuteronomy more than any other book of the Bible. Moses tells you how to test whether a "prophet" is speaking for God or just a great story teller.

Deuteronomy Chapter 18, verses 21-22: "And if thou say in thine heart, How shall we know the word which the Lord hath not spoken? When a prophet speaketh in the name of the Lord, if the thing follow not, nor come to pass, that is the thing which the Lord hath not spoken, but the prophet hath spoken it presumptuously: thou shalt not be afraid of him."

So Moses makes it clear that if someone isn't 100% correct, then the story they are telling is spoken presumptuously. He doesn't say that if the story sounds similar, then it is from God. The "thing has to follow." That means that it must come to pass exactly.

So let's test it. The Old Testament was translated from Hebrew into Greek somewhere around 300 BC. This is called the Septuagint. All the prophesies that were foretold before this time and happened after this time can be validated to ensure that they were actually prophecy and not retold history. It is obvious that the Book of Daniel was written during the Babylonian Empire but tells about the Medes and Persians, the Greeks and the Romans. Does this pass the test that Moses has laid out? There are many, many prophesies and many ways to ensure that they are prophesy and not just retold history. The Old Testament is very strong. I have no doubt in it's trustworthiness. Test each book if you have doubts.

This only leaves us the New Testament to question. Is it as solid as the Old Testament? First, was the Old Testament an accepted document to the Jewish people that were governing the nation? Of course it was and they defended it. If you read Deuteronomy Chapter 18, you will see that each King of Israel was instructed to write a copy of the Law himself. How about the New Testament? Let's look at the New Testament more closely. If you reflect back on what we know of how a Christian lived in the earliest days, were Christians accepted by the rest of the Jews? Of course not. So, did their writings have clout? That would be ridiculous. The early church was persecuted from the very beginning. Just the mere fact that any letter would have survived would be a miracle.

Paul, in his writing to the church at Colosse in the Book of Colossians tells them: "And when this epistle is read among you, cause it to be read also in the church of the Laodiceans; and that ye likewise read the epistle from Laodicea." This is a real good example of how they were disseminated. It was written and then read to many other churches. It is obvious that there were other letters that have not survived. What was in the letter to Laodicea? We will never know.

You should not judge the entire Bible on the accuracy of the odd passage that may be incorrect. It was 66 separate books that the Roman Catholic Church pressed together and called the Holy Bible. Some of these books are Holy, but you will easily see that some are not. This should not hurt your faith, it should strengthen it. You should not throw out the entire Bible as "blabber" just because one, two or three books contained in it are wrong, and obviously not from God. Just because these may have been added to the Bible doesn't mean that the entire Christianity thing never happened.

Case in point: if someone had an agenda and wanted to slant history, does it mean that the history never happened. Let's say that you wanted homosexuality to be better accepted and so you wrote a book about how George Washington and his entire cabinet were gay. Just because it was written, does it make it true? If you want to refute this history, do you have to say that George Washington never existed? Look, it is simple, you discount the book. Many things in the book may be truthful, but the fact that there are false claims about George Washington forces you to not trust any "new facts" found in the book. The author had an agenda, so you discount the author and his book.

This is why you have to remember that the Bible was not written by one author, or at one time in history. It was 66 separate books that were forged together around 300 AD, some 1700 years ago, but 300 years after Jesus was on the earth. It isn't an all or nothing total book. It is an all or nothing "each separate book" contained within a book. You have to judge each separate book found between it's covers separately. Some are God ordained, but you will find that some are not. All you have to do is judge them with the righteous judgment that Moses taught you to use in Deuteronomy Chapter 18.

Have you ever noticed that very few books in the New Testament are signed or show authorship? Why do you believe that the Books of Matthew, Mark, Luke and John were written by these men? The only books that are signed in the New Testament are the books from Paul, minus the Book of Hebrews, and the Books of James, Jude, 1st and 2nd Peter and Revelation.

But were all of the letter we call the New Testament books, that were supposedly written by the apostles, even in that day, really letters from the supposed sender? What about the gnostic gospels? Paul warns in II Thessalonians Chapter 2, verse 2 "That ye be not so soon shaken in mind, or be troubled, neither by spirit, nor by word, nor by letter as from us, as that the day of Christ is at hand" He is telling them that what they thought was a letter from him about the end times was a forgery. He explains how to tell if the letter is really from him in the same letter at the close.

II Thessalonians Chapter 3, verse 17 "The salutation of Paul with mine own hand, which is the token in every epistle: so I write." It has to do with the closing of each of his letters. They are all signed! They also open in the same manner. He has a style. That is why I find it hard to believe that Paul wrote the Book of Hebrews. It is commonly felt by modern Christian theologians that he wrote Hebrews, but disguised it, as it would not be accepted by the Hebrews, if they knew it was from him. That's ridiculous, if they didn't know who it was from, then why would they give it two cents?

This is the problem with unsigned work. Why would you say that the Book of Hebrews was authored by Paul if it doesn't meet the test that Paul himself has told you to test any forgery by? Paul has a classic opening and closing. If they are not there, you may want to credit him with the work, but he has already told you not to credit it to him. So, why would you? All of Paul's work is signed in some way, except the Book of Hebrews. That is why it is placed in the New Testament at the end of Paul's work. No one is sure.

Which brings you to the gospels, Acts and 1st, 2nd, and 3rd John. Who wrote them? More importantly, who do they tell you wrote them? You don't know. There is no mention of the authorship in any of them within the words of the book. The only book with a clue is the Book of John. The clue can be found in John Chapter 21, verses 20 through 24 when the author of the Book of John appears to tell you that this book was written by the Apostle "whom Jesus Loved."

This statement "the apostle whom Jesus loved," is attributed to John, but then, the name of the apostle John, is never used in the Book of John. So, when you see the discrepancies between the two different gospel accounts, you really can't take something from the Books of Matthew, Mark and Luke and then apply it in the Book of John. We will cover in depth the authors of the gospels in the next chapter.

So the authors of the gospels, the Book of Acts, Hebrews and 1st, 2nd and 3rd John are all unsigned. Why would you believe that they are Spirit filled documents? How did they get into the Bible? Paul has already told you that he is being forged, so don't believe anything that is attributed to him if it doesn't have his classic opening and closing. And, of course, you know that the church at this time is an underground church, afraid of persecution.

When did the Church come out from under the brutal treatment of the governments that were over them? It was about 250 years later. Think about it. It was about 300 years later when the church was blended with the pagan religions of the day to form the Roman Catholic Church. Have you ever thought of the significance of that fact?

Who put the Bible together into what we call the Bible today? It was the Roman Catholic Church. What was the concept? Take a little here, from the Christians, and a little there, from the pagans, and presto, you have the Roman Catholic Church.

Do you really believe that the pagans of the day would have sat calmly by, when the Roman government built their new state church and used only Christian "stuff?" No, it was a compromise. What was the compromise that the pagans received? This is where the unsigned books come in. I do believe that the Book of John was written by an Apostle. But that leaves the other three accounts out. When we get done covering the gospels and the Book of The Acts of the Apostles, I will ask you to draw your own conclusion as to who or why they were written.

But think about the facts. This book that we have in our hand, called the Bible, was put together by a government that wanted to control their subjects through religion. They had to capture the imagination of all their people, not just the Christians. Don't you think that there was a chance, that they may have wanted to slant their Bible towards the books that helped in their endeavor?

Back to one of my central questions, "If God is so great, why would He let this document stay around for 2000 years to teach bad doctrine?" I can't exactly answer that, but I can ask a question to help you understand that the question itself is faulty. Do you really believe the Bible you hold in your hand today is a 2000 year old book?

The Bible wasn't put together for hundreds of years after Jesus died on the cross. When it was put together, the Roman Catholic Church had to weed out what they felt were false epistles. Take the Gospel of Mary or the Gospel of Judas. Do you believe that either are really a gospel that was written by either Mary or Judas? These were known to be fraudulent and were dismissed as trash even in the 3rd century by the Roman Catholic Church. Even the early Roman Catholic Church Bible is very different from the one that you read today.

First, the Catholic Bible has the Apocrypha. After the Reformation, which began in 1517, the Protestants threw it out. So about five hundred year ago, the then known Bible was whittled down by the reformers. This means that if you have a Bible that is not at least 600 years old, some the the "Word of God," was removed. Do you question the removal of the Apocrypha? Do you believe that the Bible is any less relevant without the Apocrypha?

Take the King James Bible. Do you read it today? I do. It is at my bedside. Open the book and read what revision it is. It is the 4th revision. Does this make the first three revisions wrong. Obviously something was wrong or they wouldn't have revised it! So, really, mankind has been questioning what man originally began to call the "Word of God" long ago.

Once again I am a solid Christian. I believe in God the Father and His Son Jesus Christ who died for me. But, after you have read this book, and read your Bible at the same time, you will know that some of what is found in the New Testament is not written by the Spirit of God. Should this shake your faith? No, it should relieve the frustration and fear that is felt when some scripture passages are found to conflict with other scripture passages.

The New Testament, the Facts and the Fiction

The Authors of the History Books: Matthew, Mark, Luke, John and The Acts of the Apostles

The authors of the Books of Matthew, Mark, Luke, and Acts will only be discussed in the history books, as these are the only books that they wrote. John on the other hand wrote the gospel of John, maybe John I, II, and III, as well as the Book of Revelation. This makes John the second most prolific author of the New Testament, second only to Paul.

Have you ever wondered who the authors of the Bible were? I still remember when I was very young, probably 6 or 7 years old telling my mother "when I grow up I will write a book of the Bible." I wanted to write my own "section" or what we call a Book of the Bible. My mother explained that it had all been written. How innocent, how naive I was. After all, these New Testament authors had been disciples of Jesus Christ. That is what I believed during all my early Christian life, but had they, did they, really "walk" with Jesus?

It is important to understand who these authors were and their relationship to Jesus. As all four gospels tell different stories of the same event from time to time, you have to establish who was the first-hand witness to an event. The gospels are the best source of fact that the New Testament was not written by the hand of God. Why? Because if God had written these stories through a man's hands, it would tell the same story, but it doesn't. None of the gospels profess to be a vision of what transpired in the life of Jesus Christ. They are written as a witness to what transpired and there is no revelation or vision mentioned anywhere in the pages.

Let's take a quick overview of the authors that are credited with these works. The Apostle Matthew supposedly wrote the Book of Matthew. He was one of the twelve apostles of Jesus Christ. We know that he should have been an educated man as he was a tax collector (publican). He had to at least be able to document who, and how much each patron had paid to the Roman State, and others that he may have managed. This writing ability may explain why he has such lengthy dispositions on the events that he writes about.

As an apostle he would have had first-hand knowledge of many of the events, but when did he become this very important witness? The author of the Book of Matthew explains that Matthew doesn't become a follower of Jesus Christ until Matthew Chapter 9, verse 9. The author of the Book of Matthew identifies him as "Matthew sitting in a receipt of custom." This is why we link Matthew, here in this story, to the author of the Book of Matthew. The Books of Mark and Luke identify the man in the receipt of custom as "Levi the son of Alphaeus." Even if this was the same person, where did Matthew get the information that he shares with us in the preceding chapters and verses? This is an important question for you to answer. Was it just a story that he heard, or was it revealed to him by God as so many Christians want to believe?

Matthew flees with the other disciples at the garden when Jesus is arrested, and then locks himself away with most of them until after the resurrection had already happened. Where does he get the information that he passed on about the arrest, trial, and crucifixion? Remember these time frames when you want to contemplate his credibility to an event he writes about, when it disagrees with other recordings of the same event. This is why you have to ask yourself, does God actually want you and me to believe that the Bible is the inerrant word of God?

If Matthew's gospel story is from God, then it would be 100% correct. But as my last paragraph implies, and will easily be proven in the next several chapters, the Book of Matthew will be at great odds when it is stacked up against the other gospel accounts. So either the Book of Matthew's account is from God and the others aren't, or the Book of Matthew's account isn't from God. But then, where does the Book of Matthew tell you that this gospel is given to the author by God? For that matter, where do any of the New Testament writers tell you the New Testament book that you are reading is from God?

It is pretty simple to answer that question. Read an Old Testament prophesy. Those prophets all tell you that they receive a vision. All except Moses. God tells you in Numbers Chapter 12, verses 6-8, that visions are given to a man at night, but He spoke directly with Moses. In each of these Old Testament visions the prophet gives the glory of the prophesy to God by revealing that it was given to them in vision. We see it again in a few places in the writings of Paul and then again in the beginning of the Book of Revelation.

But you don't see anyone in the gospels giving the glory of "this vision" to God as a revelation given to them by Him. Read how the Apostle John opens Revelation: "The revelation of Jesus Christ, which God gave unto Him..." Who gave the revelation? John tells you that God delivered it! Does John tell you the same thing at the beginning of the gospel of John? No! That is because none of the gospel accounts are revelations given to them by God. They are recounts of the events that they believe are important to tell the story of Jesus Christ.

Not only do the authors not tell you that they received a revelation or vision from God, they don't tell you who wrote them. I was over 10 chapters into writing this book when I realized that the Books of Matthew, Mark and Luke do not give any hint as to who wrote them. The Book of John implies in the last chapter that the author was an apostle. If you didn't have the titles that are at the beginning of each book, and who knows where the titles came from, you wouldn't have a clue who wrote them.

But do you really believe that if Matthew wrote a book about the life of Jesus Christ he would have called it "The Book of Matthew?" No, he might have called it the "Testimony of Jesus Christ by the Apostle Matthew."

The Book of Matthew is the one gospel that tries to link Jesus to much of the Old Testament so-called prophecy. He pulls a stretch to do it on most occasions. He is the one author that brings you the virgin birth, Jesus living in Egypt, and so many others, supposedly fulfilling required Old Testament prophesy. But when you scrutinize the Old Testament scripture that these are referenced from, you have to ask, "What is the author talking about?"

To be even more sly, the author of the Book of Matthew will say that Jesus said "thus and thus as foretold by Isaiah (or some other prophet)." This way it isn't the author of Matthew telling you that it was fulfillment of scripture, it is Jesus telling you that it is a fulfillment of scripture. Here is an excellent example of this. Read Matthew Chapter 13, verse 14. It goes like this: "And in them is fulfilled the prophesy of Esaias (Isaiah), which saith, By hearing ye shall hear, and shall not understand; and seeing ye shall see, and shall not perceive..." This quote is supposed to be from Isaiah Chapter 6.

But if you read Isaiah Chapter 6 you will learn that the words are indeed there, but this was a message that Isaiah was delivering to Israel in that day. And, that message was valid until they were overthrown by Assyria, which they were a few years later. It kills me why Christians don't look up the references to the Old Testament to see if they are valid.

Why would Jesus want to say that He was fulfilling scripture that had already been fulfilled. He could have said "Just as Isaiah had to fulfill this prophesy, it is valid also today." But that isn't what the author of the Book of Matthew will record. No, Matthew will state that something Jesus is doing, or saying is a fulfillment of scripture. The only problem is, most times that scripture has already been fulfilled. Instead of showing the many times that it happens here, watch for them as we proceed through the Book of Matthew and you decide if prophesy was actually fulfilled by Jesus or whether it was already fulfilled beforehand.

John Mark supposedly wrote the book of Mark or so it is said. The Book of Mark is pretty much a "Matthew light." I mean by this that Matthew will tell, let's say, 6 stories, all long accounts. The author of the Book of Mark will tell you five of them in a condensed version. And again, like the others gospels, this writing gives no apparent clue from it's text as to who actually wrote it.

Many modern theologians like to speculate who wrote the Book of Mark, but then, why not trust who the book says wrote it? Mark was a youth at the time when Jesus was preaching, or maybe not even born as you learn of his youthful age, years later when working with Paul in the Book of Acts. From this simple fact, where did Mark learn all that he wrote down about the life and ministry of Jesus Christ? It had to be from stories of others. Once again, there is no passage in this book that can lead the reader to believe that it was delivered to the author by vision or revelation from God.

Let's try to work out Mark's age at the time of the Lord's crucifixion. Mark isn't mentioned in any of the gospels. The first time you see Mark in the New Testament is in the Book of Acts, Chapter 12, verse 12. "And when he (Peter) had considered, he came to the house of Mary, the mother of John, whose surname was Mark..." This event is way after the crucifixion!

Whose house was it? Mothers didn't keep the house back then, it was given to the son when the Father passed away, unless he was not of age. The age of adulthood established by God is 20 years old. It appears that he is not 20 years old at this time in the Book of Acts. How many years have occurred since the Lord died? Let's see.

Paul was not a Christian until after Steven was stoned (Acts 7-8) which was some time after the crucifixion. He then spent three years in Arabia (Galatians 1:16-19) and returned to Damascus before going to Jerusalem. Paul's own letter to the Galatians, states that the first time he went to Jerusalem he only met with Peter and James, no other disciples. He then doesn't return there for 14 more years and this time he meets with everyone. Once in Jerusalem, he caused an uproar among the Jews and was sent to Tarsus (Acts 9:30). Finally, Barnabas seeks out Paul and brings him back to Jerusalem where they assembled for a year before they take their first journey (Acts 11:25). All this happened before Mark is 20 years old!

Let's be honest, I do believe that this time frame is a little long as I have used Acts in building this time line. I believe, and so should you if you have looked closely at the author of Luke's work, that it is usually a little unreliable. But from Paul's own letters, it was many years between Jesus' death and when Paul took Mark under his wing for their first ministry trip.

I like the Book of Mark as it does add to many of the events that are recorded in the books of Matthew and Luke, but it can't be a first-hand witness to those events. Mark wimped out on his first ministry trip with Paul and Barnabas (Acts 13:13). This is why when Paul and Barnabas are to take their next trip, they separate ways as Paul will have nothing to do with Mark (Acts 15:36-41). You learn later in the Book of Acts and in Paul's later writings that Mark becomes a solid witness as he matures.

Even if you don't like my reasoning from the scriptures as to the age of Mark, you have to agree that he was not one of the 12 disciples and hence, would not have been privy to most of what he wrote about, even if he was older. The very fact that he was not there during the gospel events explains why Mark's order of events and some contradictions to the other gospels appear. The same is true with the Book of Luke.

Luke, the supposed author of the Book of Luke is said not even to be a Jew. The Book of Luke is supposed to be a legal document that was sent in defense of Paul when he was on trial in Rome. Isn't it odd that during all Roman encounters in the Book of Luke (and the Book of Acts, also supposedly by Luke) the Romans are the good guys? As a Gentile, was he a first-hand witness to any events in Jesus' life? Remember, there is no passage anywhere in the book to attribute this writing to Luke, or any other person for that matter.

Focusing more closely on the works of Luke, it can be surmised that he wrote two books, the Book of Luke and the Book of the Acts of the Apostles. Although historical, these were purposefully written books, but not meant to edify the church at all. As mentioned earlier, they were probably written in defense of Paul when he was in Rome. This is theorized by the opening in Luke Chapter 1, verse 3 "It seemed good to me also, having had perfect understanding of all things from the very first, to write unto thee in order, most excellent Theophilus..." This is a very formal opening to a Roman, possibly a lawyer.

By the time the Book of Acts is written, the author is on a less formal note starting the Book of Acts like this: "The former treatise have I made, O Theophilus..." As you can see, both the Book of Luke and the Book of Acts were written solely for the information to get to a man called Theophilus. Acts begins at the end of the Book of Luke and concludes with Paul being at Caesar's Palace awaiting trial. This does bring the point home that they were both written for an event centered around Paul's imprisonment.

So, the Books of Luke and Acts were not written for the Christian's edification at all. They were probably written as a persuasion to help explain why Paul believed as he believed, to a man named Theophilus. You can accept this argument or you can reject it, but you will have to conclude after reading the next few chapters that the events, as told by the author of Luke, are overly dramatized. Many of the stories we know in Jesus' ministry are only told in the Book of Luke. But, after you read them and the other gospels, ask yourself: "Can I be sure that they really happened?"

I have more doubts about the accuracy of the Book of Luke than I do the Book of Acts. This is because if Luke "the physician" wrote these books, he is a close associate to Paul, at least later on. The later stories he writes down about Paul would have been hearsay or possibly even first-hand witness. In the Book of Luke, he is very much in disagreement with the other gospel writers, and that is why I find the areas that only he writes about to be in question.

I know, I know, this is the beginning of the slippery slope. If we doubt here, where do we stop? It is simple, look at it for what it may have been: a defense document written by a man that had no first-hand knowledge of the events he is writing about until later on in the ministry of Paul. He is only mentioned two times in the New Testament. Paul writes of him in Colossians Chapter 4, verse 14 and in II Timothy, Chapter 4, verse 11.

In the Book of Colossians, Luke is mentioned at the close. This is common in most of Paul's letters to give credit to those that are working with him at the time of the letter. If you read Colossians Chapter 4, you will see that Luke is not mentioned with the group known as the circumcision. This is how you know that Luke was not a Jew. Even if he was a Jew he would not have been accepted by Jews being uncircumcised. Hence, he would not have been with or around Jesus in Israel or Judah. You will also note that Paul tells you that Luke is a physician.

So, if Luke the physician did write the Book of Luke, where did he get all of those stories of Jesus Christ's life and the early church? Most of it had to be from Paul, who was also not a first-hand witness to anything that Jesus did or said. Remember, the first time you see Paul mentioned, is at the stoning of Steven and in that action he was working against the church! Does the Book of Luke ever tell the reader that this was a revelation given to him by God? No.

Go back to your Bible and read the opening to the Book of Luke. He states "Forasmuch as many have taken in hand to set forth in order a declaration of those things which are most surely believed among us..." This statement alone tells you that this is not "vision" or revelation from God. It also tells you that the order of those things that he is about to write down is solid and it is "believed among us." Where is the "eyewitness." There isn't one. This is a story that the author believes to be true and he is very sure of the order of events as he is about to write them. Unfortunately when lined up with the other gospel accounts, at least half of the accounts are out of order with the other gospels.

So, the million dollar question is this: is the Book of Luke accurate? If Luke was a Gentile, would he have the same understanding of Jewish custom, as say, one of the apostles? Let's test him. Go back and look up what type of woman a priest could marry in the Old Testament. She had to be a virgin of the Levitical line. She could have been previously married, if it was to a priest that had died and they had no children. Zacharias the priest was Elisabeth's husband.

The author of Luke explains in his first chapter that Elisabeth, the mother of John the Baptist, and Mary, the mother of Jesus, are cousins. Please read the story for yourself. If Mary was a virgin, she has to be of the tribe of Judah if Jesus is the Lion of the Tribe of Judah. Elisabeth had to be of the tribe of Levi to be the wife of a priest. There is no possible way that they could be cousins. But, as a Gentile, Luke would not have understood the significance of Elisabeth being a Levite.

I'm not saying that his accounts should be discounted at this point, but they have to be looked at closely. His books are written the way they are, because he never saw anything first-hand. These were letters to persuade a Roman, not meant to edify the Christian church. Mark and Luke are great documents to help clarify an event. If it is in one of their gospels, it proves that they at least trusted the source that told them the story of the event before they wrote it down themselves. Just remember, if they were the authors, they were not there.

This is why hearsay is usually not permitted in a court of law. Although hearsay may be based in truth, it is partial to errors. Modern Christian leaders try to explain the differences in the gospels by saying that they are written to different audiences. That is just nonsense. If you look at the Books of Matthew, Mark and Luke closely you will see many stories were told several times and they begin to blend together, or change, and definitely fall out of sequence with each other. Parts of one story are blended with parts of another from a different author.

So, as men, the authors of the Books of Matthew, Mark and Luke wrote of many events that they had no first-hand knowledge of. This brings up the Christian belief that the Holy Spirit placed it on their hearts and then they wrote it down. Could this be how they learned and then wrote of the events? If so, then each author would have written the same event but might have missed out on some of the supporting facts. In other words, each story would have been supporting of the other.

Take, for example, a football game. After the game, four spectators may give a slightly different recollection of how the game went, but they would still conclude with a similar conclusion. This isn't like politics where each writer is looking out for their own candidate. They are all voting for the same guy to win, but you will see that they all tell a different story. Many times these stories are totally contradictory. If the Holy Spirit was in-charge, does this make sense? Not at all. So, if the stories are as dissimilar as I am suggesting, you must rule out the Holy Spirit as the author.

I know, I know, you think that they are all very similar and that they tell the same story. Have you ever tried to line up the gospels? It is impossible, but I will show you the closest possible alignment in the next few chapters. That is why you have to discern between fact and fiction.

Before we go any further, go back and open your Bible to the Gospels and find for me one reference in Matthew, Mark or Luke that hints to who wrote them. You can't! How about when they were written? You can't. It's not in the text. So even though I have just given you a brief history on these biblical figures, I am not telling you that Matthew, Mark or Luke wrote any of these books, because it is not possible to even hint that they did from the text. That is why I refer to the author of these books as the authors of Matthew, Mark, and Luke.

If the Apostle John was the author of the Book of John, this would be the only pretty-much first-hand account of all of the gospels. As you know, John was with Jesus shortly after He was recognized by John the Baptist. John doesn't write of things that he has not seen. This is why he doesn't write of Jesus Christ's early life. John also chronicles events in relationship to known celebrations to help place them accurately on a time-line.

We know that the Book of John was written by either the Apostle John or his brother James. This is in the text found in John Chapter 21, verse 20 and verse 24. Peter is talking about the author of the Book of John leaning on the breast of Jesus at the Last Supper. The author tells you that it is he who is writing this gospel. Peter sat across from Jesus, leaving James and John to sit next to Him. The author had to be either James or John, both who are there for all the major events and inseparable to Jesus during His ministry.

From what we know about the life of Jesus, John was with the Lord during 99% of his gospel account. The author of Matthew, if he was the Apostle Matthew, joined up with Jesus in Matthew Chapter 9, verse 9. but flees before the end of his account. I would give him 40% of his gospel account, if the author was indeed the Apostle Matthew. Mark was there for 0% of his gospel account and Luke happened to be a Gentile, so he wasn't even aware of Jesus until at least 20 years after His death!

With that said, don't you believe that if the Apostle Matthew wrote the Book of Matthew, it would line up with the events found in the Book of John at least 40% of the time? We will see how this works out as we read through the gospel accounts.

Since the gospels and the Book of Acts all tell different accounts of Jesus' life and life in the early church, who's account do you think will hold more water? Remember, the Bible may have been written by Spirit-filled men, but it isn't all prophecy. Prophesy is given by God. For it to be prophecy it has to be 100% correct. And since these authors were not there, it is either prophecy or just stories that they heard and wrote down. Some correct, some less correct, and some just plain wrong!

If you go back and reference all the times Jesus Christ quoted from the scriptures you will see that He affirms Moses as a prophet and quotes from Deuteronomy more than any other book of the Bible. Moses tells you how to test whether a "prophet" is speaking for God or just a great story teller. Deuteronomy Chapter 18, verses 21-22: "And if thou say in thine heart, How shall we know the word which the Lord hath not spoken? When a prophet speaketh in the name of the

Lord, if the thing follow not, nor come to pass, that is the thing which the Lord hath not spoken, but the prophet hath spoken it presumptuously: thou shalt not be afraid of him."

So Moses makes it clear that if someone isn't 100% correct, then the story they are telling is spoken presumptuously. He doesn't say that if the story sounds similar, then it is from God. The "thing has to follow." That means that it must come to pass exactly.

Once again remember that none of the gospel writers wrote that the gospel they are about to tell is a revelation from God. If you can step back from the bad doctrine that is festering in the Christian church, you could plainly see that the gospels and the Book of Acts are just man's best effort to write what they believe to be true, or as you will learn, what they want you to believe is true. But since none of them line up, Moses has told you that at least some of it is definitely not from God!

The History Books

When I was a young Christian I thought that I had a handle on the Bible. I had been in regular church attendance. I listened intently and read the passages that would be discussed in the next weeks lessons. Back then, I believed that the Bible was an integrated message system (coined from another author) that was self-supporting.

As I matured I began to read the Bible for myself. I started at Genesis and concluded in Revelation. The first time through, I might have still believed that it carried a single message. But, for sure by the second time through, I had doubts. The gospels really bothered me. I had noted that the assention was very different in all four gospels.

I also noted many areas that were obviously taken out of context by most Christian denominations. After much discussion with Christian friends that I had at church, I began to wonder why, if I saw these areas where a Christian was not living as God the Father had directed, why didn't any other Christian? As I would discuss these problem areas found in the Bible, I noted that no one really wanted to know. One friend that I held in high regard actually told me that he didn't know if he loved God the Father or His Son Jesus enough to change. That was eye opening to me.

After some time I began writing about various topics and placing them on the internet, but as no one really wanted to know about these topics, who would ask to research them on an internet search engine? With time I published my first book about these topics. As I would debate these topics with Christians, I noted that many would use many out-of-context passages found in the New Testament to justify bad doctrine.

If you had read my first book, one of the chapters showed that the Bible wasn't the inerrant word of God. There are errors all through it. I had shown that the gospels had many contradictions. If you have a contradiction between two passages, then one of the passages is in error. Hence, it is not the inerrant word of God. When I started this present book I really wanted to open the eyes of anyone that was professing to be a Christian to the fiction that had been brought into the Christian religion, by the way that churches through the years had manipulated the scriptures.

I originally had two objectives. First, I was going to show the errors that are found, and the second objective was to make apparent the way that passages are taken out of context. There is no better way to learn, than to try to teach a subject.

When I began to write this book, I was going to include the entire New Testament. I started writing about the gospels. It was a very thorough study. If you try to line up each of the gospels with the others, you will see that they really don't line up at all. This was a chronological study, focusing on all areas recorded in the gospel events. With the original knowledge I was armed with from writing about it in the past, I was ready to start. I was sure, without a doubt, that anyone reading it would know for certain that all the gospels couldn't be inspired.

This was imperative as most Christians think that they are. If they are inspired, then why wouldn't I want to use them to guide my life. I would! But, if they are not inspired, then they are not a comprehensive message system sent by God to guide my life. Why wouldn't I want to delve deeply into each of them to see if they are inspired? The easiest way to do this is to line them up with each other and see if they really tell the same story.

I was not ready for what I found. There isn't one gospel story that is missing a little here-and-there that can be made up by looking at another gospel. There are two almost totally different gospel stories. One is told in the Book of John. The other is told by the other three gospels. They are two totally different stories. How different you may ask? Well, let's see what I had to go through, and you will too, if you want to really compare them.

Trying to line up each chapter of the gospels and the Book of Acts together is quite a chore. They chronicle differently. That fact alone tells you that something is wrong when we want to say that they are given by the Holy Spirit. Your chore will be to read the chapters in your Bible as I proceed through these next chapters and verify the message. Unfortunately there will be a lot of disagreement between the authors. Just remember who was there at the time that the event happened. More importantly, when none of the gospel authors are recorded to be there, note the major discrepancies between the stories.

What are you looking for when you are reading your Bible anyway? It should be to understand what God the Father wants in your life. When two or more passages are not in agreement, you need to ask why? The gospels are the best example that a Christian should use to understand that the New Testament, although may have been penned by God fearing authors, was not written by God.

Remember we are looking at fact or fiction, inspired or presumed, it can't be both. When you look carefully at the order that each author provides in the ministry of Jesus, you may want to say, "well, the order really doesn't matter that much." But then when you look closely at the event and note that they are different, you may also want to say, "well the message is similar enough." Does it really matter if the chronicle of events is different, or that the authors' stories are different in the details of each event?

I could agree that they are stories given to each author by God if the four authors tell four stories that are very similar but each leave out a little here and there, but that isn't what happens. Look carefully, and you will see that the first three authors of the Books of Matthew, Mark, and Luke tell a story with similar events, although still different and totally out of order from each other.

But then there is John. John was there, and he tells a totally different story than the others. Sometimes John will tell about the same event happening as the other authors, but that is on rare occasions. How rare you may ask? From the time that Jesus is baptized, until the feeding of 5000, there is no event in common between John's gospel and the other three gospels. That is about 1/4th of the Book of Mark and 1/5th of the Book of Matthew. This isn't to say that the rest of the gospel story lines up, because it doesn't. But that is a large chunk that has nothing in common.

But wait, it gets worse. John never tells you that Jesus is baptized. Read his account slowly. There is no mention of Jesus being baptized in the Book of John, only that John the Baptist recognizes Him as having a dove descend upon Him. Most Christians say that John left that part out. Did he? After reading the comparison between the gospels, come back and ask yourself: "Was Jesus baptized?" What sins did Jesus need to have washed away? Wasn't He sinless?

But let's look at the things that Christians feel are held as "truth" that you will see are not collaborated by the Book of John. If you didn't have the other gospels, can you tell me what the name of Jesus' mother was from the Book of John? No. Was Jesus' mother a virgin when she conceived Jesus? No. Can you tell me that John the Baptist baptized Jesus? No. Was there a voice from Heaven proclaiming that Jesus was the Son of God at the Baptism? No. Did Jesus immediately go into the wilderness for 40 days to be tempted by Satan? No. Did Jesus meet Peter, James and John at the Sea of Galilee and tell them to drop everything and follow Him and He would make them fishers of men? No.

The list goes on and on. Like I said, until I tried to write this book I wasn't aware of the major differences between these books. Now, to be fair, the Book of John doesn't tell you that Mary wasn't a virgin, or that John the Baptist didn't baptize Him either, but the fact remains that the Book of John doesn't tell you most of what the other gospels tell you about the life and ministry of Jesus. What is even more bizarre, is what you find in the Book of John, isn't in any of the other gospel accounts.

From the feeding of 5000 until the triumphal entry, how many events line up between John's account and the rest of the gospel authors? You guessed it, that would be zero. You do have the walking on water right after the feeding of 5000, but that isn't recorded in the Book of Luke. I knew that there were problems before I undertook this book, but I really didn't know it was as bad as it would turn out to be.

What this one little tidbit tells you is that from the recognition of John the Baptist until the triumphal entry into Jerusalem, just before His crucifixion, there is only one event where all of the other gospel authors agree with John. Remember, John was there during Jesus' entire ministry. His account is pretty much in total disagreement with the other authors.

Think of that statistic. This is a major part of what we believe to be true about Jesus. When you look closely at each gospel, many to most events happened in a different order and when the order is similar, they tell you that the event happened differently. Isn't it time to use a little discernment to help understand what is happening. Much is just a retold non-inspired story.

You have been told by modern Christianity that the New Testament carries just as much clout as the Old Testament, maybe even more, but when you take a close look at the books and their authors you have to ask yourself, how could God have written this? This isn't to say that none of the New Testament is inspired. The Book of Revelation is one big non-ending inspired story. But we are talking about the gospels.

None of the gospel authors tell you that their story is inspired! One more thought about John's account verses the other three gospels. Was John conveying that Jesus was the Son of God? Of course he was. And, at the close of his books he makes a note that it would take volumes to write all that Jesus had done on earth, but....If you were writing a book to show that you had walked with the Son of God, don't you think that you would write those things that proved that you did? Of course you would.

But John doesn't write about the most supernatural, incredible occurrences that the other three authors write about that supposedly happened during Jesus' life, especially while he, John, is with Jesus. He doesn't write of the virgin birth (not an Old Testament requirement for the Messiah). He doesn't write of hearing God the Father speak to Jesus from heaven, you know "this is My Son..." although he is there in the other three gospel accounts. He does record a voice from heaven, but the other three gospels do not write of it. He doesn't write of the Mountain of Transfiguration, or the raising of Jairus' daughter of which he is one of three disciples supposedly there for both events.

No, John doesn't really write about any of the greatest events that are credited to Jesus' ministry and miracles. This isn't to say that John doesn't write of powers that Jesus had while on earth. He does tell of Jesus doing things that are supernatural, just not as many and as great as the others.

The History Books

In fact, John only shows Jesus bringing one man back to life. That was Lazarus. It was at the close of Jesus' ministry. Read John's account. Mary and Martha are in mourning and filled with grief because Jesus hadn't come early enough to save their brother. Think a little here. If Jesus had brought back others like Jairus' daughter or the man at Nain, would this be so impossible? Mary would have just said, "Jesus, please bring my brother back to life."

But they were grieved because this was not an option as far as John's account goes. This is why John makes such a big deal about it. It was a big deal! Later in John's gospel the Jews decide to kill Jesus and also Lazarus, because the raising of Lazarus brought many to follow Jesus. You don't see the Jews deciding to kill Jesus, Lazarus, Jairus' daughter and the man from Nain.

Why I make a big deal about the raising of Lazarus is because John doesn't make mention of the raising of Jairus' daughter, found in Matthew, Mark, and Luke. The author of Luke attests that Jesus also raised a man at the city of Nain. This also isn't found in John. But in the three gospels, it is Jesus, Peter, James and John that are there for the raising of Jairus' daughter and the man from Nain. Why would someone who wasn't there record this supernatural event and the guy that witnessed it wouldn't?

What makes this even more bizarre, is that none of the other three gospels tell of the raising of Lazarus. It's almost like there are two different stories of Jesus' ministry. There is John's account and then there is this other account that has been verbally told and several guys write it down. Since they only heard it, when they write it down it is similar, but different. Sometimes the accounts are the same, but many times they aren't. And, as it is a long story that they only heard, they place events in a different order.

No, the three gospels, Matthew, Mark, and Luke tell one story and the Book of John tells a totally different story. This isn't to say that you should totally discard the first three gospels, but remember what Moses tells you in Deuteronomy Chapter 18, verses 21-22. Moses states that if the story teller isn't 100% correct, then he has presumed what happened, and it is not a message from God. Events out of order and disagreements of the event constitutes error.

So, when there is a disagreement between Bible authors, one author could be right, but that makes the others wrong. Let it sink in. If there is any error, then the message is not from God or it has been polluted from the message that God had sent.

Remember, just because the four gospels tell a different story, shouldn't make your "salvation" questionable. It is this kind of knowledge that should free you from bad doctrine. Take the gospels for what they are. They are four stories of Jesus Christ's life. John wrote a pretty much first-hand account of what happened. The other three wrote about things that they had either heard, or, as Moses told you, presumed what happened.

To show without question that there are two different stories, we will try to line up the gospels. Note how Matthew, Mark, and Luke will track, but how John is pretty much his own story. Remember what you are trying to do, learn of God. If there is a problem with the gospels, why make excuses? Just use a little discernment to allow the true facts to rise to the top, and then skim them off and keep them. Let the fiction settle to the bottom.

I've used the term discernment several times. What is it? Let's add a few more words to the pool. All knowledge, wisdom and discernment comes from God. Knowledge is just plain facts. The Bible is filled with facts which are found in each verse. Some facts are good facts, and some facts are incorrect.

Wisdom is the ability to apply knowledge. But if you apply knowledge that is from bad facts, then you will have bad outcomes. Discernment is the ability to discriminate between good facts and bad facts. With discernment, your wisdom will produce correct decisions.

Up to and Including Jesus Christ's Baptism.

The entire reason for a Christian to read his or her Bible should be to learn. But what are you trying to learn? The birth of Jesus is recorded in the Books of Matthew and Luke. There is no other reference found in the New Testament, but there are several prophecies that are attributed to His birth found in the Old Testament. If you look closely at each of these prophecies, you will see that they are too vague, or they are obviously taken out of context.

This applying of the Old Testament to Jesus is not only found here at the birth, but many times throughout the gospels. Do we need these Old Testament prophecies to apply, to really believe that Jesus is the Son of God? I don't believe so. There is plenty of real proof, but these "proof texts" are added by the authors of Matthew, Mark and Luke to give credibility to their version of the life of Jesus Christ. Let's look at my favorite example of wrongly applied prophecy.

When Matthew asserts that Judas made a deal with the Chief Priests to betray the Lord, it was for 30 pieces of silver. When he gives it back, the Jewish leadership buys a potter's field with the money. He tells you in Matthew Chapter 27, verse 9 that this was to fulfill the prophecy of Jeremy (Jeremiah). The only thing remotely close to this, found in Jeremiah, is located in Chapter 32, verse 9. Sounds good and most Christians would just hold that for "gospel." But when you read the prophesy in Jeremiah, it was for "Jeremiah to buy his nephew's field for 17 shekels of silver."

This is where you have to dig deep and ask yourself, do I really want to know? Would I be better off just sitting in church and keeping my head in the sand like an ostrich, or, do I really want to know what parts of the Bible are trustworthy, and what parts are not?

Here is the strange twist. There is a place where it shows a prophecy where someone is betrayed for 30 pieces of silver. It is found in Zechariah Chapter 11, verse 12. But, that is the rub. If the Book of Matthew is written by the Holy Spirit, through a man's hand, why wouldn't the Holy Spirit tell us the right prophet? You have to say that either the Holy Spirit got it right, but the book has become polluted through the years, or the author of the Book of Matthew got it wrong. Either way, when we agree that one of these two events happened, it brings into question what is trustworthy and what is not.

I will note every time that the author of Matthew tells you something in his story is prophetic proof of Jesus Christ. Then we will reference it. You will have to decide for yourself if the author of Matthew is pointing out real prophetic references to Jesus from the Old Testament.

Remember, I believe that Jesus is the reason for my joy, I just want you to judge for yourself when you read each of these passages if the reference is valid.

Which brings us back to the birth and early years of Jesus Christ. Remember, only the authors of Matthew and Luke will write about it. Look at their renditions closely. Look up their references to Jesus from the Old Testament. Do they really apply? More importantly, where do each say Jesus' family is living at each moment in time. Who sends the wise men to Bethlehem? Read these texts carefully. Why? Because they will not line up!

You may want to rely on Christian apologetics here in the beginning, but after you have read through several chapters in the gospels, you will have to conclude that the gospels won't line up, no matter how hard you try to make them. Then you will look back on this chapter and see it a little more clearly.

Matthew Chapters 1-3 takes you through a known lineage of Jesus and explains how the virgin Mary was to have a child and how the angel explained it to Joseph, the Father. Matthew Chapter 2 tells the story of Jesus' birth in Bethlehem, and the story of the three wise men. In this chapter we find the story of Jesus going to Egypt after the wise men had left. Verse 16 explains that the wise men had been traveling to see Jesus for two years, so Herod kills all children that are under two years of age in the area around Bethlehem.

By the end of the chapter, Joseph is bringing his family back to Israel, but "turned aside into the parts of Galilee." It is clear that according to Matthew, this is the first time that they have lived in Galilee. Chapter 3 is set at least 20 years later when John the Baptist is preaching in the wilderness and ends with Jesus Christ being baptized of John and the Voice from Heaven saying, "This is My Son in whom I am well pleased."

Mark Chapter 1, verses 1-11, starts many years later with John the Baptist in the wilderness preaching to prepare the way for the Lord. In verses 9-11, Jesus is baptized by John and a voice comes from heaven that states: "Thou art My beloved Son, in whom I am well pleased."

Luke Chapter 1-3, starts as a greeting to a Roman and begins his story with the birth of John the Baptist. Late in Chapter 1, Mary, the mother of Jesus, who resides in Galilee becomes pregnant and stays with her cousin who is also John the Baptist's mother. Chapter 2 begins with Joseph and Mary leaving their home in Nazareth and heading for Bethlehem where Jesus is born.

This is where we see the shepherds that came to worship. From here the little family goes to Jerusalem after Mary's purification (41 days later). While there, they meet two people that prophecy about Him. This chapter also explains that Joseph took the family to Jerusalem <u>each</u>

year for passover. Once during this celebration when Jesus was 12 years old, He stayed behind to debate with the doctors in the Temple.

Chapter 3 starts with the preaching and baptizing of John the Baptist, to include Jesus Christ's Baptism and a voice from Heaven proclaiming "Thou art My beloved Son, in thee I am well pleased." The chapter concluded with a different lineage of Jesus Christ than the one found in the Book of Matthew.

John Chapter 1, verse 1-33 begins with John telling the story of Jesus as the creator of all things and being with God before time. It then moves through the testimony of John the Baptist and concludes with John declaring that the Spirit descended from Heaven in the form of a dove, and it abode on Jesus. This was the sign John the Baptist was told to look for, according to John's gospel.

To sum up the events concluding with Jesus Christ's baptism we know for certain that Jesus had a mother. Sounds like a silly fact, but only three of the gospels tell you her name is Mary. The Books of Matthew, Mark and Luke tell you that Jesus was baptized by John the Baptist. The Book of John never states that Jesus' mother's name is Mary and never states that Jesus was baptized. Read it carefully.

Before we dissect the verses that you have just read, lets look at the Christmas story, modern Christians talk about today. Jesus' family is forced to go to Bethlehem, by the Roman government, where Jesus is born in a manger, on December 25th. What is the weather like in December at Bethlehem? It is the dead of winter. I lived on the Island of Crete for two years. They have the same weather. Would shepherds be out with their sheep in the fields grazing? No, you don't graze in the winter. In the two accounts of the birth of Jesus found in Matthew and Luke, they don't affirm that it was winter, or December for that matter.

The December 25th date was ordained many years later by the Roman Catholic Church. Why might they give us this date? It happens to be pretty close, if not exactly, to the day of the winter solstice. The Roman Catholic Church was a blending of the Christian and pagan beliefs of the day. Pagans still hold the winter solstice as a "special" day.

It isn't exactly that date, but if you take the time to look it up, you will see that the "date" of our calendar was changed a couple of days when they learned that the world took 365 1/3rd days to travel around the sun instead of 365 days. They had to make up for the lost time and moved the calendar date a little. This isn't to say that Christmas is a bad thing, but we should not loose sight of the fact that the 25th of December has nothing to do scripturally with the birth of Jesus. Now back to the scriptures.

Only Matthew tells the story of the wise men and the journey to and from Egypt. Only Luke tells the miraculous birth of John the Baptist. John the Baptist's father was of the tribe of Levi as he was a priest. A priest could only be a priest if he married a woman that was also of the tribe of Levi. The author of Luke tells you that Mary, the mother of Jesus, and Elisabeth, the mother of John the Baptist are cousins. Is Jesus the Lion of the Tribe of Judah? For Jesus to be of the tribe of Judah, if Mary is a virgin, then she has to be from the line of Judah. So, if Mary is of the line of Judah, and Elisabeth is of the Levites (required to be a priest's wife), it makes it difficult, if not impossible, for them to be cousins.

Luke also declares that Mary and Joseph are from Nazareth before Jesus' birth and lived there continually, to include going to Jerusalem each year for Passover. According to Luke, Bethlehem is a destination spot just before the birth, and then they return home to Nazareth. There is no mention of wise men and a trip to Egypt in the author of Luke's account.

The author of Matthew makes no mention that Jesus' parents made a journey to Bethlehem, and it sounds clear that they are living there when the wise men come to visit. He explains that they fled to Egypt for some time in fear of Herod. When they returned to Israel they "turned aside into Galilee" to avoid Archelaus on their return home from Egypt. It is clear that this "new" location is one of necessity.

The author of Matthew starts Jesus' life in Bethlehem. There is no mention of any other beginning point for Mary and Joseph. Herod sends the wise men to Bethlehem to worship the child. The wise men find Jesus in a house. The angel visits Joseph and warns him to go to Egypt to protect Jesus from Herod. Herod lives in Jerusalem. When Herod dies, the family returns, but hides out in Galilee to avoid Herod's son.

The author of Luke explains that Mary and Joseph live in Nazareth. Before the birth, they have to travel to Bethlehem, where Jesus is born in a stable. Approximately 41 days later they are back in Jerusalem and then head back to Nazareth. They attend Passover each year at Jerusalem. Which of these two accounts sounds more dramatic? The author of the Book of Matthew tells you that they have always lived in Bethlehem and are in a house. The author of Luke tells you that they lived in Nazareth, traveled to Bethlehem, where Jesus is born in a manger and then return to Nazareth. You will see this dramatic style throughout the Book of Luke.

So the two guys that give you the virgin birth and the details about Jesus' earliest life can't agree on the basic facts. The author of Luke affirms that Mary and Joseph were originally from Nazareth before the angel gives the "good news." The author of Matthew tells you that they were

Up to and Including Jesus Christ's Baptism.

not from Nazareth, and in fact went to Egypt for a while in fear, but when they return to Israel, they hide out in Nazareth to avoid Archelaus. Why would you hide out in your home of origin?

How could Jesus' parents have always lived in Nazareth according to the author of Luke, while fleeing to Egypt according to the author of Matthew, and yet visit Jerusalem each year for Passover as affirmed by the author of Luke, and still hide out in Nazareth when they come back from Egypt according to the author of Matthew? Either they always lived in Nazareth as affirmed by the author of Luke, or they lived in Bethlehem, fled to Egypt and finally hid out in Nazareth some time later as told by the author of Matthew. One or both of these renditions is in error. One is wrong, or better put, fiction.

Next, take the immaculate conception. It is also only told by the authors of Matthew and Luke. No other place in the Bible is it mentioned. None of the real players in the New Testament make note of it. Why do I say real players? Remember, Luke was a Gentile and not around for any of this and if the Book of Matthew is authored by the Apostle Matthew, he comes in much later in the game. The most prominent figures in the New Testament are Peter, James, John and Paul. How do all other New Testament books except Matthew and Luke reference Jesus? He is a man, yet still the Son of God. This is a Spiritual thing. The author of Matthew does try to pull out an Old Testament scripture from Isaiah with the Emmanuel reference. Matthew Chapter 1, verse 22: "Now all this was done, that it might be fulfilled which was spoken of the Lord by the prophet, saying, Behold a virgin shall bring forth a son, and they shall call his name Emmanuel..."

This may be hard to take, but the author of Matthew has just given you a 99% truth. That exact verse is in Isaiah, but not the prophesy that the author of Matthew has affirmed. He has told you that the virgin birth was "spoken of the Lord (Jesus)," And the child will be **NAMED** Emmanuel. The child in the prophesy of Isaiah is a prophetic "sign" from God. Let's see what this prophetic sign was to be a sign of. Read Isaiah Chapters 7-9.

Since most readers will not read this prophesy for themselves, I will give you the exact verse, but add the two following verses that prove when this "Emmanuel" would be on the world's scene. Isaiah Chapter 7, verses 14 through 16: "Therefore the Lord Himself shall give you a sign; Behold, a virgin shall conceive, and bear a son, and shall call his name Immanuel. Butter and honey shall he eat, that he may know to refuse the evil, and choose the good. For before the child shall know to refuse the evil, and choose the good, the land that thou abhorrest shall be forsaken of both her kings."

Who are the kings and the land that "thou abhorrest?" If you read from the beginning of Isaiah Chapter 7 you learn that Judah is under attack from Israel and Syria. Both of the kings are named.

Immanuel, the son of a virgin, was a sign to show that Israel (not Judah) was to be overthrown by the Assyrians. Later in the Book of Isaiah, they are. You really have to read Isaiah to better understand the prophesy. In the same chapters of Isaiah, he visits a prophetess who has a son. "And before the child could cry father or mother, the riches of Samaria shall be taken away." Was this the child of the virgin? Either way, the sign was to <u>show</u> that Israel was to fall, and they do. It has no reference to a coming Saviour, Messiah or the Christ. The virgin having a son was a sign from God. It was a proof positive sign that only God could do. This sign, when it happened was a foretelling that God was going to bring to an end the Nation of Israel by Assyria, and then He does!

A "sign" is proof that an event foretold by God <u>will</u> happen. If the event already happened, what good is a sign coming later? So the sign Isaiah was talking about had happened, the virgin had a son, and then the Assyrians overthrow Israel. So where in the Bible does it say that the Messiah was to be born of a virgin? The only sign where a child is born of a virgin was to show that Israel was to fall to Assyria, and they did, hundreds of years before Jesus is born. We Christians make such a big deal about the virgin birth, and yet it is not a requirement, nor a prophecy. We only make a big deal about it because the Books of Matthew and Luke tell you it happened, but the prophetic link isn't there.

One more important thought about Immanuel. The angel that delivered the prophecy told Isaiah that the child would be <u>named</u> Immanuel. It wasn't to be a title of the child, or a nickname, but that the child will be "<u>named</u>" Immanuel. Go back and read the event. When the angel supposedly told Joseph and Mary what to name the child, our Lord, it was Jesus, not Immanuel. So once again, it isn't fulfilling anything prophetic!

Why Bethlehem? Why the two stories about Jesus being born in Bethlehem in the Books of Matthew and Luke? First, for either of these authors to write their stories they would <u>have</u> to be prophetic. In the Book of Matthew he is telling you what Herod was talking about in his court. In the Book of Luke you spend some time with shepherds in the hills. So, were they prophetic? To be prophetic it has to be 100% accurate. Let's test them!

The birth in Bethlehem is being referenced from Micah Chapter 5, where a deliverer is to free them from the oppression of the Assyrians. Remember, when Micah wrote this, they were being oppressed by Assyria. Micah takes you back in time and then forward in time to include the last days. Then he talks about "that prophet" that is to be from Bethlehem Judea, that will free them from the oppression.

Up to and Including Jesus Christ's Baptism.

This is the "messiah" that the Jewish people in Jesus' day were looking for. Only, it isn't the Assyrians that are oppressing them as referenced in Micah, it is the Romans. Either way, the Jews believe that it is "this guy" from Bethlehem that will deliver them. You really have to read the entire Book of Micah to understand what his prophesy is fulfilling. So the authors of Matthew and Luke think that this is the end times, and want to prove that Jesus is "that prophet." But, as they were not there, is this story of the birth of Jesus in Bethlehem fulfilling the prophesy?

Read all of Micah. It will take about 15 minutes. You will see that Israel is besieged and they have called the troops out when this individual from Bethlehem appears, and he becomes their savior. Is this how Jesus appeared on the scene? If you want to believe that this is prophetic, then you have to finish the prophesy. It has to be 100% correct!

Where else do we see a reference to "that Prophet" coming from Bethlehem? Why not read John Chapter 7? In it, you will see that many want to think Jesus is "that prophet" but then question. Isn't "that prophet" supposed to come from Bethlehem? After all, Jesus is from Galilee. John doesn't give you the caveat that Jesus was born in Bethlehem and no one knows. No, John makes it clear, if they want to say that Jesus is "that prophet" he would have to come from Bethlehem, but doesn't. Take it for what it is. John is agreeing that Jesus isn't the guy that Micah was referring to, that must come from Bethlehem!

Even later on in the other gospels, they will tell you that when they come back to Jesus' home, it is always in Galilee.

The author of Matthew asserts that Jesus had to live in Egypt, when he again tells you that Jesus is fulfilling scripture, in Matthew Chapter 2, verse 15. By fleeing to Egypt and then coming to Israel, the author of Matthew is asserting that Jesus is fulfilling Hosea Chapter 11, verse 1, "Out of Egypt have I called my Son." But when you read Hosea you will note that it is a lament from God, how when Israel was young, He, God, brought them out of Egypt. There is no way that the verse in Hosea was prophetically talking about a Messiah to come, that spent time in Egypt.

But did the parents of Jesus live in Bethlehem or Nazareth before the birth? The author of Luke is the only one that tells the story of the decree from Caesar Augustus that forces Joseph to take his family to Bethlehem to be counted. The author of Matthew leads you to believe that they have always lived in Bethlehem and makes no mention of the journey from Nazareth to Bethlehem, nor the return back to Nazareth. In the Book of Matthew, even Herod sends the wise men to Bethlehem where they find the child. There is never a mention of Nazareth in the Book of Matthew until the return from Egypt.

Think about the fact that a large train of foreigners came to worship Jesus. It caused an uproar in Jerusalem. They left gold, frankincense and myrrh. What happened to all that money? Why is Jesus' family poor? Do you think they just left a small contribution after all that travel?

This moving, not moving, to Egypt to avoid Herod is accentuated if you look closely. In the Book of Matthew, Joseph keeps his family away from Herod until his death. Herod lived in Jerusalem. The author of the Book of Luke declares that Joseph brought his family to Jerusalem each year for Passover. How could Joseph avoid Herod while bringing Jesus to the Passover annually in Jerusalem?

But how does Caesar Augustus validate or discount the author of the Book of Luke? Caesar Augustus ruled Rome from January 16, 27 BC until his death on August 19, 14 AD. So he died when Jesus was 14 years old. Here is the problem. After his death there were Caesars Tiberius, Caligula, Claudius, Galba, Otho, and Vitellius ruling until 69AD. Jerusalem was sacked in 70 AD. The man that records the Book of Luke also records the Book of Acts. I believe that Augustus ruled during the time of the birth of Jesus Christ, but then how can Paul appeal to Caesar Augustus in Acts Chapter 25, focusing on verse 25? Remember the same author wrote both stories. That had to be way after the death of Augustus in 14 AD, with Jesus dying around 32 AD. What I am trying to show is that this author has a credibility issue, even if he gets some of the facts correct, others are way off.

Now I know that someone will point out the fact that most emperors of Rome at that time have the name Augustus in their name somewhere, but then, that wasn't what those Caesars were called. There was only one Caesar Augustus, and he died in 14 AD. So when the author of Luke records that Festus stated Paul had appealed to Caesar Augustus in Acts Chapter 25, Paul was appealing to a dead guy!

Remember what you should be trying to learn: Is the New Testament, and even more focused, the gospels, really gospel? As you will learn, The Books of Matthew, Mark and Luke generally tell one story, while John tells another. You either believe that they are "from God" or, as I assert, they are not. This does not make them "evil," just not from God.

Let's look one more time at one of Matthew's "proof texts" from the Old Testament and decide if his version of the events of the birth of Jesus Christ pass the discernment test. When the wise men come to Jerusalem in Matthew Chapter 2, they confer with Herod. Then Herod sends them on to Bethlehem, Judah. The wise men supposedly go home a different route and Herod is mad. He slaughters all the children of two years of age and under. Matthew quotes Jeremiah Chapter 31, verse 15: "Thus saith the Lord: A voice was heard in Rama, lamentation, and bitter weeping: Rahel weeping for her children refused to be comforted for her children because they were not."

Use your Bible and do some homework. What was this passage about. The message from Jeremiah begins in Chapter 31, verse 10, and ends in verse 17. If you read it, you will learn that Rahel is lamenting over the fact that her children have been taken away to other countries, but the Lord will bring them back. It has nothing to do with a slaughter of children by anyone, not even the possibility of Herod.

But, it gets worse. What is the town mentioned? It was Rama. Herod slaughtered the children in, and around Bethlehem. Bethlehem is in Judah. If you look back in Joshua Chapter 18, verse 25 you will learn that Rama is located in Benjamin! So how could this prophesy have anything to do with a slaughter by Herod in Bethlehem. Use some discernment, the author of Matthew is flat out wrong!

There is another reference to Jesus from prophecy in this portion of reading in the Book of Matthew. It is found in Matthew Chapter 2, verse 23 where the author asserts that because Jesus is from Nazareth this makes him a Nazarene. This is referenced back to Judges Chapter 13, verse 5 and 1 Samuel Chapter 1, verse 11. Read both texts, but expand your reading to understand the stories. In Judges it is about the birth of Samson, where his mother is being instructed not the allow her new son to cut his hair or drink wine. This is the oath of a Nazarite.

In Samuel it is a Nazarite vow once again that Hannah, the mother of Samuel is making for her son. Neither of these stories has anything to do with living in a town called Nazareth. It is a vow of a Nazarite in both of the referenced stories, where they do not cut their hair or drink wine. We all know that Jesus drank wine, and living in a town does not automatically place you under a vow.

There is one last reference to Old Testament prophecy by the author of Matthew found in Chapter 3, verse 3. Basically it is referencing the fact that John was a messenger preparing the way for Jesus. This is referenced from Isaiah Chapter 40. This is a valid reference to the Old Testament, but it is not about Jesus, it is about John the Baptist. Oddly enough it is also referenced by the Apostle John in John Chapter 1, verse 23. In fact, you will see that the only times that the author of Matthew has a relatively accurate reference to the Old Testament, it is always found in the Book of John.

Have you ever taken a close look at the lineage found in the Books of Matthew and Luke? Once again, these books are from God, or they are not. Both authors of the Books of Matthew and Luke record "directly" that they are providing you Joseph's linage, the father of Jesus. In the Book of Luke it even calls Joseph the "supposed father" of Jesus. Follow Joseph's father in each account. It is a different man in both, and then stays different back through King David, when they miraculously have the same lineage again.

To drive this point home further, the author of the Book of Matthew tells you that it is 14 generations from King David to the captivity in Babylon. He then tells you that it is an additional 14 generations from the captivity in Babylon to Jesus Christ, for a total of 28 generations between King David and Jesus Christ. If you look at the Book of Luke's genealogy it is a total of 40 generations between King David and Jesus Christ. Christian apologetics try to tell you that one is the lineage of Joseph and one is the lineage of Mary. But sadly, the text states that it is Joseph's lineage in both books.

If you want to state that the text became polluted through the years, then again you have to say that it is possible that all areas where the New Testament contradicts the Old Testament may be polluted also! I do believe that much of the New Testament could be polluted, and that's the point. How can you base doctrine on a single verse or chapter, or believe that you are saved because you find one author that will tell you that "this way of believing is all that you need?"

Why do I say the New Testament could be polluted and not the entire Bible? The Old Testament was recorded over and over. There was a copy of it in every synagogue. They could compare them. It was translated into Greek and distributed around the known world many years before Jesus was even born. But the New Testament is a couple of letters that we believe to be "real." Early Christians were hunted down along with these letters. Just the example of the lineage of Joseph, the father of Jesus, should make the point. At least one of these lineages is dead wrong, and they may both be wrong!

Finely, at the Baptism of Jesus, the Spirit descended on Jesus Christ in the first three gospel accounts and there was a voice that proclaimed from heaven. In all three vocal accounts, it is a different, although similar statement, supposedly from God the Father. Once again, was this prophecy, as none of the authors were there, or was it a presumed story? Moses tells you it is presumed since all three tell of a different sentence telling you what the voice from heaven said. John says it never happened!

Let's say that God spoke and revealed it to the authors latter in life. For sure, you would have to say that the authors did not take down the words "exactly" as there are three different supposed statements from God. So, if God told the authors what He said in a vision, and they can't write it down accurately, what makes you think that the author will be correct on anything else that God tells them? Unfortunately I believe that Moses has already told you what to think. It was presumed.

Please note also in the author of Luke's account of the baptism, that John the Baptist is already in prison (Luke 3:19-20) before he makes mention of Jesus being baptized. This begs the question, who baptized Jesus in Luke's account? You may say that Jesus was baptized first and then John was imprisoned, but in the Book of John's account, John the Baptist isn't imprisoned until much later in Jesus' ministry.

But then, you have to look closely at John's account. John the Baptist is being harassed with questions from the Pharisees. John tells them that he is not the Christ. Next, He states that there is someone among them that he, John the Baptist, is not worthy of tying His shoes. The next day, John sees Jesus and states "Behold the Lamb of God" and tells those there, "this is He whom I spoke of (paraphrased)."

But he, John the Baptist, also makes mention twice that "And I knew Him not," and then states: "I saw the Spirit descending from heaven like a dove, and it abode upon Him...but He that sent me to baptize with water, the same said unto me, Upon whom thou shalt see the Spirit descending, and remaining, on Him, the same is He that baptizeth with the Holy Ghost."

Do you see John the Baptist affirming "Wow, I saw my cousin coming and the Spirit descended upon Him?" No, John hasn't a clue who this guy is. And when the dove descended, was it at a baptism? John does not tell you this! In fact, John doesn't tell you that he, John the baptist, is baptized, just that he is sent to baptize with water. He also doesn't tell you that Jesus Christ was baptized. Just that he, John the Baptist, saw the Spirit descend upon Jesus and this was the sign that shows that Jesus will baptize with the Holy Ghost. So does the story of the baptism in the Book of John actually affirm anything from the gospels of Matthew, Mark and Luke? No!

Look at the name "John the Baptist." Who calls him this name? Only the authors of Matthew, Mark and Luke. John and all other New Testament authors only refers to him as John!

What Christian truths should be learned at this point? Nothing, other than the fact that the four gospels are very inconsistent to this point. None of the supernatural events from each of the gospels that we hold as truths are collaborated by any other gospel. What they all do agree on is: Jesus was born of a woman and was recognized by a man named John as having the Spirit descend upon Him.

Oh, did you note that the author of Matthew has affirmed his story has been foretold of in the Old Testament five times so far. Did you see one reference in the Old Testament that really foretold of an event as portrayed by the author of Matthew? Only once, and that was also told by the Apostle John. This isn't to say that the author of Matthew will always be reaching with the Old Testament, just that his proof texts so far, are not very sound.

One last thought. Why not read the original Greek from the first 10 verses in the Book of John. This would be a great way to become more familiar with the interlinear scripture analyzer and the Westcott and Hort compilation. It can be found on the web at www.scripture4all.org.

From your reading in the printed Bible it is clear that the first several verses in the Book of John are talking about Jesus. Do you really trust the individuals that translated the Greek to English? Remember, we are trying to differentiate between facts and fiction.

What you will find is that the beginning of the Book of John does not sound like he is talking about Jesus at all in the Greek. It is more like the preamble for the "word" that is spoken of in the Old Testament that would come before the "Prophet" arrived. And then we have John the Baptist introduced in the Book of John. I believe the Book of John starts with the "Word" that is "in" John the Baptist! Read it yourself.

I am afraid that what I have presented so far will shake most Christians. The sad part is that this is only the beginning, it only gets worse. Religious leadership have a vested interest in not showing you how badly the gospels line up. Instead they use apologetics to try to meld these stories together, even though they obviously do not, under close scrutiny. After the third or fourth time through the Bible I was shattered. But, with time I began to understand that maybe God had allowed these errors in here for a reason.

Look, the early church wanted to prove that Jesus was the Messiah. You will learn that the Book of John is totally scriptural to the Old Testament. It shows that Jesus was the Son of God without all the hoopla that the authors of Matthew, Mark and Luke want to add. The Book of John will flow with a Jesus that appears from humble beginnings and will perform miracles that become more and more awesome. They begin with changing water into wine and conclude with the bringing back of Lazarus from the dead.

Religious leadership want to give the Books of Matthew, Mark and Luke the same authority as the Book of John so that they can "claim a verse here and there," that suits their needs. There are many things found in the first three gospels that are counter to the Old Testament, and I will present them as they appear. Should it really matter if God has revealed to you that some of what we used to believe to be true, found in the gospels, doesn't pass the discernment test?

If you have questions at this point, go back and read these opening chapters of the gospels again and ask yourself: "Do they really teach the same story?" If they don't, and if you are truthful to yourself you will say that they don't. Have an open mind and try to learn through discernment how God wants you to live.

After the Baptism

Did you ever think about what happened directly after the baptism of Jesus? Most people would say that Jesus went out into the wilderness and was tempted by Satan. Then he does a few things and travels back home to the Sea of Galilee where he calls Peter and his brother Andrew followed shortly by James and John by saying, "follow Me and I will make you fishers of men."

This was what I thought, before I wrote this book. It is an interesting time to look at the difference between the stories found in the Books of Matthew and Mark to the Book of John. Please remember that John never told you that Jesus was actually baptized. Note how John's message is so different. Where is Jesus three days after the supposed baptism? Does Jesus find Peter, James and John, or do they find Him? Is it fishermen at the Sea of Galilee or is it John the Baptist's disciples walking by the Jordan River?

What about the Book of Luke? It will begin following the Books of Matthew and Mark, but then side steps some of this story. The author will later tell most of these stories but much later in the ministry of Jesus Christ. If what I have just written is true, then only one can be correct. Only one can be the inerrant word of God, if any.

Matthew Chapter 4-5 Starts directly after the baptism with the fasting in the wilderness for 40 days and the temptation of Jesus by the Devil, followed by His return to Galilee. Jesus preaches in several towns and ends up at the Sea of Galilee where He says "Follow me, and I will make you fishers of men," to Simon Peter and his brother Andrew. Shortly after, He meets James and John. When He calls both pair, they drop what they are doing to follow Him. He begins in earnest to preach the gospel of the Kingdom of God and healing all manner of sickness.

Matthew Chapter 5 begins with the beatitudes and expands into what is called the Sermon on the Mount. Jesus gives a "disclaimer" in verses 17-18 where He affirms that He has not come to destroy the Law and the Prophets (Old Testament), but to fulfill. "For verily I say unto you, Till heaven and earth pass, not one jot or one tittle shall in no wise pass from the Law, till all be fulfilled." The chapter concludes with Jesus explaining that the Law was not to be followed just physically, but mentally. It isn't just the physical act that God is looking at, it is the desire to do that act that really counts. One good example He gives is adultery. Just the desire to have sex with another man's wife is adultery in your heart!

Mark Chapter 1, verse 12 – 45. Jesus has entered the wilderness and is tempted by the Devil. John the Baptist has been cast into prison, and Jesus has returned to Galilee to begin preaching. As He is walking by the Sea, He meets two men, Simon (Peter) and Andrew, casting nets and says to them "Come after me and I will make you fishers of men." Shortly after, He meets James and John and they too follow Him. They leave everything and follow Jesus.

The next Sabbath He is recognized by an evil spirit. After they left the synagogue, He enters Peter's house where He finds Peter's mother-in-law sick and heals her. From this point on in the chapter He is healing many different types of uncleanness.

Luke Chapter 4, Verses 1-37 Jesus enters the wilderness for 40 days and is tempted by the Devil. Jesus returned in the power of the Spirit to Galilee. He had fame throughout the region, but returned to Nazareth. He reads in the synagogue on the Sabbath and remarks about some past Gentiles that were blessed in the time of the Judges, which incites an uproar. The people try to cast Him off a cliff, but He miraculously walks through them. As He teaches in Capernaum, He casts out an evil Spirit that identifies Him as the Holy One of God.

John Chapter 1, verse 34,- Chapter 2, Verse 11. The very next day after John the Baptist affirms who Jesus is, John the Baptist tells two of his followers "Behold the Lamb of God," and they followed after Him. One of these followers was Andrew, who brings Peter to meet Jesus. The next day Jesus goes into Galilee and finds Philip. Philip brings Nathaniel to Jesus. Chapter 2 opens the third day after Jesus' supposed baptism with the turning of water into wine at Cana. This miracle is affirmed by John as the beginning of Jesus' miracles.

So, from the Baptism until the beginning of His miracles and ministry what did we learn? This is the problem with taking a critical look at the New Testament gospels. The closer that you look at them, the more bizarre the stories are. The Books of Matthew, Mark and Luke all tell of how Jesus calls His disciples at the Sea of Galilee. They three, all tell of the 40 days in the wilderness and temptation.

The author of the Book of Luke adds a supernatural observation of Jesus walking through a crowd that wants to kill Him by thrusting Him down a hill. Unfortunately, if the author of Luke was the gentile physician Luke, he was not a Jew and doesn't understand that when Jews believe someone to be blasphemous, as they felt He was, or just plain want to kill someone for a crime unto death, they <u>STONE</u> them. Look it up. It is the sentence of death for a Jew. Instead, the author of Luke picks a sentence of throwing Him down a hill, which no other gospel makes note of.

John on the other hand tells you that three days after His supposed baptism, Jesus is in Cana where He does His first miracle, turning water into wine. No voice from Heaven leading Him into the wilderness, no temptation, no meeting fishermen on the banks of the Sea of Galilee, no casting out demons who know who He is. No, John tells you of disciples being drawn to Jesus

After the Baptism

the very next day, who follow after Him. To be fair, John isn't totally clear when Jesus is baptized, if He is baptized, by John the Baptist. But John the Baptist does testify that Jesus is the "Lamb of God" and then two of his own disciples follow after Jesus. They are Andrew, the brother of Peter, and another. Andrew goes and finds his brother Simon (Peter). So you know for sure that the story of Jesus calling James and John as well as Peter and Andrew by the Sea of Galilee to make them fishers of men is all wet! Peter and Andrew seek Jesus out at the Jordan River!

Peter and Andrew, James and John are two sets of brothers and are inseparable. John never tells you when he began to follow. He is never mentioned by name in the Book of John, but we know that he was always with Peter and James. At this point John, who was probably there, tells a totally different story that does merge from time to time with the other gospels. We will follow with the first three gospels to see how they track, and then follow up with John's account when they do intersect.

The fact that we have to do this should set alarms off in your head. Why don't the stories line up if it is the inerrant word of God? This is why the book is called *The New Testament, the Facts and the Fiction.* There is no way that it can be fact if it is this messed up. But what do you trust? How do you explain that you believe the Bible to your friends, when in these few verses you can see that it is easily picked apart?

Did you note the author of the Book of Matthew drew four more references to the Old Testament during this reading? Let's see how he did. Turn to Matthew Chapter 4, verse 6. In this verse Satan is talking with Jesus and telling Him that if He is really the Son of God, He should throw Himself down off a very high place as God the Father would protect Him from harming himself. This is referenced from Psalm Chapter 91, verse 11 and 12.

Psalm Chapter 91 is a beautiful Psalm about the care God the Father has for those that trust in Him. The key to understanding who this Psalm is written about is found in verse 9. "Because thou hast made the Lord, which is my refuge, even the most High, thy habitation." It makes no reference to someone that is to come that could be a supernatural being living among us. It is a trust that we all can have if we trust in God to care for us. If you read this Psalm for the first time and did not know that the author of Matthew had made the connection in his story, you would never doubt that this was written to you, if you trust in God for your salvation.

The second prophetic Old Testament reference is found in Matthew Chapter 4, verses 15 and 16. This is a reference to Isaiah Chapter 9, verses 1 and 2. The author of Matthew is trying to show that when Jesus moved to Capernaum it was foretold in these passages of Isaiah.

The story in Isaiah Chapter 9 began much earlier in Chapter 7. It is about the foretold destruction of Israel. It has one main sign that is to prove that God will bring this about. It is the birth of the son to the virgin, which we spoke about in the last chapter. Again, here in the beginning of Chapter 9 we see that the author of Matthew is again taking Isaiah out of context. It doesn't have anything to do with Jesus moving to Zebulun or Naphtali, it is about the destruction of these areas as they are about to be destroyed by the Assyrians, and a little latter in Isaiah, they are.

There was also the reference to man not living on bread alone and the reference to worship the Lord thy God only. These are very generic in the scripture and apply to all of us at all times, just like "thou shalt not steal." Since Jesus never stole anything, does this mean that this message was written of Him? No, it is a generic message or statute that God expects all of us to live by.

So during this chapter's reading we have two generic messages that were referenced and two prophetic references by the author of Matthew from the Old Testament. The prophetic references are to be of Jesus found in the Old Testament scriptures, but they are not. I'm not saying that Jesus isn't foretold in the scriptures, just that the author of the Book of Matthew has taken the Old Testament totally out of context for both of these references.

Thus far in the Book of Matthew, there has been one excellent prophetic reference to John the Baptist, which coincidentally the Apostle John has given you, and six references to Jesus Christ that are just wrong! There has not been one single in-context reference provided by the author of Matthew to Jesus from the Old Testament.

Why not try a little discernment for a change? The Bible makes it perfectly clear that all knowledge, wisdom, and discernment comes from God. You must do your best, and let God do the rest. Knowledge is just plain facts. Some facts are good facts and some facts are bad facts. Wisdom is the ability to use facts. But discernment is the ability to choose between good facts and bad facts, to understand what is "true."

So, to do your best you must read the scriptures, then reread the scriptures and pray to God for wisdom and discernment. With time you will learn of God. All truths that we know of Him will line up with what we know of Him. He is never changing.

How do we use discernment with the gospels? Well, you already know the history of the four supposed authors. You also know that Moses told you how to test if it was prophecy. You also know that none of them state anywhere that what they have written was delivered by God. So you have to agree that these are recalled stories that you, the reader, will need to ponder on. Who was the first-hand witness? Usually it was John.

Since John will not collaborate anything that the other three gospels are about to tell you, you have to ask yourself, am I willing to hang my salvation on the next few stories in the Books of Matthew, Mark, and Luke? Remember, they were never there! After all, John too is trying to show that Jesus is the Son of God. He is trying to give proof-positive to his readers, but he has not made any of the elaborate and over exaggerated claims that have come out so far from the other three gospel writers.

John has stated that Jesus was born of a woman, was recognized by John (the Baptist) and a dove landed upon His head. He then was followed by several of John the Baptist's disciples that asked to follow Him. Jesus has done one miracle and it was a big one if you ponder on it. He changed water into wine. Who do you know that can change water into anything other than vapor?

The other three gospel writers who were not there, have told you that Jesus was born of a virgin, had a father with two different lineages, was spoken of by God, spent 40 days fasting in the wilderness and tempted by the Devil. According to these authors, Jesus called James and John, as well as Andrew and Peter, at a location that the Apostle John himself disagrees with, and Jesus has already incited a riotous movement against Himself that He miraculously moved through.

I would like you to re-read the event when Jesus was back in his own city found in Luke Chapter 4, starting in verse 16. I want you to note that only the author of Luke has written of this story. You will note in this author's story of the life of Jesus Christ that Jesus does not have any disciples yet. This author will bring you more supernatural stories than any of the other authors, and if he is Luke the physician, he is not on the seen for many, many years. In this story, Jesus is stating from the scriptures that He is claiming that the Spirit of God is upon Him. Then He insults those in the synagogue by telling them that in the time of the prophets, many Jews needed help but only two gentiles were helped by God. They want to kill Him and decide that the best way to do this is to throw Him down a cliff. This would be a major event in anyone's life. The other three gospel accounts have all got disciples by now. Why would this event to kill Jesus be ignored by the other authors? More importantly, Jesus has claimed boldly to have the Spirit of God upon Him. This claim is not noted until many chapters later in the other gospels.

Did you note that the Apostle John never agrees with God speaking from heaven when the other three gospel authors will record it. If you can't tell, I have issues with the first three gospels. If the Book of John had not been written, then at least the stories would be close, but then you have to ask yourself, which gospel story do I trust? After all, they all tell a different story if you read them critically. You have John, the apostle that walked with Jesus through His entire ministry and stood by Him at the Cross, and you have three others that were there, at best, part-time.

You have John, who not only wrote the Book of John, but also the Book of Revelation. In the Book of Revelation you have John talking with Jesus, the elders in heaven and seeing the Being or Presence of God the Father. If you don't believe John, then you have no reason to trust the Book of Revelation.

So, this far in the gospels, where do you draw the line between fact and fiction? Is the message of the four gospels from the Holy Spirit? I would have to conclude that a statement like that has to be fiction. I believe that all four gospel writers were writing what they believed to be true or at least sort of true in Luke's case, but only one can be fact when all four tell a different story. Remember, what we call the Bible, never claims to be the inerrant word of God. That is a recent Christian thing. But as you read farther you will have to answer whether you truly agree that it is the inerrant word of God for yourself.

The New Testament authors wrote "Epistles," which simply translates into letters. But, if Christians can change the epistles to be "Scriptures" then they would carry equal weight.

Before I continue with the gospels I must expand this explanation again. I have said the word "scripture(s)" several times when referring to the New and Old Testament. This is a bad habit. It is a false doctrine picked up through the years from attending church. It would be fair to say that I am arguing with Paul if I am not "trusting my scriptures."

I know that some will say, "but what about when Paul states in II Timothy Chapter 3, verse 16-17: All scripture is given by inspiration of God, and profitable for doctrine, for reproof, for correction, for instruction in righteousness: That the man of God may be perfect, thoroughly furnished unto all good works." This is true and I would not want someone asking if I felt closer to God than the Apostle Paul.

But that is not what Paul is saying at all. He is not referring to the New Testament when he is using the word "scripture." At the time of Paul's death there was no New Testament, but there were scriptures. I'm not hammering on the scriptures, I am hammering on the epistles, or early letters. Paul wouldn't have a problem with that. Why not read Paul's own words on what he referred to as scriptures. Read II Timothy Chapter 3, verse 15: "And that thou from a child hast known the Holy Scriptures, which are able to make thee wise unto salvation through faith in Jesus Christ."

Read II Timothy Chapter 3, verses 15 -17 and you will agree that the New Testament wasn't written when Timothy was a child. The Old Testament were the scriptures of the day. The New Testament were only letters of encouragement at the time Paul wrote this letter to Timothy, if they were even written yet!

The Bible is made up of the Holy Scriptures (Old Testament) and some letters by early church members organized together by the Roman Catholic Church (RCC). The RCC named these letters "The New Testament." The only reference in the New Testament that "we should live by the scriptures" was referring to the Old Testament.

So lets not forget that when we read a New Testament author talking about scriptures, he is talking about the Old Testament. What did Paul tell Timothy would make him wise unto salvation through faith in Jesus Christ? The Old Testament! He doesn't say a new truth that you may try to pull out of his or any other New Testament brother's writings.

Now, let's get back to covering the gospels. Lets follow the Books of Matthew, Mark, and Luke's account through the calling of Levi, or also referred to as Matthew, the supposed author of the Book of Matthew.

The Calling of Matthew

This chapter only includes passages from the Books of Matthew, Mark, and Luke. As noted earlier in the history books, John does not write of these events. We will pick up with John in the next chapter. And, in that chapter again, he will not write of the events that these three authors will write about until the very end, at the feeding of 5000.

Please note that the order of these events are very different. The author of Matthew will attribute many stories here of Jesus' ministry as they happened before his calling. Many of these same stories can be found later after Matthew's calling according to the authors of Mark and Luke.

But then, who should know when they happened with reference to Matthew's calling? Matthew, the guy that was supposedly called, or two other guys telling the same story, but were not there? Not that we are sure that the Apostle Matthew wrote the Book of Matthew. Two examples of these stories are Jesus calming the Sea and the two possessed men of the tombs in the country of the Gergesenes. The author of Matthew affirms that these events happen before his calling, but the authors of Mark and Luke tell you that they happen much later, after Matthew's calling.

More importantly, the Book of Matthew tells you that the event in the land of the Gergesenes is of two men that are devil possessed and Jesus casts the devils into the swine. The authors of Mark and Luke tell you that the devils are in one man of the tombs. Either the author of Matthew is correct or the authors of Mark and Luke are correct, but, even if it was one man, don't you think that Matthew would know if it was before or after he was called?

This is one problem with thinking that the Book of Matthew is written by the Apostle Matthew. If it is he that wrote this book, this totally discounts the events recorded in the Books of Mark and Luke. More notable to this fact, if the authors of Mark and Luke are wrong here in these stories, how many other stories that they write are wrong also?

As to the order of events surrounding the calling of Matthew, it is obvious that Matthew should know if it happened before or after his calling. But this assumption requires the Matthew, in the receipt of custom, to be the disciple Matthew, and also the Matthew that wrote the Book of Matthew. You will see from names given to the man in the receipt of custom and the naming of the 12 disciples that it brings into question if they are the same guy.

As mentioned earlier, John does not make mention of any of these events at all? I hate to keep beating the same drum, but if you were trying to show that you believe that Jesus is the Son of

God, and He is awakened on a stormy sea, then "silences" the weather, don't you think that this is a story that you would want to tell?

John does tell of Jesus calming the Sea after the feeding of 5000 along with two of these authors, but they make reference to this event here, which is earlier in Jesus' ministry. Don't you think that if you were John, you would record it? Maybe this wasn't an important incident to John. But the other three gospel writers say that those on the ship were in "fear." Oh yeah, the author of Matthew will tell you that he wasn't there, and the author of Luke tells you that Matthew was!

Let's take a quick look at the events concluding with the calling of Matthew.

Matthew Chapter 6 to Chapter 9, verse 13. Chapter 6 opens with a few more lessons that Jesus taught at the conclusion of the Sermon on the Mount, about not doing things religious in front of man for man's recognition, but doing them in silence where God only will know.

In the middle of this teaching Jesus instructs the disciples in the Lord's Prayer. The Book of Matthew follows it with some more teaching about not looking good before man, but to God, and if you do, God will take care of you.

Chapter 7 starts with showing the condemnation of judging others when you may have committed the same sin. There are many more excellent examples of how God wants you to live taught by Jesus that the author of Matthew wants to give Him credit for saying at this time. "And when Jesus had ended these sayings, the people were astonished."

In Chapter 8, He heals a leper and instructs him to offer the gift that is required under the Mosaic Law for the cleansing of leprosy. As Jesus enters Capernaum, a Centurion asks Him to heal his sick servant. When Jesus agrees to go to his house the centurion shows the great faith that he has in Jesus' "word." Jesus is amazed and heals his servant without visiting.

As they come to Peter's house, He finds Peter's mother-in-law sick and heals her. She then ministers to Him and the disciples. In the evening He heals all those with sicknesses and casts out devils that have possessed many. As the multitude grows, He tells his disciples to depart to the other side of the sea.

While at sea, a bad storm arises and His disciples fear for their lives, but we find Jesus asleep. When they awaken Him, He explains that they are short of faith. Then He rebukes the storm and it subsides. His disciples marvel.

As they arrive on the other side, they arrive at the Gergesenes' shore, where they meet two men possessed with devils coming from the tombs. Jesus casts the devils from the two men into a herd of swine that then run down into the sea and perish. The people of the land ask Him to depart and He does.

In Chapter 9, He leaves their shores and lands back in His own city. Jesus tells a sick man with the Palsy, "Son, be of good cheer; thy sins be forgiven thee." Many think that He blasphemed. So Jesus asks a question, which is easier, to make that statement or to say, stand up and walk? Then He states, " But that ye may know that the son of Man has power on earth to forgive sins, (Then saith He to the sick with the palsy) Arise, take up thy bed, and go unto thy house." And, as the man did, the people watching marveled.

As He left them, He instructs a man to follow Him, named Matthew sitting in a tax booth. He dines at Matthew's house that evening and is spoken ill of by those that are unhappy that He is dining with sinners (tax collectors). Jesus explains that it is not the "well" that need a physician, but the sick.

Mark Chapter 2, verses 1-17. Jesus comes back to Capernaum after several days. A palsy stricken man is lowered down through a roof to Jesus. Jesus tells him, "Son, thy sins are forgiven thee." The reaction and conclusion is the same as in the Book of Matthew Chapter 9. Jesus then meets Levi sitting in a receipt of custom and instructs Him to "Follow me." Jesus dines at his house that evening as in the account by the author of Matthew.

Luke Chapter 4, verse 38 through Chapter 5, verse 39. Jesus enters into Peter's house and finds his mother-in-law sick with a fever. Jesus heals her and then she waits on them. That evening He heals all that are brought to Him and many devils cry out, but Jesus rebukes them not to speak. In the morning He departs into a desert place, but the people find Him and stay with Him. The chapter closes with Him preaching in the synagogues of Galilee.

Chapter 5 starts with Jesus entering into Peter's boat and preaching to the people on the shore at Lake Gennesaret. After he has preached, Jesus tells him to let down his nets to try to catch some fish. A reluctant Peter does, and the nets are overfilled with the catch. Peter is amazed and falls at Jesus' feet. His brother Andrew and two partners James and John feel the same. Jesus tells them, "Fear not, from henceforth thou shalt catch men." They leave all and follow Jesus.

Jesus enters another city and heals a man with leprosy and instructs him to show himself to the priest and offer the offering in the Mosaic Law. This increases His fame and the multitude that follows Him. So He withdraws to the wilderness.

The Calling of Matthew

While Jesus is teaching, a man with Palsy is lowered down through a roof to Him and Jesus tells the man, "Man, thy sins are forgiven thee." As in Matthew and Marks' recount Jesus shows that He has the power to forgive sins by saying, " I say unto thee, Arise, and take up thy couch, and go into thine house."

After this, He finds Levi at a receipt of custom. Levi throws Jesus a great dinner where Jesus is questioned about the company that He is keeping. Jesus explains that it isn't the well that require a physician, but the sick. Jesus is questioned as to why His disciples didn't fast and give themselves to prayer. Jesus explains that soon they will.

Three more parables are attributed to this dinner by the author of Luke. These are the adding new material to an old garment, the new wine in the old wine skins and how you wouldn't drink new wine after you had drunk old wine as the old wine is better.

So, what have we learned so far?

You will note that many of the stories are similar, and yet not the same. The order of events is definitely off, but then, who was there? None of these authors were there. Take the story of the man at the tomb in the land of the Gergesenes'. Was it one man or two? This story will be told again later in both the Books of Mark and Luke, but next time it is only one man that is possessed, and the devils are sent out into the pigs, then they drown themselves.

Does it matter? Only if you want to believe that the Bible was penned by men under the Spirit of God's direction. This can't be fact as they are not the same, so at least one of the stories is wrong, hence not penned by the Holy Spirit.

How about the man stricken with the palsy that Jesus said, "Son, your sins are forgiven thee." Was He sitting there when Jesus walked up to him as the author of Matthew describes, or was He lowered down to Jesus through the roof as in the Books of Mark and Luke? The stories are all similar, but are actually very different. The similarities are too similar to say that they are different happenings, but the story is different enough to say that the author obviously heard about it, but no one is certain what actually happened. Are the stories inerrant? At least one is incorrect.

The only witness at this point in the life of Jesus Christ is the Apostle John. If John wrote it, it probably happened. If he did not write it, why would you call it gospel? After all, John has told you definitively that some things that are in all three of the other gospels never happened! Did Jesus really go into the wilderness for 40 days and fast, while being tempted by Satan? Go back and read John, he was there! On the 3rd day after His supposed baptism, Jesus was in Cana changing water into wine! That would be 37 days before the Books of Matthew, Mark and Luke try to convince you that Jesus comes out of the wilderness.

The author of Luke tells a story about Jesus at Lake Gennesaret. This is where Jesus tells Peter, Andrew, James and John that he will show them how to "catch men." Doesn't this story sound eerily like the one recorded in the Books of Matthew and Mark that tells of how Jesus walks up to the same four fishermen at the Sea of Galilee and states "I will make you fishers of men?" Same guys, same type of statement, different sea shores, and definitely a different time in the ministry of Jesus Christ.

What makes this story so bizarre, is that it is a conglomerate of Matthew and Marks' story and one that you will see John (John Chapter 21) telling of after the resurrection. John will be fishing with the same people, and Jesus, in His resurrected body, will tell Peter to lower his nets. A reluctant Peter will, and then catches so many fish that he needs his partners to come help haul it in.

It is very important to note the name of "Matthew" in the gospels. As John does not make reference to this story at all, we have to look closely at the name given to this man by the three gospels that do. The author of Matthew identifies him as "Matthew sitting in a receipt of custom." This is why we link Matthew, here in this story, to the author of the Book of Matthew. The Books of Mark and Luke identify this man as "Levi the son of Alphaeus." Up until I studied this closely, while I was writing this book, I over looked it. It isn't so important now, but when you see the names of the 12 disciples it becomes very important. We will cover this in the next chapter.

The last discrepancy comes from the Book of Luke at the end of the dinner that Matthew or Levi holds for Jesus. The author of Luke explains that Jesus tells three parables at the end of dinner. It is part of a conversation about why Jesus' disciples are not fasting and praying like the disciples of John the Baptist and others.

During this chapter of reading, the author of Matthew has only tried to squeeze Jesus one time into the Old Testament. It is found in Chapter 8, verse 17. Jesus has been healing many people. The author of Matthew quotes Isaiah Chapter 53, verse 4 to say that this healing is a fulfillment of the prophesy by Isaiah. I believe that Isaiah Chapter 53 is a foretelling of Jesus, but not in this context.

Isaiah Chapter 53, if read in one sitting, is about the coming gift by God to man that was to grow up before God, be rejected by mankind and then crucified. It has no reference to the "sign" to look for is that this gift was to be healing people in his ministry. In fact, this chapter in Isaiah looks like Jesus is to be totally despised and rejected. Can you fit this chapter of Isaiah into the healing that is going on in the Book of Matthew at this time? No, so this shows the author of Matthew to be zero for 7 references to Jesus to this point.

Here in Matthew Chapter 8 we see Jesus calming the wind and sea. This is before the calling of Matthew. The disciples are amazed. Who wouldn't be? Jesus has just displayed the power over nature. This event is recorded in Mark Chapter 4 and Luke Chapter 8 much later in Jesus' ministry after the calling of Matthew. They record that Matthew is there for this miracle although the Book of Matthew shows here that he is not. This would be a great power that would be very supernatural. Unfortunately the Apostle John does not make any mention of it.

We will open the next section with this same conversation in the Books of Matthew and Mark, but in Mark it sounds like it is at a different time, and if you look at what is happening, it would appear that it wouldn't have happened at Matthew's house.

In the author of Matthew's account, he makes it clear that at the end of these three parables, the rich young ruler comes to ask Jesus to save his daughter. If the author of Luke is correct, the only way it could flow is that at the end of the dinner, Jesus leaves for the rich young ruler's house. But then, this would wreck the other two stories. Read the three accounts carefully and you will conclude that although they are in the same order, the three gospels are showing them to be occurring at different times.

Shouldn't it seem strange to you that when you read the gospel of John, none of this is in his gospel. What is worse, John, the guy that was there, tells you a totally different story of Jesus Christ's ministry that the others do not. Although I would like to show John's recollection of these events, there is nothing in the Book of John to compare it to.

The Feeding of 5000, and Walking on Water

This is a very long chapter as there is no place to make a good break. The first three gospel writers have the events in this section in a completely different order. In this chapter we have all four gospel authors concluding with the feeding of 5000 and three of them rendering the story of Jesus walking on water. This chapter is very long because there is no earlier point where the first three gospels have all the events completed. It also happens to be where John's gospel and the first three converge.

The authors of Matthew, Mark, and Luke will begin just after the calling of Matthew. But, in the Book of John we begin just after Jesus turns water into wine. Not that the first three gospel authors agree with the water into wine miracle either, but that is where we left off on John's gospel, two chapters back.

Do you remember the purpose of this book? As the title implies, *The New Testament, the Facts and the Fiction,* For the New Testament to be factual, the stories have to line up. This isn't to say that just because they don't line up they are lies, on the contrary, they may be based in truth, yet not correct. More importantly, the gospels, at best, sort of tell the same story. Hence all four accounts cannot be totally credible, or at best, one is credible. Ask yourself, over and over, "Can this really be written by the hand of God?" Is God a God of order or confusion?

Once again, the first three gospels do tell most of the same stories, but they will be in a very different order. And yes, again, there are many differences to each of their stories. Look for the condition of Jairus' daughter when Jairus first comes to Jesus for help. Is she sick and alive, or dead?

You will again note that only the author of Luke tells a story of Jesus bringing back a man to life in the city of Nain. Does any other gospel author write of this? When Jesus heals the man with a withered hand, the author of Luke affirms that it happened on a different day than when Jesus' disciples have eaten corn in a field on a Sabbath. This directly disagrees with the Books of Matthew and Mark's account.

The author of Luke also tells the story of the Beatitudes and the Sermon on the Mount. The only other recording of this is in the Book of Matthew, and the Book of Luke states that it happened after Matthew's calling, even though the author of Matthew affirmed earlier that it happened before Matthew was called. Line the Beatitudes up in Matthew Chapter 5, and those found here in Luke Chapter 6. They are not the same. So, what are the correct Beatitudes? Who is blessed by them? You really can't be sure as they are different. Moses will tell you that at least one of these accounts is presumed!

There is much more to talk about, but we will try to hit it all at the end of this chapter. What should you take away from your reading so far? All four gospels tell a different story and hence can't be the actual inspired word of God! But then, they don't claim to be. Let's get back into the books.

Matthew Chapter 9, verse 14 through Chapter 14, verse 32. Sometime after Jesus had eaten with Matthew, the disciples of John come to Him and asked why His disciples don't fast. Jesus explains through three examples that they won't fast until He is taken from them. At the end of this conversation, a ruler comes and worships Him and explains that his daughter is dead. Jesus goes with him.

On the way, a woman touches Him, that had an issue of blood, taking virtue from Jesus. Jesus explains that her faith has healed her. As He arrives at the ruler's house He finds the funeral ceremonies have begun and He tells them to leave. Jesus then brings the girl back to life and the fame of this event went abroad unto all that land.

After leaving the ruler, two blind men follow Jesus and He heals their lack of sight. This is followed by Jesus casting out a devil in a dumb man and the people marvel that "was never so seen in Israel." Jesus is accused that He is casting out devils through the prince of devils by the Pharisees. He continues to heal and preach and is moved with compassion as He sees the people and states to His disciples, "The harvest truly is plenteous, but the labourers are few; Pray ye therefore the Lord of the harvest, that He will send forth labourers into the harvest."

Chapter 10 starts with Jesus sending forth the twelve chosen disciples with power over unclean spirits, sickness, and all manor of disease. It is important to note that they are sent only to Jews in Israel. They were to take nothing with them to heal and cast out devils. In His sending them off, He makes a statement in verse 22: "And He that endureth to the end shall be saved."

Actually, Chapter 10, verse 16 on, for several verses, looks more like Jesus is talking about end times, or at least some time in the future as none of these predictions occur during the sending forth. But, these verses would be excellent advice at the end of His ministry to prepare His disciples for what is about to happen to the church. You will see this same type of verbiage used later on in the Book of John.

Chapter 11 opens with the conclusion of the sending forth, and Jesus departing to teach and preach in their cities. John the Baptist sends two of his own disciples to ask: "Art thou he that should come, or do we look for another?" Jesus assures them that He is "He" by explaining and showing the powers that He possesses.

He then explains concerning who John the Baptist is to the multitude. The conversation moves to Jesus telling them that John is the Spirit of Elijah (Elias), as was predicted in the Old Testament. But, even though John is a great prophet, he is not respected by the nation. Jesus too, has shown great powers and the "wise and prudent" people call Him a gluten and winebibber.

With that, He moves to upbraid all the cities that He had been doing miracles in, because they did not believe. Jesus then thanks the Lord in front of the people for revealing who He is, to these less wise and prudent people. He follows it with explaining His relationship to the Father, the Father's to the Son, and finally mankind. Jesus closes this chapter with explaining that all that come to Him, He will give them rest.

Chapter 12 is set on a Sabbath day with Jesus and His disciples walking through a field and His disciples eat some of the grain as they walk. When questioned about this action, Jesus asks about David and his men eating food meant only for the priest when they were hungry and then questioned why the priests work in the temple on Sabbath and yet are counted blameless. He then explains that He is Lord of the Sabbath!

On the same day He enters into the synagogue and sees a man with a withered hand and asks: "Is it lawful to do good on the Sabbath?" He heals the man and the Pharisees want to destroy Him for this act. Jesus slips away and the multitude follow Him and He heals the sick. The author of the Book of Matthew draws you to believe that this is prophecy from Isaiah (Esaias).

Jesus heals a devil possessed man that was both blind and dumb, and the Pharisees again state that His powers are from Beelzebub, the prince of the devils. He then justifies how He is not from Satan as that would be Satan against Satan. Besides, their sons could cast out devils also, so who are they getting their power from.

Then Jesus warns that they can blaspheme Him, but they should not blaspheme the Holy Ghost, who was obviously doing these miracles through Him. After all, as His works are for the good, then He is good, "for the tree is known by its fruits...A good man out of a good treasure of the heart bringeth forth good things; and an evil man out of the evil treasure of the heart bringeth forth evil things." So our words will either condemn or justify us.

The Pharisees ask for a sign and Jesus tells them that the only sign that He will give is that of Jonah (Jonas), "so shall the Son of man be three days and three nights in the heart of the earth." He then follows with a condemnation of the present generation for not recognizing who He is.

The end of the chapter shows Jesus explaining that "His" family are those that follow Him.

In Chapter 13, Jesus went into a ship and taught those by the sea shore. He taught three parables. At the end of the chapter He explains the meaning of these parables to His disciples. The first was the parable of the four soils. This parable shows that there are four distinct types of people that hear and receive the word, but only one of these categories of people will become prosperous from hearing the word.

The author of the Book of Matthew tells us that Jesus explains that He is telling these parables to the Jews so that He will be fulfilling prophecy that explains that the people will see but not perceive and hear but not understand. But His disciples will perceive and understand and be saved.

The next parable was the wheat and the tares. This parable explains that the devil will sow bad people next to good people and God will leave them there until the end times. Then the tares will be "harvested" and thrown into the fire for destruction. The last parable was two parables in one, where Jesus explains the greatness of the Kingdom of Heaven. It is likened unto a mustard seed and also unto leaven. Jesus did not explain these final parables.

After Jesus explains to His disciples the meaning of these earlier parables, He tells them several others about the Kingdom of Heaven and end times. He asks them if they understand and they agree that they do.

Following these parables, He comes back to His own country where he teaches to the astonishment of those that know Him. Because of their unbelief He does only a few miracles and remarks, "A prophet is not without honor, save in his own country, and in his own house."

Chapter 14 opens with Herod believing that Jesus is a "risen" John the Baptist, as he, Herod, had put John the Baptist to death. When Jesus heard this, He departed by ship to a desert place. The multitude followed on foot and Jesus healed them. In the evening Jesus blessed five loaves and two fishes that were split into baskets and fed 5000 men plus women and children. There were 12 baskets of pieces left over.

Jesus straightway sends the disciples ahead of Him in a ship before He sends the multitude away. Then He goes into the mountains to pray. At evening time the boat was in the middle of the sea and was being driven by the wind. Later that night, Jesus walks across the top of the water, to the boat and the disciples think He is a Spirit and are fearful, but Jesus reassures them.

Peter tells Jesus that if it is really Him to call him so that he can come to Him on the water. Jesus does so, and Peter begins to walk on water to Jesus. But Peter becomes fearful and begins to sink so Jesus rescues him. As they enter the ship, the wind subsides.

Mark Chapter 2, verse 18 through Chapter 6, verse 52. The author of Mark starts this section with what appears to be a pause, with a new story. Jesus is being asked why the disciples of John the Baptist and the Pharisees fast often, but Jesus' disciples don't appear to fast. Jesus explains that His disciples are celebrating with Him, as do the children of the bride chamber with the bridegroom, but soon they will fast also. He uses two more analogies as did the author of Matthew with the old and new garment and the new wine in the old wine skins.

He completes the chapter with Jesus and His disciples walking through the grain field eating as they go. The Pharisees question Him and He uses the analogy of David feeding His men with the shew-bread and concluding the discussion stating, "the Son of Man is also Lord of the Sabbath."

Chapter 3 opens with Jesus healing the man with the withered hand on the Sabbath. Jesus asks if it is OK to do good on the Sabbath to those that are angry with Him for healing on the Sabbath. The Pharisees take council with the Herodians against Him.

So, He withdrew and went to the sea where He healed the masses that followed after Him. He then went into the mountains with all His disciples and ordained 12 to have power to preach and heal. They entered into a house where Jesus is accused of casting out devils in the name of Beelzebub.

Jesus explains that Satan cannot cast out Satan, as that would be a house divided. He then explains that blasphemes will be forgive that are made to man, but by saying He is casting out the devil by the power of the devil, they are not giving the glory to the Holy Spirit. This won't be forgiven. This conversation is followed by Jesus being informed that His family are outside asking for Him. He explains that His real family are those that do the will of God.

Jesus is again by the sea when Chapter 4 opens. He is teaching from a boat to the people on the shore. He teaches several parables. The first was the sower who sowed seed into four types of ground. Later in the chapter he explains what these parables mean. In the parable of the sower, people hear and accept the word of God gladly, but only one category of individual really accepts the word, although all four appear to accept it at first.

The second parable is what you do with a candle, once lit, is it hidden? Nothing will be hidden that you think is secret. He then made some comparisons of what the Kingdom of God is like. It is like a man that grows a crop of corn, or it is like a mustard seed that grows from nothing to something great. That evening He takes the disciples to the other side of the sea. A great storm occurs and Jesus stills the storm. This brings fear to His followers.

When they land in Chapter 5, in the Land of the Gadarenes, they meet a man that has been living in the tombs that is spirit possessed. This man is unbelievably strong and feared by the locals. Jesus casts out the devils that are within him into a herd of pigs, that run violently down into the sea and choke to death. The local people were afraid and pray Jesus to leave, so He enters again into His ship and passes back to the other side.

When He lands, a ruler named Jairus falls at His feet and asks Him to come and heal his daughter that is very sick. On the way to Jairus' house a woman, which had an issue of blood touched His garment in the belief that she would be healed. Jesus felt the virtue leaving His body and tells her that her faith had healed her.

During that incident, a man from Jairus' house comes to tell him that his daughter had died, but Jesus is not deterred. Jesus, although scorned by those at Jairus' house, tells them that the child is not dead, but asleep. He takes the girl by the hand and says, "Damsel, I say unto thee, arise." And straightway she begins to walk.

In Chapter 6 Jesus has come back to his own town and teaches on the Sabbath in the synagogue. They know that He teaches beyond what His background should deliver and His works are mighty, and yet they do not believe, hence He "could not" do mighty works other than heal a few sick.

So Jesus sends out 12 disciples, two by two to preach, to heal the sick and cast out unclean spirits. He gave them instruction not to take anything for their well being, that where they healed, the people there should support them.

Herod hears of Jesus' fame and believes that it is John the Baptist, risen from the dead. About this same time, His disciples come back and tell Him of all that had happened to them. Jesus takes His disciples and departs to the desert for a rest.

The multitude sees Him leave and follows Him, so He has compassion on them and teaches them until the day is spent. His disciples ask Him to send them away so that they can find food and Jesus tells them that they should feed the multitude. After a short discussion He asks them to sit in the grass. After asking a blessing over five loves and two fishes, Jesus brakes them and places the pieces before the people. There were 12 baskets of fragments left over after all 5000 men were fed.

Jesus immediately sends the disciples away in a boat, but stays behind to send the people away. He then goes into a mountain to pray. At evening the boat was in the middle of the sea and was being driven by the wind. Later that night, Jesus walks across the top of the water, and appears to almost walk by the men in the boat. They think He is a Spirit and are fearful, but Jesus tells them who He is and climbs into the Boat.

Luke Chapter 6, verse 1 through Chapter 9, verse 17. On the second Sabbath after the first, Jesus went through a corn field with His disciples and they eat from the field as they walked. This was criticized by the Pharisees as it was done on the Sabbath. Jesus asks them about how they felt about David and his men eating the priest's shewbread. He then states "that the Son of Man is Lord of the Sabbath."

Also, on another Sabbath, He entered into a synagogue where there was a man with a withered hand that He healed. Since He did this on the Sabbath they were filled with madness and communed what they might do to Him.

So Jesus went out to pray all night and in the morning He called together all His disciples and chose 12 that He named apostles. He went out from there to a great plain where there was a vast multitude that came to be healed. This is where the author of the Book of Luke affirms that Jesus delivers the Beatitudes and many of the sayings that the Book of Matthew affirms He taught at the Sermon on the Mount, although this is a great plain and not on a mountain.

At the beginning of Chapter 7, Jesus enters into Capernaum where a centurion sent elders of the Jews to ask Jesus to come and heal his servant. But before Jesus could arrive at his house the centurion sent a friend to say to Jesus, "I know your power and all you have to do is speak the word and my servant will be healed (paraphrased)." Jesus is impressed with his faith and states there is no one in Israel with the faith of this man.

In the Book of Luke, the next day Jesus brings a man back to life in the town of Nain. And when the fame of Jesus had traveled through the land, John the Baptist sent to Jesus to ask, "Art thou he that should come? Or look we for another?" So, Jesus healed and cast out evil spirits before John's disciples and then told them to report back to John what they had seen and heard.

Then He spoke to the people about John the Baptist, who was a messenger that was sent to prepare the way for Jesus. Then He railed on them for not accepting John or Himself. At the end of this long discussion a Pharisee asks Him to come and dine at His house.

As Jesus is dining, a woman sat at Jesus' feet wiping them with her hair and tears, and anointing them with ointment. The Pharisee believes that Jesus couldn't possibly be a prophet or He would know that the woman was a sinner, and so Jesus remarks, "Her sins that are many are forgiven; for she loved much: but to whom little is forgiven, loveth little."

Mary and several other women are ministering to Jesus and His disciple's needs at the beginning of Chapter 8. Jesus then teaches the parable of the sower, and the candlestick as in the Books of Matthew and Mark. He is then told that His mother and brethren are outside asking for Him. He states that "My mother and brethren are these that hear the Word of God and do it."

On another day, He and His disciples enter a ship and He falls asleep while they are traveling. A storm arose and they felt in jeopardy, so they awaken Him. He then rebukes the storm and it calms, leaving the disciples afraid and wondering who this is that can command the weather.

When they arrived on the other side they were in the country of the Gadarenes where He met a man that lived in the tombs. He was devil possessed for a long time. When Jesus asked the devil his name, he said it was Legion. So Jesus cast out the devils into a herd of swine that ran down the hill and drowned in the lake.

The people of the area were afraid and asked Him to leave their country, so Jesus gets back in the boat and returns to the other side. When he arrives he is met by a man named Jairus who besought Jesus to come to his house because his daughter was dying. A lady with an issue of blood touched Jesus on the way and He felt virtue leaving His body. When asked "Who touched me," the woman came and fell down at His feet and confessed. Jesus blesses her and while He was still speaking, one came from Jairus' house with the message that his daughter is now dead.

Jesus simply tells Jairus to "believe only" and so He takes Peter, James, John, Jairus and his wife only, to the maiden. After dismissing everyone that is with the maiden He tells her, "Maid, arise." The daughter rises straightway.

After this in the beginning of Chapter 9, Jesus gives the power and authority to the 12 disciples over sickness and devils and sends them to preach the Kingdom of God. He instructs them to take nothing as they should be rewarded for what they do by the city that they enter, with food, shelter, and clothing.

Herod hears of Jesus and wonders who He is. He is perplexed because he hears so much of what Jesus has done. He hears that many think He is a risen John the Baptist. After all, he had beheaded John the Baptist, so he knew that it was not John, but he desired to meet Him. After Jesus' disciples return, He takes them to a desert place.

While there, Jesus taught the masses about the Kingdom of God and heals them. In the evening, the disciples want Jesus to send the multitude away, but Jesus tells His disciples to "Give ye them to eat." He then has them sit down in 50's, and after blessing, breaks five loaves and two fishes placing them in baskets, that are fed to 5000 men.

John Chapter 2, verse 12 through Chapter 6, verse 21.

After Jesus changes water into wine in Cana, Jesus with His family and disciples enter Capernaum for a while. It is Passover and Jesus goes to Jerusalem where He finds venders in the temple selling oxen, sheep and doves for profit and drives them out with a whip, turning over tables as He went, condemning their actions.

When questioned for a sign to show that He had the authority to do this, Jesus explains that when they destroy "This" temple (His body), He will bring it up again in three days. They, thinking that He is talking about the actual temple structure, explain that it took 46 years to build. Jesus continues there through the Passover and performs many miracles.

Later in Chapter 3 a man named Nicodemus comes to Jesus to ask for understanding of who Jesus is. Jesus explains that no one will be saved if they don't learn of Him and are born of the Spirit (born again). Jesus explains that we understand nature around us and yet they cannot understand what they are witnessing. Jesus explains His crucifixion and it's payment for sin through an analogy of the brass serpent that was lifted up in the wilderness by Moses. He explains that God sent Him to die for our sins to save the world, but we must believe in Him to receive this gift. Man will have to choose to love the light or darkness. It is his choice.

After this, Jesus departs into Judea where He begins to baptize near where John the Baptist has been baptizing. John's followers ask about Jesus and John testifies that Jesus is from above and will increase while he, John the Baptist, will decrease. At the beginning of Chapter 4, Jesus departs from there and travels through Samaria on His way to Galilee.

As He is traveling, He sits down at a well where He meets a Samarian woman. He asks her for a drink of water and she questions why He would even speak to her, He being a Jew. Jesus speaks of spiritual things to the woman. At first she thinks He is speaking in the physical, but soon understands the spirituality of the conversation and understands that Jesus must be the Christ. So she goes back into the village and tells everyone to come see Jesus.

His disciples had left Him at the well while they went looking for food to eat. When they return, they are perplexed when He doesn't want to eat. He would rather look forward to meeting the people of the city than to eat. So Jesus stayed with the Samaritans for two days, and many there believe on Him. After this He continues to Galilee.

Once in Galilee, He was received openly because of all that they had seen Him do in Jerusalem. A nobleman meets Him who was from Capernaum and asks Jesus to heal his son. Jesus tells Him to go his way, "thy son liveth." Later the man's servant comes and tells the nobleman that his son has become well, and he knew it was Jesus that healed him.

Chapter 5 opens with Jesus again going up to Jerusalem for a feast. He heals a man that was by the pool Bethesda with the words, "Arise and take up thy bed and walk." The man was questioned why he was carrying his bed on the Sabbath. The healed man states that the man that cured him told him to do so. When the Jews found out it was Jesus that had healed the man, they wanted to persecute Him for healing on the Sabbath.

Jesus explains that His Father works on the Sabbath, thus making Himself equal to God. He testifies to them that all things that He does comes from the Father and greater things they will see, to include the power to bring back the dead. He then explains that if you believe on Him, you will have everlasting life. Soon there will be judgment on those that are dead; to those that have done good, unto life, and those that have done evil, unto damnation.

Jesus then explains that the miracles that He has been doing are witness to who He is, and that the Father had sent Him, and yet they still reject Him. Even the scriptures that they trust in, tell of Him. Jesus then explains that these same scriptures will testify against them, as they are written by Moses. If they don't believe what Moses wrote, then why would they believe His words either.

Opening in Chapter 6, Jesus went over the Sea of Galilee and then up in to a mountain with His disciples, while being followed by the multitude. He asks Philip to feed the people, to test him. Five loaves and two fishes are brought to Jesus and He blesses them and breaks them into pieces. These are fed to 5000 men who believe Him to be a prophet and want to take Him to make Him a King, but Jesus leaves them and goes into the mountain.

At evening, His disciples go down into the ship and travel towards Capernaum, although Jesus is not with them. After they had rowed a great ways, Jesus comes walking to them on the water. The disciples are afraid, but Jesus assures them "It is I; be not afraid." They immediately receive Him into the ship and the ship was immediately transported to the land where they went.

What have we learned from these passages? As you can see from our study of the gospels, John, who was there, tells a very different story to the other three gospel writers that were there, at best, part time. If the stories they tell are in contradiction to the one that John tells, are they gospel? No, of course not. They are the stories of the recollection that these other three authors have, either from stories of stories, or maybe a little first-hand witness.

You might feel I am being flippant, but I asked you to use a little discernment earlier in this book. Do you remember what discernment is? It is the ability to choose between good facts and bad facts.

If it looks like a duck, sounds like a duck, flaps it's wings like a duck, and how about "tastes" like a duck, then it is a duck. It is the real thing. The Books of Mark, Luke and much of Matthew were written by people that were not there and hence, tell a different story than John. You really can't be sure if any of the Book of Matthew is first-hand witness either. If John is the real thing, he is the duck. The others, although probably founded on good principles are not "duck." That would make them "good for you," but not "duck." I think of them more like"duck flavored tofu," definitely good for you, but not the real thing!

So, does this mean that I feel the first three gospels should be thrown out. No, but we have to use discernment in understanding that they are not "fact!" This isn't the infallible word of God we are reading. If you can get over the bad doctrine that has been drummed into Christians about the inerrancy of the scriptures then you have a chance of being able to explain to others why the Bible appears to argue with itself. And, it does! But by now you should be better able to explain why it does.

In this section we see Jesus calling the 12 disciples to Him and giving them extraordinary power. As you are aware, the Apostle John never makes that claim. John does tell you several times that Jesus called 12 close followers to Him under different circumstances, but they are never mentioned by name. Look closely at the names that are given in all three lists. Are they the same names?

The Books of Matthew and Mark give you one of the interesting names. It is Simon the Canaanite. The Book of Luke calls him Simon called Zelotes. So Simon had a nick name called Zelotes, just as Simon, the Brother of Andrew, had the nick name of Peter. But what was a Canaanite? It was an unclean Gentile from Canaan, just as a Moabite was from Moab. Later you will read the story of the woman from Canaan that wants Jesus to heal her daughter. What is this person equated to? A dog! Read Matthew Chapter 15, starting at verse 21. This is just something to ponder. The real meat is the apostle with the name Matthew.

The Apostle Matthew is commonly believed to be the author of the Book of Matthew, and he is commonly thought of as the publican that was sitting in the receipt of custom from our last chapter. Does he pass the majority rules test here? Not that majority rules, but this is one more "melding" of the stories to make them blend by apologetics. When you look at it closely, it doesn't.

The Book of Matthew identifies the guy in the receipt of custom as "Matthew sitting in a receipt of custom." The Book of Matthew never called him a publican, just that at the dinner he threw that night, there were publicans there. The Books of Mark and Luke identified the guy sitting in the receipt of custom as "Levi the son of Alphaeus." But when you look at all three lists of the disciples you have the Book of Matthew identifying Matthew as a publican, but the Books of Mark and Luke identify the Apostle Matthew as just Matthew.

Here is the rub. The man in the receipt of custom was identified as Levi the son of Alphaeus, in both Mark and Luke's account. The Books of Matthew, Mark and Luke all tell you that there is a son of Alphaeus that is an apostle, but it isn't Matthew, it is a guy named James. So James the son of Alphaeus _is_ the brother of Levi the son of Alphaeus, but there is no Levi the Son of Alphaeus in any of the lists of the Apostles!

Are you really sure that the Apostle Matthew is the guy sitting in the receipt of custom? It isn't him according to the Books of Mark and Luke. And Matthew calls him a publican. There is no reference to the Apostles Matthew and James being brothers! Can you really be sure that the guy that wrote the Book of Matthew is Levi the son of Alphaeus? The only three books that tell the story of the calling of the 12, all tell a different story.

Take the story of the sending forth of the 12 to heal and cast out devils. This is a very supernatural power that Jesus has supposedly given to the disciples, including John, but as you can see, John does not make mention of him or any other person having this power, only Jesus. One note as I did focus on Matthew Chapter 10, verse 22, if you read the verses that come before it, and what comes after it, it is very blunt that only "those that endure to the end will be saved."

Look at the significance of that statement. If you believe that this story happened, the author of Matthew is telling you that some who think they are saved will not be able to continue in their faith and will fall away. Those who are in that category are "not saved!" What ever happened to once-saved-always-saved? It is a Christian myth, just like the old belief that the "world is flat!" Both statements are not fact, they are fiction.

Let's carry the thought through that once-saved-always-saved is fiction, by using the parable of the sower. As the authors of the Books of Matthew, Mark, and Luke all tell the story of the sower, let's look at it closely. This is why I don't believe that you can throw out the baby with the bath water. I do believe this parable was believed, even though John doesn't tell it. All three versions are a little different, but have you ever read what Jesus' explanation was for the four types of soils? Go back and read the author of Matthew's extensive rendition of this in Chapter 13.

Jesus Himself explains that there are four types of people that respond differently to hearing the "word." All four types accept the word gladly but the first looses the "word" because of a lack of understanding (those that fall by the way side). The second hears the word with joy, but when troubled by what or how the "word" wants you to live, becomes offended (those that fall by the stoney ground). The third are taken away by the cares of the world (those that fall by the thorns).

Only one category of individual will actually become fruitful (those that fall by the good ground). Did Jesus sound like He felt that all four categories would be saved? No, in fact He makes it clear that three out of the four are "snatched away be Satan!" So, just because you or someone you know has asked Jesus into your life, does that make you or them saved? No, you're still one of the four types of soils. You have to bare fruit to be saved. Read the parable again and again.

Most so-called Christians fall into the second category, not the fourth. When a Christian reads in their Bible that they should change their behavior, do they change? God has directly told His children to live contrary to how most are currently living. I have been a member of many churches and a willing participant in Bible study. <u>I have never met a single church member that will stand up for the Bible over bad doctrine in that church</u>.

This is the second category. "Yet hath he not root in himself, but dureth for a while: for when tribulation or persecution ariseth because of the word, by and by he is offended." This is a truth in the Bible that proves most Christian lives are fiction themselves. If you truly study your Bible you will have to agree that keeping the Sabbath is a Commandment of God that is inconvenient to live by today. Same with the health laws. God says that eating any sea food that doesn't have both fins and scales is an abomination. Do you like lobster, shrimp and crab?

Don't take my word for it. Do an extensive study of the Bible, or, live with your head in the sand. Ignorance will not be an excuse when we are judged. Most so-called Christians willingly follow their church "Mission statement" over the truths written in the Bible. Why if it is so obvious how we should live, do church members follow bad doctrine? Because no one wants to rock the boat. No one wants to be thrown out of their "church club." I know. I have many times asked why we won't change doctrine, even in small community churches, and no one wants to hear.

What is really bad is when everyone will agree that the scripture proves they are living wrong and no one will vote to change. Do they sound like they are in category two or four? They don't want the "trouble" that comes with changing for God. They are "offended." They are not saved according to this parable! Once again, don't take my word for it, it's in your Bible.

Back to the accuracy of the gospels. Remember where this parable was taught? It was in a ship to those at the sea shore in the Books of Matthew and Mark, but just to a multitude in the Book of Luke, and as you should know, not in John at all. But in Matthew and Mark, He tells additional parables with the parable of the sower. These additional parables are different in both Matthew and Mark's author's accounts, and in Luke it is only the one parable.

Matthew Chapter 11 shows why discernment is so critical. Matthew is already a disciple and walking with Jesus when John the Baptist asks a question through his disciples to Jesus, "Art thou he that should come, or do we look for another?" Why do we need discernment here?

Go back to the author of Matthew's own story of Jesus' baptism by John the Baptist in Matthew Chapter 3, starting at verse 13. John the Baptist identifies Jesus for who He is, and tells Jesus that he, John the Baptist, isn't worthy to baptize Him. According to Matthew, so far Jesus has healed all kind of illness and deformity, cast out every type of devil, and even brought back the dead. All these are famed of Him if you read the author of Matthew's account, and yet John the Baptist has doubts. According to the author of Matthew, John the Baptist should have heard God proclaim who Jesus is/was during Jesus' baptism!

But to be fair to Matthew, he should have been gone at this point, being one of the 12 sent forth to heal and cast out devils in his gospel. This is the problem. When he is not there, he still has these great stories that just don't add up. But, you will note that the author of Matthew never explains when they get back as in the Books of Mark and Luke.

The author of Luke also shows John the Baptist sending His disciples to ask Jesus if He is the Christ. This is even more bizarre when you remember back that Luke is the author that tells the story to you of the pregnancy of John the Baptist. While in his mother's womb, John leaped when Mary, who was carrying Jesus in her womb, came into the same room. And of course, there was the dove and voice from heaven when Jesus was brought up out of the water by John the Baptist. All this is found in the Book of Luke's account.

Compare the doubt by these two "John the Baptists" with the simple story told by the Apostle John. John doesn't tell the same supernatural events that the other three gospel writers do of Jesus and John, only to say that John saw a dove descend upon Jesus showing him who it is that will baptize with the Holy Ghost. This was the sign that John the Baptist was to look for according to John Chapter 1. The following day, John the Baptist identifies Jesus as the "Lamb of God."

The last we hear of John the Baptist from the Apostle John is in John Chapter 3. This is before John is thrown into prison, while he and Jesus are both baptizing in the same location. John the Baptist is explaining to his followers that he, John, will decrease as Jesus must increase. He has explained to his followers that he is rejoicing in Jesus' rise, similar to how a friend of the groom rejoices when the groom becomes married. Where is the doubt in John the Baptist's voice? There isn't any in the Apostle John's account, nor should there be in the other accounts if what they had written earlier was fact!

John Chapter 4 tells the story of the Samaritan woman at the well. Even the text tells you that Jesus is speaking to an unclean person, and a woman at that. Think of the significance of this story. A Samaritan was about as unclean as they got for a Jew. The woman even states in John Chapter 4, verse 9: "How is it that thou, being a Jew, askest drink of me, which am a woman of Samaria?" Do we see a Jesus that will not converse or "work" with those that are unclean? This is a major difference between the story told by the apostle John and the one found in the other gospels. Later on in their rendition you will see Jesus calling them "dogs." This condemnation is not found in the Book of John. According to John, Jesus lives with them for 2 days before moving on.

As with many times before, the author of Matthew has again reminded us of Old Testament prophesy during this reading, two of which are supposedly referenced by Jesus. These are found in Matthew Chapter 11, verse 10; Chapter 12, verse 17; Chapter 13, verse 14 and lastly Chapter 13, verse 35. let's see how the author of Matthew will fare when his story is compared to the Old Testament that he is referencing.

In Matthew Chapter 11 we see Jesus telling the crowd about John the Baptist. It is supposedly Jesus who is telling you that John the Baptist is referenced in Malachi Chapter 3, verse 1. If you read the close of Chapter 2 and follow it with the beginning of Chapter 3 it looks more like a reference to Jesus in the end times, not John the Baptist just before Jesus is to come. Read it for yourself.

The next reference is found in Matthew Chapter 12, verse 17. This is referenced to Isaiah Chapter 42, verse 1. If you read Isaiah Chapter 42, verses 1 through 5, it does have many of the same words, but not exactly the same. So what! Isaiah Chapter 42 is about the "servant" bringing forth judgment to the Gentiles. How does judgment being brought to the Gentiles have anything to do with Jesus being persecuted by the Jewish ruling class, as found here in Matthew Chapter 12? There is no reference to Gentiles in the entire story by the author of Matthew, except this supposed reference. This passage from Isaiah Chapter 42 is totally out of context to the story in Matthew Chapter 12.

I do believe that Isaiah Chapter 42 is about Jesus, but it doesn't fit in this part of the author of Matthew's Story. Remember to this point, Gentiles are not in the picture. It isn't until Matthew Chapter 15, when Jesus heals the Canaanitish woman, that Jesus heals his first Gentile, according to the author of Matthew. And, in that story, Gentiles are equated to dogs! So why quote about judgment to the Gentiles here? It makes no sense.

But note that the author of Matthew felt that the passage applied to Jesus, and so do I. But what great truth is told in Isaiah Chapter 42? Jesus is a servant to God whom the Father has chosen. Jesus is not God living among us like so many Christians want to believe. Once again, He is the Son. The Son prays to the Father while He, the Son, is on earth, but He is not God. The author of Matthew understood this. Read Isaiah Chapters 41 and 42 and you will better understand.

The author of Matthew, in Chapter 13 has slyly woven in Old Testament prophecy to bolster Jesus' position as the fulfillment of prophesy. Did you catch it? This time the author of Matthew will say that Jesus said "He was the fulfillment of that prophecy." This way it isn't the author of Matthew telling you that it was fulfillment of scripture, it is Jesus telling you that it is a fulfillment of scripture. Go back and read Matthew Chapter 13, verse 14. It goes like this: " And in them is fulfilled the prophesy of Esaias (Isaiah), which saith, By hearing ye shall hear, and shall not understand; and seeing ye shall see, and shall not perceive..." This quote is supposed to be from Isaiah Chapter 6.

But, if you read Isaiah Chapter 6 you will learn that the words are indeed there, but this was a message from God for Isaiah to deliver to Israel in that day. And, that message was valid until they were overthrown by Assyria, which they were a few years later. It kills me why Christians don't look up the references to the Old Testament to see if they are valid. This reference in Isaiah has nothing to do with why Jesus is speaking in parables.

The last scripture passage by the author of Matthew to the Old Testament in this chapter of reading is found in Matthew Chapter 13, verse 35. It is supposed to be a reference to Jesus found in Psalm Chapter 78, verse 2. In Matthew Chapter 13, Jesus has been telling several parables. The author informs you that Jesus will never again speak to the crowd unless it is in a parable. This statement alone is not true. Jesus does speak many times to the crowds in common language. But, supposedly in this verse we see that Jesus only speaks in parables to fulfill this verse in the Psalms.

In Psalm Chapter 78 you will read about how God will "open my mouth in a <u>parable</u>: I will utter dark sayings of old, which we have heard and known, and our fathers have told us." Does this Psalm have anything to do with the teachable moments that supposedly Jesus was giving at the time? No, this Psalm is telling you that it is about to tell a story (<u>parable</u>) of the history of the

Jews. Then, right after Psalm Chapter 78, verse 2, you will see the entire history of how the Jews came to be. So what does this Psalm have to do with Jesus Christ's supposed teachable moments? Nothing. By the way, how many parables are found in the Book of John?

There is only one parable found in the Book of John. It is found in John Chapter 10, verses 1 through 5. It is about the sheep following their Shepard. Unfortunately, it is not found in the Books of Matthew, Mark or Luke.

Thus far the author of Matthew has made two references to the Old Testament that were supposedly to reference John the Baptist. One is sound, but the other is very weak and should have been made to reference Jesus Christ in the latter days. The author has made 10 references to Old Testament passages that were to support his story of the ministry of Jesus Christ. All 10 have been found to be out of context or just plain wrong.

The events of Jesus and His disciples eating in the field of corn and then healing the withered hand are classic. First the Book of Mark tells you at the end of Chapter 2 that Jesus goes from dining with Levi directly into the field of corn where His disciples begin to eat on the Sabbath causing an argument with the Pharisees.

The Book of Luke tells you that the eating from the field on the Sabbath event began on the second Sabbath after the first. Whatever that means (I can't tell you), but it shows that it is happening some time after the last event, which was the dinner at Levi's. He then says that the withered hand event happens on "another" Sabbath.

Finally the Book of Matthew's account occurs much later in the book and both events happen on the same Sabbath day. So all three accounts were on Sabbaths, but yet all three events happened at different times. These times are chronicled differently by each author. But the story is even more bizarre if you look at the defense that Jesus was to be using in this story.

When Jesus and his disciples are walking through the cornfield they are plucking and eating on the Sabbath. This is considered work to the Pharisees and they point it out to Jesus in Matthew Chapter 12, verse 2. This story was told in Mark Chapter 2, staring in verse 23 and again in Luke Chapter 6, verse 1. Jesus refers them back to scripture and explains that David and his men ate the priest's shewbread that was holy, when they were hungry. If you use your center reference in your Bible it will lead you to I Samuel Chapter 21, verse 6.

It's really not a big deal unless you have read all of I Samuel Chapter 20 and 21. David has fled for his life from Saul. He is all alone and without any men, weapons or armor. He enters into Nob and sees Ahimelech the priest. David makes up a story of being at haste to do the kings business, but it is all a lie. Although Ahimelech identifies that David is without any men in Chapter 21, verse 1, David explains that there are others. But, if you read the story you will see that David is alone.

He is also alone when he gets to his first destination, Gath, where he has to fake that he is mad as he is in fear for his life. You don't see the King of Gath stating that David and his men are mad, just David. David gets followers when he finally reaches the cave Adullam, in the beginning of the next chapter. So what is my point?

The originator of the story who told that "David and his men" were hungry and ate the shewbread was not familiar enough with the "real" story in I Samuel to know that David was alone. The originator of the story took the lie told by David as truth. That means the originator of the story didn't really understand the story of David's encounter with Ahimelech the priest. So the originator of the story wasn't Jesus Christ, the Son of God.

Have you noticed that some of the same quotes are given in John's account that are given in the other three gospels? Jesus will give a quote when an event is happening, but it will be at a different event. Take the words: "Rise, take up thy bed and walk"

Do you remember reading this statement by Jesus? What was it in reference to? The early gospels will tell you it was about the man with palsy. John will tell you it was a man by the Bethesda pool.

But the similarities in where the statements are attributed don't end there. Remember the sign that was asked of Jesus? You know, the Jews ask Jesus to give a sign and He states "The only sign I will give you is the sign of Jonah in the belly of the fish." Well, in John you see a similar statement about what authority Jesus has to cast out the money changers in the temple. Only in this statement it is "In three days I will build up the temple." But look more closely at the happening around this statement by John.

Jesus has just cast out the money changers and those that are selling oxen, sheep and doves in the temple. This, according to John is again early in Jesus' ministry. The other three gospels tell the same story at the end of Jesus' ministry, just before the crucifixion, after the triumphal entry.

Did you look for the account of Jairus' daughter? Was she originally sick or was she dead when Jesus was first asked to go to his house? She was dead in the author of Matthew's account and very sick in the authors of Mark and Luke's. You could make the case that Mark and Luke were mistranslated, but then in the middle of their stories a servant from Jairus' house comes to inform Jairus not to trouble Jesus as the child had died. But since this was supposed to be the first person that Jesus brings back to life, who does the author of Luke say was there at this miraculous event? It was Jesus, Jairus, his wife, Peter, James, and John. But John doesn't tell of this event. As you will see from John's account of Jesus' ministry, Jesus only brought back Lazarus, and that, just before His crucifixion.

In the middle of the story of Jairus's daughter you have the woman with the issue of blood. She touched Jesus and virtue left Him. First remember that John doesn't tell you any of these stories, but if you have faith, you can take virtue from Jesus without His approval according the the authors of Matthew, Mark and Luke. That is what this story has taught. So in the Books of Matthew, Mark and Luke (also Acts or Luke II) if our Saviour is not aware, and you sneak up to him you can "take" virtue from Him by touching Him.

This is a major problem or difference between the story told by John and the one told by the authors of Matthew, Mark, and Luke. In their story you have powers from God given by Jesus to His disciples, taken by strangers for their own healing (here), or utilized by others who do not follow Him just by using His name (later in the book). But, the apostle that was there does not record this anywhere.

Did you also look for the account of the man from the tombs? Yes, I know that the author of Matthew already told you it had happened much earlier, but was it one man as the author of Matthew professes, or two as in the story by the authors of Mark and Luke, that lived at the tombs that were devil possessed? Was it before the calling of the 12 or after? The author of Matthew tells you it was before and the other two authors tell you it was after!

Do you remember the Beatitudes and the Sermon on the Mount in the Book of Matthew? Yes, that was before Matthew was called, but now the author of Luke is telling you that it occurs. This is much later than the calling of Matthew, in fact, according to the author of Luke it is after the sending forth of the 12 to preach, heal, and cast out unclean spirits. Many of the teachings are the same, but they are different. Even the location is different. The author of Matthew tells you that it was up on a hillside, hence the name "The Sermon on the Mount," but the author of Luke tells you that it is on a great plain.

How about the centurion in Capernaum. The author of Luke tells you that the centurion sent the elders to Jesus and then sent friends to state that all Jesus has to do is give the word and his servant will be healed. The author of Matthew tells of the centurion himself coming to Jesus and asking for His help, but explaining that all Jesus needs to do is give the word and his servant would be healed. You may note that the Roman didn't lower himself to come and ask Jesus, but instead asked the Jewish elders to do so in Luke's account.

All four gospel accounts give you the feeding of 5000. This is the first place where all four gospels tell a similar story since the identification of Jesus Christ by John the Baptist. I say similar because they are close, but not the same. This is one story where you could make the point that you need to have all four stories to put the pieces together, but there are still problems between the accounts. The author of Luke tells you that the place where this takes place is a desert place that belongs to the city of Bethsaida. At the end of his account you do not have the disciple entering a ship and Jesus walking on water, but it is plain as to the starting point.

At the close of this reading we find Jesus walking on water. Well, we do in the Books of Matthew, Mark, and John. Again, the author of Luke somehow left this story out. But are the stories the same? First, remember that in the Books of Matthew and Mark, Jesus sends the disciples away before he dismisses the multitude. In John, He and His disciples go into the mountain until the evening. Then His disciples depart. Matthew tells you that Peter actually tries to walk on the water to Jesus, but through fear is not able to, and Jesus has to save him. Neither the authors of Mark or John make any reference to it.

But remember what has happened in the life of the disciples by the time we have Jesus walking on the water. In the Books of Matthew, Mark, and Luke you have Jesus sending the disciples with power to cast out all manner of spirits and devils. Why would they be fearful if they have power over devils when they see Jesus, presuming that He is a spirit? They are supposed to have power over spirits? John doesn't make any of the claims that he or any other disciple has been given this great power and hence, when they are fearful in John's account it makes sense. Oh, did you notice, the author of Luke forgot to tell you that Jesus walked on water?

A ways back in the middle of Matthew Chapter 12, Jesus cast out a devil that had made a man blind and dumb. He is accused of casting out devils by the power of Beelzebub. Jesus' defense is that their children cast out devils, so who are they casting out devils in the power of? This means that it isn't the Name or Power of Jesus that is casting out these devils, as they would not have been casting out devils in His name. This supposed power is key to remember later on in the book. Think hard here, the story is implying that if devil possession is real, as taught in the Books of Matthew, Mark, Luke and Acts, Jews too could cast out evil spirits without the Name of Jesus!

I was actually proofing my book and got to this chapter before I came to a great realization. Why can't Jesus perform healing in His own town? The authors of Matthew, Mark and Luke will all tell you that Jesus is unable to perform many miracles in His home town because the town folk have unbelief. You have also seen that Jesus tells many that their faith has healed them. Is Jesus' power of healing directly linked to the recipients faith? Why would it be?

In the books authored by Paul, you read plainly that God is the potter and we are the clay. Paul even questions what "right" we have to question the potter, no matter what the potter wants to do with us. So why would our faith have any thing to do with a healing God may want to perform, even if we don't want Him to perform it?

Look up the word "faith" in the concordance. It isn't in the Book of John a single time. John never tells you that an individual's faith has any consequence in the actions of Jesus Christ. In all accounts in John, Jesus just walks up to the individual and chooses to heal that individual. What a different Jesus, and a different type of power, than the one found in the Books of Matthew, Mark and Luke.

Isn't my drum beating beginning to wear out the old myth that the gospels are "gospel?" They can only be gospel if they are all factual, hence, the same. They don't even give the same message. The first three show a super, supernatural Jesus. John shows you a "teaching" Jesus that does miracles, but not the constant casting out of "super devils" and bringing back the dead. He will bring back the dead in John's account, but not until Lazarus, just before His crucifixion.

Have you got it yet? Have you begun to shed some of that bad doctrine that teaches that the "entire" Bible is the "Word of God." God is orderly, not disorderly. If you can't discern between good facts and bad facts, you may want to pray for discernment. Is this scary? It is if you hold to bad doctrine. It would or could be life shattering, but it shouldn't be.

Let's try one more. The authors of Matthew, Mark, and John all bring you the walking on water after the feeding of 5000. Do you see any differences in the stories? The author of Mark states that Jesus walks on the water and then climbs in the boat. No big deal other than the walking on water. John tells you that Jesus walked on water and then the boat is moved through space and time to the other side of the sea as He stepped in the boat. Finally, Matthew tells you that as Jesus approached, Peter asks the Lord, "if it be thou, bid me come unto thee on the water."

We all know the story, Peter starts to walk on the water, but because his faith is lacking, he begins to sink and Jesus has to rescue him. Why does Jesus state that Peter began to sink? "O thou of little faith, wherefore didst thou doubt?" Think hard here. Whose power was allowing Peter to walk on water? If this story recorded only by the author of the Book of Matthew is true, who did Peter ask to help him to walk on water? The sentence read, "if it be thou, bid me come unto thee on the water."

Who is doing the bidding, Jesus or Peter? Whose faith is it that must provide the power, Jesus' or Peter's? This is the problem with the Books of Matthew, Mark, Luke and the Acts. They teach that if you have faith you can do anything, but if you do not, God does not have the power to save you. Is it your faith or His will? You do not see this anywhere in the Book of John. It is Jesus and Jesus alone that performs all miracles with the power given to Him from the Father. Remember, the word faith is not located anywhere in the Book of John. Take out your concordance and you will see that the word "faith" is noticeably missing from the entire text.

Where were the disciples headed when they left the feeding of 5000? Remember, according to Luke they started somewhere around Bethsaida. According to the Books of Matthew and John they are heading to Capernaum. They have been battling the rough seas and traveled "about 5 and 20 or 30 furlongs" when Jesus reaches them. Lets round it off to 25 furlongs. They land on the other side of the sea of Tiberius (Galilee) when it is all over. Twenty five furlongs is over 3 miles. And then they still have a distance to go to get to Capernaum. Only Bethsaida and Capernaum are only 1 mile apart according to the map in the back of your Bible. They are next to each other, not across the Sea of Tiberius from one another.

The Bible is a book that was put together some time back and is made of Holy Scriptures that the Apostle Paul tells you to live your life by. Paul tells you that the scriptures are the Old Testament. It also has several letters written after the Resurrection of our Lord. But these are not scripture. These are the New Testament. The New Testament has some correct facts and some stories that many would like to believe are fact, but can't be, as you have already witnessed.

If you are confused, should you go to your pastor and ask for help? No, go to God. Your pastor or church leader is "paid" to sell you their version of events. Why not let the Bible tell you all that you need to know. The entire New Testament isn't wrong, but as you can see, at least three out of four versions of Jesus' early life and ministry are.

Should that shatter your belief? Why would it, if you use a little discernment? It will help explain why there are so many conflicting accounts. Look, the gospels are written by four guys with four reasons for writing their account of what they believe to be true about the life and ministry of Jesus Christ, nothing more, nothing less. They were all trying to show how they knew that Jesus was the Son of God. Jesus is worthy of worship. But it becomes harder to believe that many of the stories that we hear of Him are founded.

Why not just take the Book of John and focus on that? There is plenty in the Book of John to build doctrine or the life that Jesus Christ and God the Father want you to live. John is in full agreement with the rest of the New Testament without all the "extra" stuff. Have you begun to see why I call this book *The New Testament, the Facts and the Fiction?*

This isn't to say that none of the stories written in the first three gospels are correct. But you have to agree by now that they are questionable. More importantly, you have to agree that they can't be visions given by God to the authors. Go back and read Moses' thought on this issue. If the text has eluded you it can be found in Deuteronomy Chapter 18, verses 21-22: "And if thou say in thine heart, How shall we know the word which the Lord hath not spoken? When a prophet speaketh in the name of the Lord, if the thing follow not, nor come to pass, that is the thing which the Lord hath not spoken, but the prophet hath spoken it presumptuously: thou shalt not be afraid of him."

Mountain of Transfiguration

This is a chapter where we will only be covering the Books of Matthew, Mark and Luke again. The Books of Matthew and Mark will track identical story lines from Jesus walking on the water until the Mountain of Transfiguration. The Book of Luke will follow the same story, but leave out many of the events. This would be a great example of how all three can be telling the same story, but one just left out some of the events. Does this mean that this part of the ministry of Jesus Christ is sound? No, it just means that the authors of Matthew, Mark and Luke all believed in these stories and for once, tell of the same events. You are missing one thing to make it believable.

John doesn't make reference to any of these events. You could say that these events were not important enough for him to write about. If this is your apologetic, ask yourself why? Why would John never write of God speaking to Jesus from heaven when the other three gospel writers write of it? Isn't John trying to prove that Jesus was the Son of God? Think about the importance of these stories.

Remember what the point of this book is. We are learning whether the Bible is the inerrant word of God. Is the entire Bible error free? By now you should know that it isn't. Do the verses in the Book of Matthew actually reinforce the verses found in the Books of Mark, Luke and John. For that matter, do any of the books really reinforce any of the others? Obviously Matthew, Mark and Luke do follow a similar track, but do they really reinforce each other? They have contradicted each other many, many times. This is the real point of the book.

Modern Christianity hangs its salvation on the point that each verse is infallible. This way, they can claim a verse here and a verse there to explain why they do what they do. Only, as you have already seen, there are many verses that contradict other verses. That is the point, if two verses tell a different story, which one is correct. More importantly, when only one author tells a story, is it really accurate?

In the Mountain of Transfiguration story, only Peter, James and John are there. This is one of the most supernatural events credited to Jesus while He is on earth, and yet, John does not feel that it is important enough to mention it. This is where, once again, God speaks from heaven.

Why would John who was supposedly there, not write of it, while the three other gospel authors, who were not there, wrote of it? I can't fathom it, and yet, it is written. This is the story used to "prove" who the two prophets are in the last days, found in the Book of Revelation. But, did the

The New Testament, the Facts and the Fiction

stories of this chapter really happen? If they did, why doesn't John tell us? With no more discussion, lets read the passages.

Matthew Chapter 14, verse 34 through Chapter 17, verse 13, begins with Jesus and Peter entering the boat and they that are in the boat worship Jesus. When they landed at the land of the Gennesaret, they were met by many that wanted to be healed. While there, they were met by those that questioned why Jesus' disciples did not wash their hands before they ate, as it was a tradition of the elders.

Jesus asked why they concerned themselves about the traditions of the elders, when they were knowingly braking the commandments of God, citing honoring their mother and father. In His rebuttal He shows that they are hypocrites in that they follow visible actions, but are far from God in their hearts.

Jesus explained to the multitude, that was gathered, that what goes into a man's mouth is not what defiles him, it is what comes out of his heart, to include evil thoughts, murder, adulteries, fornications, thefts, false witness, and blasphemies. He concludes that "These are the things which defile a man: but to eat with unwashed hands defile not a man."

He then departs to the coasts of Sidon and Tyre and is met by a Canaanite woman who has a daughter vexed with a devil. When Jesus resists curing her daughter by saying "It is not meet to take the children's bread and cast it to the dogs." She agrees, but then say's "yet the dogs eat the crumbs that fall from the masters' table." Jesus is so taken by her faith that he heals her child.

He then travels to the Sea of Galilee and sits by a mountain to heal and teach the great multitude that followed after Him. After they glorified the God of Israel for what He was doing, Jesus had compassion on the multitude, and asked His disciples to feed them as they had been there three days.

He then fed 4000 men plus women and children with seven loaves and a few fishes after He blessed it. When they were done, they had seven baskets full of food left over. He then sent the people away and sailed to Magdala.

Chapter 16 opens with the Pharisees asking Him for a sign showing that He was from heaven, but Jesus tells them that He won't give them any sign except for that sign of the prophet Jonah. As the disciples arrive, He explains to beware of the leaven of the Pharisees. They think He is talking about the lack of bread, but He explains that He is really talking about the doctrine of the Pharisees and Sadducees.

As they arrive at the coast of Caesarea Philippi, Jesus asks who the people think that He is. Many say different things but when asked directly, Peter states that Jesus is the Christ, the Son of the Living God. Jesus blesses him and instructs His disciples that no one is to tell that He is Jesus the Christ.

This is the point in Jesus' ministry when He began to teach His disciples that He was to die at Jerusalem, but rise again on the third day. Peter begins to rebuke Jesus for these sayings and Jesus strongly rebukes Peter, calling him Satan, and instructs the others that they must not think of themselves, but do as He has asked. After all, He will come back in glory and reward every man according to his works.

Six days later we open in Chapter 17 where Jesus takes Peter, James and John to a high ountain where He is transformed before them with His face as bright as the sun and His apparel as white as white. There appears Moses and Elijah, so Peter explains that he and the others will build them three resting areas. But as he is speaking, a cloud covers them all, and a voice from heaven speaks saying: "This is my beloved Son, here ye Him."

The disciples are obviously frightened and fall to the ground. Jesus walks over to them and touches them saying, Arise, and be not afraid. When the disciples open their eyes, there is only Jesus. So they walk down the mountain and Jesus tells them to tell no one of this event until after He is risen from the dead. During the descent the disciples ask Him about the Old Testament passage about Elijah coming again before the Messiah. Jesus explains, and they understand, that Elijah did come and it was John the Baptist.

Mark Chapter 6, verse 53 through Chapter 9, verse 13 is in lock step with Matthew's account of what occurs during the same time. They are so much in time with each other that the entire areas are written verbatim. Mark starts with Jesus and Peter entering the boat and they that are in the boat worship Jesus. When they landed at the land of the Gennesaret, they were met by many that wanted to be healed.

While there, they were met by those from Jerusalem that questioned why Jesus' disciples did not wash their hands before they ate, as it was a tradition of the elders, that included washing often to include the pots, cups, and tables that they used to prepare the food.

Jesus asked why they concerned themselves about the traditions of the elders when they knowingly are braking the commandments of God in these traditions, citing honoring their mother and father as an example.

Jesus explained to His disciples that what goes into a man's mouth is not what defiles him, it is what comes out of his heart, to include evil thoughts, murder, adulteries, fornications, thefts, false witness, and blasphemies. He concludes that "All these evil things come from within, and defile a man."

He then departs to the coasts of Sidon and Tyre and is met by a Greek woman who has a daughter vexed with a devil. Jesus resists curing her daughter by saying "Let the children first be filled: for it is not meet to take the children's bread, and cast it unto the dogs." She agrees, but then says "Yes Lord: yet the dogs under the table eat the children's crumbs." Jesus is so taken by her faith that he heals her child.

At the end of Chapter 7 and beginning again in Chapter 8 Jesus is back at the Sea of Galilee, and heals a man that had a speech impediment by opening his ears and removing a string from his tongue. In those days the multitude was very great that followed after Him. Jesus had compassion on the multitude and asked His disciples to feed them as they had been there for three days. The disciples ask where they are to get enough food to feed them.

Asking what is available they brought Him seven loaves and a few fishes that he blessed and set before the people. This fed 4000 and they had seven baskets full of food left over. He then sent the people away and sailed to Dalmanutha. The Pharisees came forth asking Him for a sign showing that He was from heaven, but Jesus tells them that He won't give them any sign!

Jesus takes ship again and explains to His disciples to beware of the leaven of the Pharisees and Herod. They think He is taking about the lack of bread, but He explains by questioning them, if they remembered how He had fed the 5000 and 4000. In Mark he does not explain what the Leaven of the Pharisees means.

At Bethsaida a blind man is brought to Him, so He leads him out of town and spits in the mans eyes and asks what the man sees. The man states that men looked like trees, so He places His hands upon His eyes again and then the man saw everything clearly.

As they arrive at the coast of Caesarea Philippi, Jesus asks who the people think that He is. Many say different things but when asked directly, Peter states that Jesus is the Christ, the Son of the Living God.

This is the point in Jesus' ministry when He began to teach His disciples that He was to die at Jerusalem, but rise again on the third day. Peter begins to rebuke Jesus for saying that He will die and Jesus strongly rebukes Peter, calling him Satan.

Jesus then explains to his disciples and the people around him that they need to stop worrying about the cares of today, focus on heavenly things, and take up their cross. Jesus then warns that whoever is ashamed of Him and His words, Jesus will be ashamed of him when He comes back in glory.

Chapter 9 opens with Jesus taking Peter, James and John to a high mountain where He is transformed before them with His apparel as white as snow. There appears Moses and Elijah and the disciples are fearful. Peter explains that he and the others will build them three resting areas. A cloud covers them all and a voice from heaven speaks saying: "This is my beloved Son, here Him."

When the disciples open their eyes, there is only Jesus. So they walk down the mountain and Jesus tells them to tell no one of this event until after He is risen from the dead. During the descent the disciples ask Him about the Old Testament passage about Elijah coming again before the Messiah. Jesus explains that he has already come.

Luke Chapter 9, verse 18 through verse 36 starts immediately after the feeding of 5000. You will note that they do not get into a boat where Jesus walks on water, much less Peter having a try.

As Jesus is alone praying, He asks His disciples, "Whom say the people that I am?" Some say Moses, some say another prophet. Then Jesus asks, "But whom say ye that I am?" Peter states "The Christ of God." Jesus tells them not to tell anyone and then begins to explain that He is to be rejected, slain and then rise again on the third day. Those that follow Christ must take up their cross and follow Him without shame. If not, He will be ashamed of them when He comes in His glory.

Eight days after these sayings, Jesus takes Peter, James, and John and begins to pray on top of a mountain. Jesus' countenance changes and His raiment becomes white and glistens. Then Elijah and Moses appear and talk with Jesus about His forth coming death in Jerusalem. The disciples are tired and fall asleep, but when they awake, and they see Jesus in His glory, Peter asks if they should build three resting areas for Jesus, Moses, and Elijah. As he yet spoke, a cloud overshadows them and the disciples were filled with fear.

A voice comes out of the cloud and says: "This is My beloved Son, hear Him." When the voice was past, they were alone with Jesus, and they kept these things to themselves.

What facts and fiction were detected in these passages? One of the main reasons I wrote this book was to debunk many of the so-called liberties taken that are "located" in the New

Testament. The statement found in the Books of Matthew and Mark where Jesus met with the Pharisees about eating with unwashed hands is one quoted to help bolster the notion that Christians are not under the Levitical Food Laws. They end the story with Jesus saying that "it isn't what goes into your mouth that makes you unclean, it is what comes out," ie a cruel tongue.

This is a story about supposed unclean food being consumed by the disciples. They are being challenged by the religious leadership, and Jesus will not have any of it. But in this story, the food that is mentioned isn't about "the what" that is being consumed, it is about "the how" they are consuming it. In other words, it isn't the consumable product, it is the preparation of the consumable product, that the leadership is challenging the disciples over.

Even though it was a much larger issue that Jesus was talking about, our hearts, He also made sure that we understood that He was referring to the "how to" eat what was going into our mouths. This is easily proven by the conclusion of the conversation with His disciples in the Book of Matthew Chapter 15, verse 20: "But to eat with unwashed hands defileth not a man."

This story is quoted often to say that Jesus did not believe that what went into our mouths will defile us, it is just what comes out of our mouths that does. This is then taken out of context to state that Jesus is telling you that you can eat whatever you want as it will not defile you. But that isn't in the text. It was only about whether eating with unwashed hands will defile a person. Eating Levitically unclean foods is an abomination to God. Read it in Leviticus Chapter 11. My God is, was, and always will be. If it was an abomination, then it still is today. For that reason I can claim the promises of old, and still know that they are valid today.

Even though the authors of Matthew and Mark are in lock step during this area of their gospels, they still differ. Who was Jesus teaching when he explained what real defilement meant? In the Book of Matthew, He is teaching the entire multitude, but in the Book of Mark it was after He had left the multitude and was speaking privately with His disciples. The Books of John and Luke do not make mention of this, but the author of Luke will tell a story about Jesus' being questioned why He doesn't wash His hands before He eats in Luke Chapter 11. Of course, none of the other gospel writers write of Luke's event.

About now you have Jesus, once again, calling the scribes and Pharisees hypocrites. In Matthew Chapter 15, verse 7 you see that Jesus tells them that Isaiah prophesied of them. This is supposed to be supported by Isaiah Chapter 29, verse 13. If you read this chapter in Isaiah you will see that it is a lament over Jerusalem (Ariel) and the way that the people are feeling towards God. Although many of the words are the same, there is no reference to this event happening in a time frame when Jesus is on earth.

The conclusion of this prophesy states, beginning in Isaiah Chapter 29, verse 23, "But when he seeth his children, the work of mine hands, in the midst of him, they shall sanctify the Holy One of Jacob, and shall fear the God of Israel. They also that erred in spirit shall come to understanding, and they that murmured shall learn doctrine." Do you see any reference in the gospels where those that were murmuring against Jesus (Jewish leadership) learn the doctrine of Jesus? Since there is not, you have to agree that this is still to be done in the future, or it happened back in the time of Isaiah.

This is another reference to things stated by Jesus or were happening in His presence that is supposed to be found prophetically in the Old Testament. The link is way to weak. Go back and look at the accuracy of the author of Matthew's supposed prophetic proof texts to what he is stating. I find it hard to believe that if anyone actually read the scriptures for content that they would give this book of the Bible too much authority.

When Jesus heals the Greek Canaanite woman (in Gennesaret), the authors of Matthew, Mark and Luke all make a big deal about the fact that she was not Jewish and Jesus did not want to waste his time on non-Jews as they were "dogs" in His own words. Now this story was probably a metaphor, but Jesus has been wandering throughout non-Jewish areas throughout His ministry by now, and one of his own disciples is Simon the Canaanite (Mark 3:18).

Remember the casting out of the "Legion" of devils into the swine. Where was that done? It was Gennesaret. It was unclean to touch pigs under the Law. How could they be Jews, and yet He healed many located there in this reading alone? So According to the Books of Matthew, Mark and Luke, Jesus has already been healing in non-Jewish regions.

Besides the fact that John does not write of this account, Jesus has not only talked with Gentiles, he has stayed with them. Remember the woman at the well in John Chapter 4? That was Samaria, the lowest of all Gentiles to a Jew at that time. Jesus has conversed with Gentiles all along in John's account of Jesus Christ's ministry.

Maybe I am missing something, but either way, for those that like to read the Lord's words "in red" in their Bibles, what did He exactly say to the Canaanite woman? Although similar, all three accounts found in the books of Matthew, Mark and Luke are different. Can you really be certain of what Jesus' exact words are from anywhere in the gospels? No!

The feeding of 4000 is only found in the Books of Matthew and Mark. The author of Matthew tells you it was 4000 plus women and children, but the author of Mark only tells you it was 4000. This type of miracle is my favorite type, next to bringing back the dead. Jesus isn't just changing one thing into another, as in water into wine, He is making something from nothing. If you understand physics, this can only happen with the infusion of enormous energy.

The Jews were looking for a Messiah that would help them overthrow the Romans. What could be better than a Messiah that could make them food out of nothing when they are being besieged or at battle? What makes this more interesting is that Jesus has already done this same miracle just a couple of days before.

This is why I have a problem with the miracle of the feeding of 4000. Why would the disciples in the Books of Matthew and Mark forget what Jesus had just done only a few days before and now seem to question how a problem like this can be solved? They question where they are going to get the food to feed this multitude. I'm not all that bright, but if I had seen it done once and Jesus said we were about to do it again, I would probably say, "Let me go find some baskets!"

Read the author of Mark's account, it is like this miracle is something new. Not only doesn't John make mention of it, neither does the author of Luke, who usually makes all supernatural events in the Books of Matthew and Mark even a little more super, supernatural.

Right after the feeding of 4000, the author of Matthew tells you that they sailed to Magdala, but in the Book of Mark it affirms it is Dalmanutha. Once there, Jesus is questioned by the Pharisees for a sign. In the Book of Matthew, Jesus states that the only sign they will receive is that of Jonah, but in the Book of Mark, He states that they will not be given any sign. Which one is it? The three days and three nights in the belly of the earth, or no sign at all. Both stories can't be accurate.

But what was the sign of Jonah? Matthew Chapter 12, verse 40, states that as Jonah was in the belly of the whale for three days and three nights, so will the Son of Man be in the belly of heart of the earth. This is critical when you look at the resurrection. How can Jesus be in the heart of the earth for three days and three nights if He is crucified on a Friday and risen on a Sunday. It can't be done. This is just a Christian myth that I will debunk and you will understand when we cover it later in this book. So, what you learn is that according to the author of Matthew, Jesus is to be in the grave for three days and three nights. We will look at this very closely in the chapter that covers the resurrection.

In the Book of Mark you see a story of Jesus entering Bethsaida where a blind man is brought to Him. Jesus walks outside town with him and spits in his eyes, but the man isn't healed the first time. It takes a second try for Jesus to heal this man. This is critical. Up until now, all Jesus had to do was say the word and someone was healed, BAM, first time. I have a hard time with this story, especially because it is only told here by the author of Mark, and Jesus needs a second pass at this miracle.

According to the Books of Matthew, Mark and Luke; Jesus has already brought back the dead, but right here He needs two tries to restore a man's sight. I find it impossible to believe. I have problems with all three of these gospel accounts, but this specific story is totally out of balance with the power attributed to Jesus by this point in His ministry. Is Jesus still learning how to use His powers, or why is God having trouble working through Him?

You will note that when Jesus asks who the people think that He is, the disciples understand that He is the Christ. It's very important that you realize that Jesus is supposed to be explaining who He is, and what His purpose is on earth. He has pointed it out <u>right here,</u> and at many other times in the near future, that He will die and be risen from the dead after three days. When Peter has a hard time with the concept, Jesus rebukes him and calls him Satan. Lets look at the exact words found in Matthew Chapter 16, verse 21 (also found in Mark 8:31) : "From that time forth began Jesus to shew unto His disciples, how that He must go into Jerusalem, and suffer many things of the elders and chief priests and scribes, and be killed, and be raised again the third day."

Do you think that the disciples would remember this incident? You will see this education again at the return from the Mountain of Transfiguration, in just a couple of days. The disciples, in the Books of Matthew, Mark and Luke's account, have been told and will be retold over and over of the coming events of His death and resurrection, and yet, they supposedly haven't got a clue when it happens. In contrast, the Book of John does not have any of this type of "education" for the disciples.

Remember that you will only see discussions like this in the Books of Matthew, Mark, and Luke. If these are fact, why would the disciples have such a hard time when Jesus is taken, slain and then resurrected? Where is their belief later, especially because He is foretelling of it here! After all, He has brought back the dead, made something from nothing, cast out devils, and will shortly appear with Moses and Elijah talking about His crucifixion.

If you look at their unbelief and fear they will have in the garden, it really gets worse. Jesus has told them plainly here what will happen. According to these three authors, each of these disciples has been given the power over spirits, can heal the sick, and have been told that they should fear no harm to themselves. One of these authors will tell you that James and John believe that they have the power to call down heavenly fire. If all this is true, why would they fear a mere mob? Why use a sword when you can call down fire? Even as a young boy I never understood it.

Another discussion or teaching point that you would have read by all three authors during this chapter is the saying by Jesus that goes something like this: "If any man will come after me, let him deny himself, and take up his cross daily, and follow me." To anyone that understands the crucifixion story, it is obvious what Jesus is talking about.

But the story is only told by these three authors and once again the story seems strange if you think about it. What would it mean at that time in His ministry for a person to take up their cross and follow Him? Who would have understood the significance of taking up the cross? He had not drug the cross from the trial to Golgotha yet. Why would you remember that statement? This again shows that it was probably a saying that was used after His death and then inserted into the story that was told and retold before it was written down.

Very few times will you see a timing between events shown in the Books of Matthew, Mark, and Luke, but for some reason they all three show the days after the "identifying that Jesus is the Christ" and the Mountain of Transfiguration event. Only, the authors of Matthew and Mark tell you it is six days later and Luke tells you it is eight days later. As they are very specific, it does bring to question, was it six or eight days? This is only a big deal if you try to say that the Bible is the inerrant word of God.

The event at the Mountain of Transfiguration is different in all three accounts. Read them again. The author of the Book of Luke has the most in-depth account and tells you that the disciples go to sleep during the event. He also tells you that Moses and Elijah are discussing the crucifixion with Jesus. This is another rub that ties in with Jesus telling His disciples that He is going to be slain and resurrected.

Think of the magnitude if you were present. Jesus, just six or eight days (depending on what book you reference) before, had called Peter, Satan, because he would not accept that Jesus was on a mission. Now, supposedly Peter, James, and John are witnesses to Elijah and Moses talking about the planning of the event. The rub is: if these accounts are fact, why would they have such a problem accepting that He was risen on the third day? Who would go to sleep during this?

At the close of this reading you have Jesus, Peter, James and John descending from the Mountain of Transfiguration. They have a discussion that is recorded in the Books of Matthew and Mark. The disciples are asking Jesus why Elijah has not come back yet, as it is foretold by the prophets. Jesus tells them that if they believe, they would understand that it was John the Baptist. Have you ever looked at the reference to this story?

It is found in the last chapter of the Old Testament, Malachi Chapter 4. Read the Book of Malachi. It will take you less than 5 minutes. It is all about end times prophesy, and the authors of Matthew and Mark believed that they were obviously in the end times. Were they? That was about 2000 years ago. If you read Malachi, Elijah does come, but it is in the Day of the Lord. Read what is happening when Elijah will appear.

According to Malachi, God will be burning the proud in an oven and the righteous people of the earth will be trampling down the wicked. Was that happening when John the Baptist was on the earth? Has that happened yet? Since the answer is obviously no, then Elijah has not yet returned and John the Baptist was not Elijah! But say that this is a true reference to John the Baptist. If it is, it flies in the face of John Chapter 1, verses 20 and 21, where John the Baptist himself declares that he is not the Christ, Elijah, or that prophet.

Now that we have hit the major points of this story, please note that John has not and will not mention any of these events. If you note in the feeding of 4000 it is an almost mirrored event to the feeding of 5000. Why I draw your attention to this, is that a short time later in the Book of Luke you will have a sending forth of 70 disciples two by two with a mirrored wording to the sending forth of the 12 disciples two by two. The Book of Luke is the only gospel story to tell you of the sending forth of the 70.

What I am getting to is John tells of supernatural events. The other three gospel authors write of even more supernatural events and then the author of Luke adds to it even greater. Why is it that John, who was there, never makes mention of these duplicate events, let alone the original supernatural event?

Remember to focus on what you should be trying to learn. Are the gospels really gospel? What I mean by this is, is each and every word in them correct? And, as you study, if they aren't, can you discern the error so that you are not led away by false Christian doctrine based on the incorrect passages that are present?

Look, we are only about half way through the gospels by now. It is obvious that they all tell the story of Jesus Christ while He is on earth, but can you say that these books are exact? Just the comparison between the Books of Matthew, Mark and Luke have shown you that the specific facts they present are different. These last chapters so far have shown hundreds of discrepancies between their stories.

This doesn't even bring John's Epistle into account. The authors of Matthew, Mark and Luke tell one story and John tells a different one that is pretty much a totally different story. Please recall back from this point, or just turn the pages in your Bible and read the headings of what is transpiring in each book. How many events actually overlap exactly by this point. Only in the actual event of the feeding of 5000 do all four accounts read the same. But not what happens directly before and what happens directly after each either, just the feeding of 5000.

There are major discrepancies between John and the other three gospels on the events that they three all agree happened. Go back and read them again. Take the baptism. Did a voice from heaven speak? If it did, why didn't John write it down? Why does John make note that the dove was the sign to look for. If the dove was the sign, why have a voice? If there was a voice, as the other three like to profess, why is the wording different in all three accounts? Why wouldn't John the Baptist "know" that Jesus was the Christ? Why does he have to send his disciples to ask Jesus if He is the Christ? But the Apostle John does not make mention of the voice or the concern from John the Baptist in the Book of John.

This is the problem with how Christians have been taught to read and understand their Bibles. Is the Bible the "word" of God? Is it inerrant? The answer is no to both questions. God's "word" can be found in the Bible, but the Bible is not entirely the word of God. And, if you haven't learned that it is not without error by now, you just plainly don't want to know. You prefer to live your life with your head in the sand. Do you think that ignorance will be a good excuse to God when you are asked why you took the traditions of men over the commandments of God?

Just take the gospels for what they are. Four accounts of the life of Jesus that may or may not be true. Many parts of the accounts are true, but it appears that many things were exaggerated over the years before they were written down. Let's just reflect back on the death of John the Baptist. Only the Books of Matthew and Mark write of the death in specifics.

Is there any chance that either of the authors of Matthew and Mark were at Herod's great dinner that supposedly happened? No, of course not. To know what happened at this dinner, the authors would have either received a vision, been told by someone they trusted, or presumed what might have happened. Did Herodias' daughter know before she danced that she wanted John the Baptist's head in a charger? Both accounts differ. Would God give two different visions to two different "Spirit-filled men?"

Although a small detail, but a detail just the same, where did the request for John the Baptist's head in a charger originate and when? In the Book of Matthew, Herodias' daughter requests the head of John the Baptist when Herod asks what she wants, as she had already been told to ask for it by her mother. But, In the Book of Mark, when Herod asks Herodias' daughter what she wants, she runs to ask her mother what to ask for. The stories are similar, as Herodias' daughter dances for Herod and he offers her whatever she wants. The outcome is still the same, but was the request prearranged as in the Book of Matthew, or was it spontaneous as in the Book of Mark?

Why this little detail is so important is that the only way that a follower of Jesus could know what was happening in Herod's castle during a party, was for it to be either a vision from God, or as Moses has told you, presumed! At least one account is presumed if both are said to be accurate.

This is the problem with trying to rationalize that the gospels are the "word" of God. God can't give different messages. If it is from God, it would have to be in a vision. To believe they are both telling their gospels from vision, would also force you to believe that your salvation can be in question. Why? If they are both in vision they have both received a different message from God. If so, God can change the "message" of what are the requirements for salvation from time to time or author to author.

But, as you know, this isn't the first time all four gospel writers have told different facts to events that they were not present to witness. In fact, I would hazard to say that you have already witnessed over 400 different inconsistent supposed facts by now.

Why I keep pounding this home, is to show that if there is error in just the tiniest area, it brings into question the "infallibility" of the entire message by the author. This is critical as so many Christian doctrines are based on a chosen verse here and a verse there from what they want to call the "inerrant word" of God. After all, they teach that the entire Bible is totally correct and there to live your life by. If it is so correct and inerrant, why are there so many errors? I know of a real Biblical "authority" in Post Falls, Idaho, that tries to explain that it was 100% correct in the original letters. But over the years it has become polluted.

What proof does he have of that? Let's say that his idea is correct. Does it make the gospels any more accurate today if that was the case? No, they are still inaccurate and hence, we need to stop building doctrine on lines that are out of bounds to what we know to be true scripture. Go read II Timothy Chapter 3, verses 15-18 again. Paul is telling you that the Old Testament is there to live your life by, not the New Testament.

If the New Testament agrees with, and is asking for behaviors that are consistent with the Old Testament, then so be it. But if you come to a passage that differs to what we know to be true in the Old Testament, you have to ask yourself: why? Not only why, but how can God change?

These errors are not throughout the entire New Testament, just the history books. There are errors found in other books, but they are usually mistranslations or out-of-context verse pickings! It is the gospels that are riddled with errors, as you should have learned by now. It is important to understand this to know that you cannot just accept verses from the gospels as messages to you from God!

Remember it isn't an all or nothing single book, it was a compilation of separate books accomplished by the Roman Catholic Church. They were supposedly trying to put together the true letters from the early church with the Old Testament. This was to be an all inclusive message system from God. Maybe they had Godly reasons for this task and maybe they didn't. We will never know, but what you should know by now, is that the Bible that you hold in your hands today has passages located in the gospels that can't pass the discernment test. One or more of these authors has a credibility issue if he was professing this to be from God.

Triumphal Entry

After this chapter, we have all four gospel authors writing about similar events. So the differences in the stories will be obvious. This is where we will see John writing in great detail and hence, we will cover a lot more from John in those closing chapters. As John will only have one thing in common in this time period with the other gospel authors, the actual triumphal entry, we will bring John forward to this time in the next chapter.

That chapter will be followed by *The Stories of Luke*. During this present chapter, the Book of Luke will cover 10 Chapters of information. To keep from loosing the comparisons between the books, just from the shear volume from the author of the Book of Luke, the stories only told by him will be told separately from this chapter. Some of the information that the author of Luke talks about, will be covered by the other gospel writers and will be contrasted in this chapter. But the Book of Luke has a lot more stories during this time frame than any other. Most of these are not told anywhere else, and some contradict what we know to be true about God.

Matthew Chapter 17, verse 14 through Chapter 21 verse 11 starts with Jesus descending from the Mountain of Transfiguration with Peter, James and John, (who doesn't record it), and they see a crowd around Jesus' disciples. A man comes to Jesus asking for help with his lunatic son that has a devil causing this problem. The man explains that Jesus' disciples tried to cast out the devil, but couldn't. Jesus answers, that they are a faithless and perverse generation and then proceeds to cast out the devil. When His disciples come to Him to ask why they could not cast out the devil, He explains that is was from their unbelief.

Once again, while they are at Galilee, Jesus explains that He will be betrayed, killed, and then rise again on the third day; making the disciples very sorry. As they arrive at Capernaum, Peter is asked if Jesus paid tribute (taxes). To this, Jesus asks Peter to cast a line and hook, and look into the first fish's mouth that he brings in. There is a coin in the mouth and Peter pays the tribute for Jesus and himself.

At this same time, in the beginning of Chapter 18, the disciples ask Jesus who will be greatest in the kingdom of heaven. Jesus explains that we have to humble ourselves to a level bestowed to children, and this person will be greatest. Then He states that if you received a child in His name, you have received Him.

Jesus then starts to explain of things that are offenses. He explains that it would be better to have cut off your own hand, or pluck out your own eye, and enter into life halt or maimed than to be cast into everlasting fire. Next, He explains not to despise children. For the son of Man is come to save that which is lost. This is followed by the lost sheep parable, where the shepherd will leave the 99 sheep and go searching for the one that is lost. He will rejoice over the one when he finds it more than the 99 that are not lost. This parable is meant to explain that the Father in Heaven does not want to loose even one little child.

Directly following, He explained that if your brother trespass against you, to first tell him about the offense and try to get him to see his error. If that doesn't work, bring witnesses to help, and eventually the entire church to witness against him. If he neglects to hear them, cast him out of the church.

Jesus expounds that where two or more come together to ask for anything in His name from the Father, it will be given you. And, "Where two or three are gathered together in My name, there am I in the midst of thee." Peter comes and asks how often should he forgive his brother, if asked? Jesus answers that it should be much more often than Peter expected.

To this Jesus tells a parable likening the Kingdom of Heaven to a certain king that took account of his servants accounts. One was brought to him that owed a great deal, but the king forgave him. Later, the same servant found a servant that owed him a very little amount, who was not able to pay it. So the first servant threw the second servant into jail. When the king was told what the servant, that he forgave, did to the servant that owed so little, he delivered the first servant to the tormentors.

After this, Jesus leaves Galilee for the coasts of Judea with a large multitude following Him, in Chapter 19. Once there, the Pharisees test Him by asking if a man can divorce his wife for any reason? After all, Moses told the people of Israel that a man could do this, if he first gave her a letter of divorcement. Jesus responds by telling them that the Father, from the very beginning made woman for the man, and that when you are wed, it is a contract between the man and woman, before God. "What therefore God hath joined together, let no man put asunder."

When pushed, Jesus further explains that Moses allowed the letter of divorcement because of the hardness of their hearts, but make no mistake, unless she is guilty of fornication or adultery, if you put her away and have a new wife, you are committing adultery. Then He says to His disciples that it might be better just not to marry.

When little children are brought to Him the disciples try to shoo them away, but Jesus rebukes them, and puts His hands on the children's heads and then departs.

A rich young man comes to Jesus to ask what he must do to have eternal life. When Jesus tells Him to keep the commandments that show love to man, the young man explains that he has done this since he was a child. Then Jesus tells him that there is one more thing he must do. Sell all that he has and follow Him. The young man is sorrowful as he is very rich.

Jesus explains to His disciples that it will be difficult for any rich person to enter into the kingdom of heaven. The disciples exclaim, "Who then can be saved?" Jesus replied, that with men it is impossible, but with God all things are possible. Peter states that the disciples had left everything and followed Him and wants to know if that is enough. Jesus explains that those that have left all to follow Him will receive these, and more, to include everlasting life.

Jesus further explains this by telling the parable of the man that wanted to hire those to work in his vineyard, starting in Chapter 20. The man hires laborers in the morning and agrees to pay them a penny for the entire day. Later in the day he finds more men that want work. Near the end of the day he finds even more laborers and sends them into the field.

At the end of the day, the owner begins by paying those that began last, a penny for their efforts. He finally pays those that started in the morning with a penny also, and they begin murmuring. The owner asks the morning hires if he had indeed paid them what they had agreed. Then he asks, isn't it his prerogative to pay those at the end of the day the wage that he felt appropriate, as it was his money to spend? "So the last will be first and the first will be last: for many will be called and few will be chosen."

As they are going to Jerusalem, Jesus takes His disciples apart from those following and explains an even more detailed explanation of the coming trial, crucifixion and resurrection. Then comes James and John's mother to ask Jesus if her sons can sit, one on His right and one on His left in His kingdom. Jesus explains that they do not know what they are requesting and that it is not for Jesus to give this position, it is the Father's.

When the other disciples hear of the request, they are filled with indignation. Jesus then has to explain that they have to get over the "position" concern between themselves. This attitude should be left for the Gentiles. If you want to be great in the Kingdom of God, you have to be a minister (servant) to others. Jesus' example should be an example to them as He came to be a minister, and to give His life as a ransom for many.

Two blind men hear that Jesus is walking by and they call "Have mercy on us, Oh Lord, son of David." Jesus asks them, what do they want from Me? They ask for their sight and Jesus obliges by touching their eyes and they can immediately see.

In Chapter 21, as they drew near to Jerusalem at the Mount of Olives, Jesus sends two disciples to get an ass and her colt from a certain village. They find them as Jesus had stated and bring them back to Him, where they put their clothes on them and set Jesus upon them. A very great multitude go before Jesus leaving garments, straw and leaves before Him as they go saying, "Hosanna in the Highest." The city asks, who is this? In response, the multitude explains: "This is Jesus, the prophet of Nazareth of Galilee."

Mark Chapter 9, verse 14 through Chapter 11, verse 10 Jesus has just come down from the Mountain of Transfiguration when He sees a multitude around His disciples, and He asks: "What question ye with them?" A man steps out of the crowd and states that he has brought his son who has a dumb spirit, but His disciples cannot cast him out. Jesus states that they are a faithless generation. Then He tells the father that if he can believe, all things are possible. The man explains to Him, help me with my unbelief. With this Jesus casts out the spirit, and the child is left lifeless, until Jesus takes the child by the hand.

When they went inside, the disciples asked why they could not cast out the spirit. Jesus explains that this kind of spirit can come forth by nothing but by prayer and fasting.

As He leaves there, on their way through Galilee, Jesus explains that He will be delivered into man's hands to be killed, but will rise on the third day. But, for some reason the disciples don't understand what He is talking about.

When they enter Capernaum, He asks His disciples what they were arguing about on the way there. It was about who would be the greatest among them. Jesus explains that the greatest will be the lesser and the lesser will be the greater. So He takes a child in His arms and explains that whosoever will receive a child in His name, receives Him, and if you receive Jesus, you receive the Father.

John then explains that they saw someone casting out spirits in Jesus' name and they forbid the person to do so. After all, he was not one of them. Jesus told them to "forbid him not," because if someone does a miracle in Jesus' name, that person could not speak evil of Jesus.

Then Jesus explains that when someone gives a drink in His name they will be rewarded, and if you offend a child that believes in Him, they will be badly punished. If your hand, foot or eye offends thee, cut it off. It would be better to have less body parts than to go to hell, where the worm never dies and the fire will never go out.

As He departs for Judea, in Chapter 10, the people follow Him, and He teaches them. The Pharisees ask Him if it is OK for a man to divorce his wife for any reason? After all Moses told the people of Israel that a man could, if he gave her a bill of divorcement. Jesus responds by telling them that the Father, from the very beginning made woman for the man and that when you are wed, it is a contract between the man and woman, before God. "What therefore God hath joined together, let no man put asunder."

Once inside, the disciples ask about divorcement. Jesus explains that unless she is guilty of fornication or adultery, if you put her away and have a new wife, you are committing adultery. Likewise for her.

When little children are brought to Him, the disciples try to shoo them away, but Jesus rebukes them, and put His hands on the children's heads to bless them and then departs.

A rich young man comes to Jesus to ask what he must do to have eternal life. When Jesus tells Him to keep the commandments that show love to man, the young man explains that he has done this since he was a child. Then Jesus tells him that there is one more thing he must do. Sell all that you have and give it to the poor and you will have treasure in heaven, and come follow Me. The young man is sad as he is very rich.

Jesus explains to His disciples that it will be difficult for any rich person to enter into the Kingdom of Heaven. The disciples exclaim, "Who then can be saved?" Jesus replied, that with men it is impossible, but with God all things are possible. Peter states that the disciples had left everything and followed Him, and wants to know if that is enough. Jesus explains that those that have left all to follow Him will receive these, and more, to include everlasting life.

As they were going up to Jerusalem, the disciples were afraid. Jesus takes His 12 aside and explains that when they are in Jerusalem that the chief priests and scribes would take Him, and spit on Him, and mock Him, and crucify Him, and in three days He would rise again.

James and John come to Him and ask if they can sit on His left and right in His glory. He explains that it is not for Him to give, but it is for whom it is prepared. When the others find out, they were very displeased. Jesus explains that they are not to be like the Gentiles that rule over others. To whom will be great, needs to be as a servant to others, and whosoever will be chiefest, will be servant to all, just as Jesus had come to give His life as a ransom for many.

As they left Jericho on the way up to Jerusalem, a blind man yelled out for Jesus to have mercy on him. Jesus asked what he wanted from Him. The man asked for his sight, Jesus stated "go thy way, thy faith have made thee whole." And immediately the man received his sight.

In Chapter 11, as they drew near to Jerusalem at the Mount of Olives, Jesus sends two disciples to go get a colt from a certain village. They find it as Jesus had stated and bring it back to Him, where they put their clothes on the colt and set Jesus upon it. A very great multitude go before Jesus leaving garments, straw and branches of leaves before Him. As they go before Him they say, "Hosanna; Blessed is he that cometh in the name of the Lord: Blessed be the kingdom of our father David, that cometh in the name of the Lord: Hosanna in the Highest." The city asks, who is this? In response, the multitude explains: "This is Jesus, the prophet of Nazareth of Galilee."

Luke Chapter 9, Verse 37 through Chapter 19, verse 40, after Jesus, Peter, James, and John come down from the Mountain of Transfiguration, they see a multitude and a man comes out from them to ask Jesus to cast out a spirit that His disciples could not. Jesus does cast out the spirit and the people are amazed. While the people were still wondering at this, Jesus explains to His disciples: "Let this sink down into your ears: for the son of Man shall be delivered into the hands of men."

The disciples have a concern as to who will be the greatest. Jesus explains that if we receive the least among us, we will be receiving Him, and he that is least will be the greatest. Then John explained that someone was casting out devils in Jesus' name, but John forbade him. Jesus explained that he should not forbid the practice, because if he is with us, then he is not against us.

Chapter 11 opens with Jesus praying, and when He was done, a follower asks Jesus if He will teach them how to pray. Jesus then teaches the Lord's Prayer. This is followed by a story of a man that asks a neighbor for bread discussed in the *Stories of Luke*. The author of Luke then explains that what we need, we only have to ask of it from God. He finishes this thought with a quote from Jesus that goes something like this: "If a son asks for bread or a fish, will the father give him a stone or a serpent (paraphrased)?" Jesus is trying to explain that if an earthly father knows how to give good gifts, then it is obvious that your Heavenly Father can give better ones.

As Jesus is casting out a devil, onlookers state that He is casting out devils through Beelzebub, the chief of devils. Jesus explains that He can't be casting out devils if He is receiving His power from Beelzebub. "A house divided against itself falleth." So the people want to see a sign. Jesus explains: "But if I with the finger of God cast out devils, no doubt the Kingdom of God is come upon you."

Jesus teaches that a stronger man can come into a strong man's house and take all that he has, discussed in the *Stories of Luke*, and then explains that when an unclean spirit leaves a man it may wander for a while looking for a place to stay. But after a while, he will take a few other unclean spirits and rest back in his original place. This leaves the man that originally had only one unclean spirit resting within him, worse off than before.

As Jesus was yet telling the story, a woman stood up to say: "Blessed is the womb that bare thee, and the paps which thou hast sucked." Jesus states to this that we are even more blessed when we hear the word of God and keep it. And then He explained that this is an evil generation, and that there will only be the sign of Jonah given to them. For they have received a better sign than was shown to the Queen of the South (Sheba) or the Men of Nineveh, as a greater prophet than they saw, is here with them right now.

And as He was talking, a Pharisee asks Him to dine with Him. At dinner the Pharisee marvels that Jesus has not first washed His hands. Jesus then chides the Pharisee because the tradition of the day required the washing of hands and dishes even though the people were inwardly wicked. He explains that they have missed what "clean" really means. They had worried about the most miniscule requirements like tithing and forgot about honest judgment and love for God. The present generation is only worried about their positional status among men, not true cleanliness before God.

One in the group explains that His rant sounds like it would also include the lawyers, which the man was one of. Jesus then begins to upbraid the lawyers also, by saying "for ye lade men with grievous burdens that ye yourselves would not bare, and that the blood of the prophets are upon you (paraphrased)." Woe to the lawyers for ye have removed the key of knowledge and hinder those that desire it. Needless to say, the Pharisees and scribes are upset.

Shortly after, there is a crowd that gathers at the beginning of Chapter 12, and Jesus begins to teach them to beware of the teaching of the Pharisees, which is hypocrisy. "For there is nothing hid or covered that won't be revealed." Every secret will be revealed. Don't be afraid of those that can kill you in this life, fear the One that can send you to hell. Are not sparrows sold for almost nothing? Yet they're not forgotten by God. Even your hairs of your head are numbered. Also, He taught that who ever will confess Him before man, He will confess before God and His angels, but if you deny Him, He will deny you. You may speak evil of Me, and that may be forgiven, but if you deny the Holy Ghost, this will not be forgiven you!

A man asks Jesus to have his brother divide the family inheritance. Jesus teaches the parable of the rich fool, and then the philosophy of giving every earthly possession away as God will always provide. He then delivers the parable about the servants that are ready to receive their master when he returns from his wedding. These are discussed in the *Stories of Luke*.

Chapter 13 starts with a couple of stories told only by the author of Luke, and hence are not discussed here, but one has Jesus explaining that He should be able to heal on the Sabbath as it is only loosing the infirmary of a child of Abraham. After all, they loose their ox and ass to give them water on the Sabbath. This story then leads into a further explanation of what the Kingdom of Heaven is like. It is like a grain of mustard seed, or like leaven, which a woman took and hid in three measures of meal. These both grew in size.

Then one comes and asks Him how many will be saved. Jesus explains that we should strive to enter at the Strait gate, because many will try to enter in, but will be turned away. He then tells of those that knock and call Him Lord, Lord, saying that they have eaten and drunk with Him, but He will call them workers of iniquity, closing that there will be weeping and gnashing of teeth. But many from the four corners will arrive and be accepted.

On that same day, the Pharisees warn Him that Herod wants to kill Him and He tells them to explain to Herod that He is casting out devils and doing cures today and tomorrow, but the third day He shall be perfected. Then He starts a lament over Jerusalem: "...how often I would have gathered my children together, as a hen doth gather her brood under her wing..."

Many more events happen that are covered in the *Stories of Luke,* and then, in Chapter 15, Jesus is with a crowd when some Pharisees start murmuring that Jesus is receiving and eating with sinners. So He tells them a parable about a shepherd that leaves a flock of 99 sheep to look for one that is lost. When he finds the lost sheep he rejoices more over the one that he found, than the 99 that had not left.

Jesus explains that this parable tells of the joy that is felt in heaven when one sinner repents. This is emphasized by the story of the prodigal son, the unjust steward, the rich man and Lazarus, and others. But these will be discussed in the *Stories of Luke*.

Someone brought to Jesus infants, hoping that He would touch them, but the disciples rebuked them. Jesus corrects the disciples and explains that they should be allowed to see Him and then explains that whoever will not receive the Kingdom of God as a little child, will not enter. Then a young man asks what he must do to inherit eternal life. Jesus explains that he must follow the commandments showing love to man. The man explains that he had done so since he was a boy. Then Jesus remarks that he must do one more thing, sell all that he has and give it to the poor. With this the man was sorrowful and walked away.

Peter is concerned and asks if they, the disciples, had left all to follow Him, was that enough? Jesus explains that those that had left all, will be be given more in this life in addition to eternal life.

Then Jesus takes the 12 aside and explains that they are going up to Jerusalem where all things that are spoken of by the Old Testament will be accomplished. This includes delivering Himself to the Gentiles, where He will be mocked, spit upon, scourged, put to death, but then rise again in three days. The disciples don't understand what He is talking about.

As they come close to Jerusalem a blind beggar cries "Son of David, have mercy on me." Jesus asks him: "what wilt thou that I should do for thee?" He asks for his sight, which Jesus grants by saying: "thy faith hath saved thee," and immediately he receives his sight.

At the beginning of Chapter 19, the author of Luke tells us that while Jesus was in Jericho He stayed and dined with a man named Zacchaeus. As they get closer to Jerusalem, Jesus tells the parable about the ruler that gave ten pounds, five pounds and one pound to three different servants. But as these stories are not told in the Books of Matthew, Mark, or John, they can be found in the *Stories of Luke*.

Now as He came close to Bethphage at the Mount of Olives, Jesus sent two disciples to a town to retrieve a certain colt. When they are questioned by the owner, they tell him that the Lord hath need of him. They cast their garments upon the colt and set Jesus upon the colt and spread their clothes in front of Him as He rode into Jerusalem. The crowd that accompanies Jesus begin to praise God for the mighty works that they have witnessed saying "Blessed be the King that cometh in the name of the Lord: peace in heaven, and glory in the highest."

As He rode in, the Pharisees ask Him to quiet the following, but Jesus proclaimed: "I tell you that, if these should hold their peace, the stones would immediately cry out."

What have we learned in this chapter? As you will see, there is only one event that is common between the story that the Apostle John will tell and the one that these three gospel authors have shared during this time period. It is at the conclusion of our reading, the triumphal entry, but even this account is different.

Let's not forget that the Book of Luke affirms that a whole lot more has happened. According to that gospel, Jesus has told many of the stories and parables during this time frame that are only told by the author of Luke. For that reason, these stories will be told in a couple of chapters from now, in a chapter called *The Stories of Luke*. Including them here would have made this chapter way too long.

Please note as you proceed through the "education" that you will learn from this chapter, how often the author of Luke is at odds with the other gospels in his account of this time period during the ministry of Jesus Christ. This is important as you have to ask yourself, "Did the author of Luke provide an accurate account when he was reporting on the same event as found in the Book of Matthew?" If you conclude that there is a reason to be concerned, then you have to ask yourself, "Was he accurate on the events that only he, a non-eye witness, reports on?"

Don't loose sight of the fact that if any of these three authors were not there, then where did they get these accounts? If you conclude that the Book of Matthew was indeed written by the Apostle Matthew, and he is in conflict with the stories of the author of Luke, was the author of Luke in vision to obtain these stories? Moses has already answered this question for you. Go back and read Deuteronomy Chapter 18, verses 21 and 22.

But let's go back to the beginning. The authors of Matthew, Mark and Luke have told the story of the Mountain of Transfiguration, where John was there according to all three of these authors, but found no significance in the story (maybe I used a little sarcasm). Hence, John did not write it down. Then Jesus, Peter, James and John are coming down off the mountain and they see a crowd that has gathered with Jesus' remaining disciples.

There is a man that has a son, that has an evil spirit in him, that the disciples cannot cast out. Jesus takes over, and casts out the spirit. Have you ever thought whether this story could be true, since Jesus has already given to His disciples power over spirits. If He gave them the power over spirits, as attested to by only these three authors, then this is the second time when the power given to them has failed them. First, there is the "fear" when Jesus was walking on water. They think Jesus is a spirit, and they fear! Why would you fear if you have power over spirits? Now they don't have the right type of power to cast out this spirit in the boy.

The author of Luke does not explain why the disciples cannot cast out the devil, but in the Books of Matthew and Mark it is explained that they cannot cast out this devil because they have "unbelief." After explaining what faith can do, Jesus states: "this kind goeth not out but by prayer and fasting."

Is the power supposedly given earlier to the disciples "their supernatural power," or Jesus' power that He gave them, or power from God the Father? Do you think that their power came on slowly as they were learning how to use it? Was it like witchcraft on television, where the young witch or warlock learns the magic spells? Give me a break.

If God has given you any gift, it is complete. This is why you need a good understanding of the Old Testament before you can understand or discern the New Testament. Do you see any Old Testament prophet needing two tries at a miracle? So, aren't Jesus Christ's powers at least as good as an Old Testament Prophet's?

Triumphal Entry

This is truly key to understanding if John's account is the true gospel, or if these three authors are the true witness. Jesus attests over and over that He is from the Father. He will state: "don't believe me, believe the works from my Father!" The power to cast out spirits and heal sickness comes from the Father! If the disciples had power over spirits, "poof" the spirit would be gone!

This is almost as bad as the healing of the blind man a couple of chapters back, where Jesus had to try twice to get it right. Remember the story found in Mark Chapter 8, verses 22 through 26? On Jesus' first attempt to heal him, the man-healed sees men walking "as trees." On the second attempt, Jesus finally heals Him.

These three events limit the power of the Father. Do you think the Father is just like a human-being that has special powers? No, He is in control of all energy. All things are Him, and in Him. This is why I have fundamental problems with the stories told by the authors of Matthew, Mark and Luke. They do not line up with the God of the Old Testament. It is stories like these that show that, if you believe them, you believe in limiting the power of God.

After this, the authors of Matthew and Mark tell you of Jesus, once again, telling His disciples about His coming crucifixion and resurrection. This is a theme. In Matthew the disciples are "sorry" about the coming event. In Mark they don't understand what He is talking about. This story is told in Luke, but it is part of the healing of the child as they come off the Mountain of Transfiguration, but in Luke's account, they don't understand. This story, or thread, about how Jesus is constantly telling His disciples of the coming events are crucial. In Matthew, Mark and Luke's gospel, the disciples are all aware of the foretelling of the event, but in John's account, they don't have a clue until the night that it happens!

When the disciples were instructed who would be the greatest at Capernaum, did Jesus bring up the question, or did the disciples bring the question to Jesus for explanation? It's different in all three accounts. What is important, is that it is almost exact verbiage in all three questions and the answers given by Jesus. But you don't see this question posed here in Luke. In Luke, you have this question posed at the Last Supper. What's worse, is that if they had this discussion on the way to Jerusalem as in the Books of Matthew and Mark, do you think that they would bring it up again during the Last Supper only a few days later? Someone has written presumptuously according to Moses!

At the beginning of Chapter 18 in the Book of Matthew, it does appear to be a little bit of a confusing message. It started with who would be the greatest of the disciples, then it transitions into being like a "child," followed by "Woe unto the world for offenses," to take heed not to despise children, finishing with the Son of man came to save the lost. If you read the chapter through you will have to agree that it appears to be a bunch of thoughts that really have no cohesion of thought. It is followed by the parable of the lost sheep, where the shepherd leaves the 99 to find the one lost sheep.

This parable is told in the same general time frame by the author of Luke in Chapter 15, but according to Luke, Jesus told it when some Pharisees are murmuring about the fact that Jesus is receiving and eating with sinners.

In Luke Chapter 11 we see Jesus asked by one of His disciple to show them how to pray. We call this the Lord's Prayer. Remember, the author of Luke affirms at the beginning of the Book of Luke that his account is all time-sequenced. Unfortunately, Matthew Chapter 6 explains that the Lord's Prayer was given at the Sermon on the Mount before Matthew was a follower of Jesus. So not only is the timing of this story wrong in one of these accounts, Matthew's account is a long address about prayer itself and the Lord's Prayer fits into the story nice and tidy. It appears that in Luke's account, it is just thrown in to make sure that the story is not forgotten.

Have you ever thought about how the Lord's Prayer is significant to you and your prayer time? Who does Jesus tell His disciples to pray to? It is to the Father. He never expresses for us to pray to Himself. That is a modern Christian thing that has no Biblical foundation.

Still in Luke Chapter 11, after the Lord's Prayer, it is followed by a set of verses that all Christians should be familiar with that states: "Ask and it will be given you; seek and ye shall find; knock and it will be opened unto you." He finishes this thought with a quote from Jesus that goes something like this: "If a son asks for bread or a fish, will his father give him a stone or a serpent (paraphrased)?" This entire teaching by Jesus can be found in Matthew Chapter 7, and it is verbatim.

So did Luke place the story at the right time during Jesus' ministry, or was it just thrown in here too, as with the Lord's Prayer? Remember, if the Apostle Matthew wrote the Book of Matthew, he should know if he was following Jesus when he stated these teachings. And, as you should know, Matthew doesn't meet the Lord until Matthew Chapter 9.

But not too long after Matthew becomes a follower of Jesus, we read Matthew telling the story of Jesus casting out a devil and the onlookers stating that He is casting out devils through Beelzebub, the chief of devils. Jesus defends Himself by saying that a house divided can't stand. This was also told in Mark Chapter 3 mirroring Matthew's account and time frames. Once again Luke has placed this story much later in time, here in Chapter 11.

This story of the author of Luke is followed by another that is also found in Matthew Chapter 12. It is the story of an unclean spirit that leaves a man and is looking for a place to stay. But after a while, he will take a few other unclean spirits and rest back in his original place. This leaves the man that originally had only one unclean spirit living within him, worse off than before. To be fair to the author of Luke, this story sounds like it is thrown into both the Books of Matthew and Luke with no reason to place the story in either epistle. But, as they are both time-sequenced, one is wrong.

What's worse, is that the author of Luke then tells the story of Jesus calling the present generation an evil generation that will not be given a sign. It is followed by the people of Nineveh and the Queen of the South to be in judgment of this generation, and it ends with a candle being the light that is not hidden, with the eye being the light of the body. These stories are a combination of stories, part found in Matthew Chapter 12, but told in a reverse order to how the author of Luke is telling them, with the final thought from Book of Luke, about the eye being the light of the body, found in Matthew Chapter 6.

Luke Chapter 11 concludes with a story where Jesus is asked to dinner by a Pharisee, where He upsets the Pharisees and Scribes over the eating with unclean hands and how the Pharisees and Scribes have led the people of God away from the truth. Once again this appears to be a combined story about the eating with unwashed hands found in Matthew Chapter 15 and Mark Chapter 7, where Jesus taught that eating with unwashed hands does not make you unclean, as uncleanness comes from within. It is combined with a story in the future found in Matthew Chapter 23 and Mark Chapter 12 where Jesus will be chiding the Pharisees for always wanting the uppermost position among men.

Opening in Luke Chapter 12 we again see a story delivered to a crowd that is a combination of stories recorded earlier in the Books of Matthew and Mark. He starts with not trusting what the Pharisees teach, followed by what is told in secret will be revealed. We should not worry about our present coming death, but the One that will send you to hell in the next. His proof to all these things being revealed, is explained by the agreed knowledge that God knows of the transaction of each sparrow, and the number of hairs on a person's head.

This story of the author of Luke can be read in Matthew Chapter 10. So, both the authors of Matthew and Luke believe that this story is true, but they disagree when it was told in the ministry of Jesus Christ, and there is another twist. The author of Matthew tells you it is two sparrows sold for a farthing and the author of Luke affirms that it is five sparrows for two farthings. This has to solidify to any reader that much of what they wrote was hearsay, that had already changed before it was written down.

But this story by the author of Luke doesn't end there. He explained that Jesus finished this one story with the fact that if you confess Him before man, He will confess you to God. You can even blaspheme Him and it will be forgiven, but, whoever blasphemes the Holy Ghost will not be forgiven. This is a story told in Matthew Chapter 12 and Mark Chapter 3.

In this story in the Books of Matthew and Mark, Jesus has just been told that He is casting out devils by the power of Beelzebub, and the glory for this miracle is not given to the Holy Ghost by those accusing Him. Jesus is rebuking them for this statement and this is why it is appropriate for the story to be told where it was in the Books of Matthew and Mark. Once again, the story is believed by the author of Luke and he doesn't want to leave it out, but appears to just throw it in somewhere, even though it has no purpose where he threw it in!

I know that I keep hammering on how the author of Luke has changed stories, or placed then in an order that is not consistent with the Books of Matthew and Mark, but then, what are we trying to understand? Do we want to lie to ourselves and say these gospels are delivering the same message, or do we want to read them critically and then discern what God wants us to take away from these writings? Why I ask, is that the Books of Matthew, Mark and Luke will continue to follow this same pattern.

In Luke Chapter 13 there are several stories that are only told by Luke, and then Luke adds to one of the teachings with what the Kingdom of God is like. It is like a mustard seed or leaven hidden in three measures of meal. These are told in Matthew Chapter 13 and Mark Chapter 4, but before the feeding of the 5000. This story in Luke includes a man that asks how many will be saved. Jesus explains that many will want to enter, even those that have eaten with Him, but they will be left outside where there is weeping and gnashing of teeth. Many other people from other parts of the world will be accepted. This story too, is told in the Book of Matthew, but it is from two different stories found in Matthew Chapters 7 and 8. Some things are a little different, but they are too similar to be the same story told at three different times.

At the close of Luke Chapter 13 there is a quote where Jesus supposedly tells some Pharisees to tell Herod that he is a "fox" and that He, Jesus, is casting out devils and curing people today, tomorrow and the third day will be perfected. It ends with a lament of Jesus over the people of Jerusalem. This whole ending to the chapter does not make sense. First, why would Jesus purposely torment Herod? I understand that the author of Luke is trying to link the three days in the tomb, but why call Herod a fox? Additionally, why add the lament over Jerusalem during this time period? The author of Matthew tells you that Jesus will use these very same words in a lament, but it is in Matthew Chapter 23, when Jesus is explaining how the people have missed the signs that they should have been looking for, and have been guided wrongly by the religious leadership of the day.

According to the authors of Mark and Luke, while at Capernaum, the Apostle John tells Jesus that they stopped someone from casting out Spirits in Jesus' name, and Jesus tells them not to do so. This brings back the whole supernatural power issue. Is the mere name of Jesus enough to allow someone, who isn't a true follower, enough power to cast out a devil or heal the sick? I know that Christians would like to believe this, but when have you ever witnessed a healing occurring in a Christian "Healing room?" These people at least believe that they are Christians. But, I have never seen anyone cured by going to one. Oh, they may say that they feel better, but is that how God works?

Do you remember when Elijah was sitting on the hill and the captain of 50 men came to bring Elijah to the king in II Kings Chapter 1? BAM they were vaporized. Then another captain with his 50 came and BAM, they were vaporized. Then a third captain with another 50 came and he asked Elijah to spare the lives of his men, and Elijah went with this captain.

That is the power of God. It is given to those that bring Glory to God, not to themselves. That is why the Book of John is so Biblical. Jesus never needs two tries at a miracle. Jesus uses the power given to Him to show the "works" given Him by God as proof that He is from God. In the Book of John, Jesus is educating His followers and none of them ever receive supernatural powers. Why would they? But here in the Book of Mark, not only did the 12 disciples receive the original power, but now a stranger can have the same power just by using Jesus' name.

I'm not saying that God can't heal, because He does. But in this story, the author of Mark is telling you that just because someone says that they are healing in the name of Jesus, the person being healed is healed. That would mean that anyone, without any connection to Jesus could cast out spirits and heal your ailments. Does this pass the discernment test? But remember that it is supposed to be the Apostle John that brings up the concern. In the Book of John, no one can cast out a Spirit. Jesus never casts out a spirit in the Book of John. There are no evil spirit possessed people in the Book of John, or anywhere else in the Bible but in the Books of Matthew, Mark, Luke and Acts!

In Matthew Chapter 18, verses 18 through 20 is a set of verses used over and over in churches. It implies that if two or more come together and pray for ANYTHING to the Father in Jesus' name, it will be given to them. It also states that Jesus is omnipresent, meaning that He can be in multiple places at one time. "Where two or three are gathered together in My name, there am I, in the midst of thee." It is a wonderful thought, but the Book of Revelation teaches that only the Father knows the future. To know the future literally means that you are outside of time, as we know it.

Jesus Himself tells you that no one knows the "end" but the Father, in the Book of Revelation. What does this have to do with Jesus being where two or three are gathered in His name? To be wherever two or three are gathered in His name would mean that whenever any Christian service is fellowshipping, Jesus is there. Think of all the times you have multiple services going on in just one town, let alone the world. The Father can be there. That is because the Father operates out of time. A being has to be able to operate outside of time to be at two places at the same time. Only the Father is omnipresent. The Book of John does not make this promise.

At the end of Matthew Chapter 19, in the middle of Mark Chapter 10, and in the middle of Luke Chapter 18 there is a question from Peter to ask if the disciples had left all things to follow Jesus, would that be enough to have everlasting life. Jesus explains what leaving all things includes in Matthew Chapter 19, verse 29. One of these things that you may have to leave is your "wife." It is located in all three gospels. This is where a good interlinear scripture analyzer comes in. Look the sentence up. The word "wife" is not there.

It's almost comical that this story would be taught just after Jesus has explained that no man can leave his wife for any reason except for fornication or adultery. That is because she is not her own, "and they twain shall be one flesh (Matthew Chapter 19, verse 5)." How can a man leave his wife if she is now joined to him by God? This is a sure case of scripture pollution, if this statement was made at all.

Again in Matthew Chapter 20 and Mark Chapter 10, Jesus gives a detailed explanation of what will happen to Him when He is in Jerusalem, to include the trial, mocking, spitting, crucifixion, and resurrection. I can't focus on this enough as the disciples in the Books of Matthew, Mark, Luke, and John will not understand what is happening, or worse, not expect Him to be resurrected when He is. But remember, in the Book of John, Jesus doesn't tell His disciples about this event, except for a short version just before His arrest. The authors of Matthew, Mark, and Luke have all told many times that Jesus has explained these events thoroughly, to include calling Peter, Satan, when he wants to believe otherwise.

In Matthew Chapter 20 you see that it is the mother of James and John that comes to ask Jesus if her children can sit on His right and left. But in Mark Chapter 10 it is James and John that bring up this "position" question.

As they depart from Jericho to Jerusalem we see two blind men asking for their sight in the Book of Matthew. But in Mark Chapter 10 it is only one man. In Luke it is one man also, but it is just before He gets to Jericho. The surrounding circumstances are all the same, but the number healed is different and the request and answer from Jesus is different. Hate to be a little picky, but only one of these accounts can be accurate, if any.

And finally, when Jesus comes to the Mount of Olives He sends two disciples to retrieve an ass and her colt, in the Book of Matthew. In his account the people cry, "Hosanna in the Highest." The city asks, who is this? In response, the multitude explains: "This is Jesus, the prophet of Nazareth of Galilee."

In the Books of Mark and Luke it is very similar, but Jesus instructs His two disciples to go retrieve a colt that had never been sat upon. There isn't an ass and a colt of an ass as in Matthew's account. This one event is the only thing in common between John's account, and these three gospels during this time period. Jesus does have a triumphal entry, but in the Book of John, Jesus does not send two disciples to fetch the colt, it states: "And Jesus, when He had found a young ass, sat thereon..."

In the Book of Luke you have an additional supernatural event. When the people are yelling "Blessed is the King that cometh in the name of the Lord: peace in heaven, and glory in the highest," some of the Pharisees tell Him to rebuke His disciples for saying this. Jesus responds by saying, "I tell you that, if these should hold their peace, the stones would immediately cry out." Only Luke, the Gentile that was not there, has recorded this statement! Now we are having rocks with the ability to speak if the people don't cry out for this joyful occasion.

Most Christians know the various stories of the triumphal entry and take for granted that this event is foretold in prophesy. It is sad to say that I believed much of what we were taught about the ministry of Jesus Christ was foretold in prophesy from the Old Testament. We wonder why the Jewish leadership did not understand who Jesus was.

But, as you have learned, and as I did when I was writing this book, most, if not all of what we thought that we knew to be true prophesy does not pass the discernment test. Let's look at Matthew's quote beginning in Matthew Chapter 21, verse 4. "All this was done, that it might be fulfilled which was spoken by the prophet, saying , tell ye the daughter of Zion, behold, thy king cometh unto thee, meek, and sitting upon an ass, and a colt, the foal of an ass."

This prophesy is found in Zechariah Chapter 9, verse 9. Before we go any further, you will note that this is the second time that the Apostle John tells you that this is to fulfill scripture. Both times the author of Matthew makes the same claim.

What was this prophecy referencing? His chapter in Zechariah is about a battle that is happening around Jerusalem. It reads very similar to the prophesy of Daniel when Greece would invade the Promised land. Read the entire chapter and ask yourself, "if I didn't know that Matthew and John had referenced this passage, could I draw the same conclusion that this passage would be referencing Jesus hundreds of years later?" After all, Zechariah was referring to "this king on the ass" taking on the superpower Greece, and their dominance as a world power was over. The Romans now ruled the world.

Most Christians believe that the riding on an ass was the form of transportation of a king. But alas, this isn't true, they rode on horseback. Even this passage in Zechariah explains that it is a lowly, meek form of transport. Jesus did enter into Jerusalem on an ass, but you will have to answer if you believe that it was to fulfill this scripture. Does it matter if they both got it wrong? Not really.

But, since the author of the Book of John draws the same conclusion as the the author of Matthew, I will give it a so, so reference. You will have to decide if this passage is really referenced in Old Testament prophesy. If I was keeping track of score, and I am, I say that the author of Matthew has sort of got one prophecy correct out of 12 references to Jesus. He did get one other reference correct, but that was about John the Baptist, and oddly enough it is also found in the Book of John.

Even though the authors of the Books of Matthew and John did agree a little here, can you honestly say that they have had anything credible in common?

Let's look credibly at how many Old Testament prophesies to this point actually pointed to Jesus Christ. Without stretching your imagination, can you honestly say that if you were a Jew during the time of Jesus Christ, from what has been presented to you as prophesy by the author of the Book of Matthew, that you would have known that Jesus was the Messiah? Even Paul does not try to pull Jesus out of the Old Testament scriptures and prophesies.

This is where I have to ask you to answer truthfully. Do you really believe that God could have "preserved" these gospels over all these years, and when you have a real good look at them, they are so different? Could these really be the work of God? They could have been written out of as much honesty and love that a man can have, but are they really telling the same story?

There are too many problems with the text to be "God sent." Does this mean that it is not true, that a Christian has nothing to believe in? No! But it means that you can't make doctrine on the words found in the Books of Matthew, Mark and Luke. They disagree with each other on most occasions, so why would you base doctrine on the times when only one of them tells you a certain story.

Catching Up with John

To keep us from leaving John too far behind we will take this chapter to move John's gospel forward. As you will note, there will be almost nothing in common between John's gospel and the other three authors over the last several chapters to include this one. As I have asserted from the very start, there are two different gospel stories. One that is taught by John and one that is told by the other three authors.

These two stories are not totally different. They do have a few occasions where they intersect, but to this point, if I renamed Jesus in John's epistle, and told you it was another Son of God, you might believe that it was a new story. Even the stories told in the Books of Matthew, Mark and Luke do not agree totally, but if you read the first three gospels you could make the point that they are three versions of the same story that had been handed down verbally over the years, before it was written down by three different authors at different times. John's story on the other hand is totally different.

Saying they are the same, is like saying that the story; *The Lion, the Witch and the Wardrobe*, tells the gospel story. When that book became a movie, I heard many so-called Christian pastors telling how C.S. Lewis was trying to tell the gospel story in a way that people would enjoy reading it. What a bunch of bunk. It is witchcraft and forbidden by God.

To this point there are only three actual events where John agrees with all three other authors. They are: Jesus is born of a woman; Jesus is recognized by John the Baptist; and Jesus fed the 5000 from a few loaves and a couple of fishes. Think of the magnitude of events that have happened so far and yet, only three events occur in all four gospels.

To make this point, do you see the name Mary referenced as being Jesus' mother in the Book of John? No. Do you see Jesus ever being baptized in the Book of John? No, but He is recognized by John the Baptist as the One that the Holy Spirit rested on in the Book of John. But it doesn't say that the event happened after or during a baptism. These are believed to be true because it states these things in the Books of Matthew, Mark and Luke.

John has Jesus going here and going there and the others have Jesus going to totally different places and doing totally different miracles. Remember, in the Books of Matthew, Mark and Luke, Jesus has already brought back the dead, twice if you believe the author of Luke.

John, on the other hand has progressively shown Jesus increasing the show-of-power in His miracles and they will culminate in the raising of Lazarus just before His crucifixion. Before I hammer home any more about these two very different stories of Jesus on earth, let's just begin reading in the Book of John.

John Chapter 6 verses 22 through Chapter 12, verse 19. On the very next day they arrive at Capernaum, where Jesus is teaching in the temple. The people that have been following Jesus are confused how He could be there without a ship. When He is asked, He explains to those that had followed Him from the other side, that they had followed Him, not because of the miracle itself, but because they received a full belly.

Jesus then begins with explaining that the "bread" that they should be longing for is the bread given by heaven, not that bread that will fill the belly. Jesus explains that He was sent by the Father, to do the works of the father. Those that believe the Father must believe on Him.

To this, they ask for a sign. He reverts back to the "bread" and explains that God gave bread (manna, during the Exodus) from heaven and that He is the bread that God the Father is now providing from heaven. "He that cometh to me will never hunger; and he that believeth on me shall never thirst."

Jesus then explains that those that the Father had given Him, He has kept secure and will raise them up in the last days. The Jews then murmur at Him. They are offended because they recognize that He was Joseph's son and had lived among them.

He explains that He is the Bread from heaven and that you have to eat Him, in the Spirit, if you want eternal life. This is hard for those that listen and they argue among themselves. It was hard even for those that follow Him to take, and He looses many followers. When He asks His disciples what they think, Peter states "Lord, to whom shall we go? You have the words of eternal life."

Chapter 7 explains from this point on, He stayed in Galilee as it was too dangerous for Him in the areas where the Jews lived. With all that He had done, His brethren still didn't believe in Him. So they mock Him and ask if He is going to attend the Feast of Tabernacles. In the middle of the feast, Jesus appears at the temple and begins to teach.

He explains that He does do God's miracles on the Sabbath, but what's wrong with that? After all, the Jews will circumcise on the Sabbath. "Judge a righteous judgment." Many wonder if He is the Christ, others want to kill Him. On the last day of the feast, Jesus cries: "If any man thirst, let him come to Me, and drink." This was signifying the giving of the Holy Spirit which was to come.

Many thought He was a prophet, others said that this was indeed the Christ, which brought up a question: "Shall Christ come out of Galilee? Hath not the scriptures said, That the Christ cometh of the seed of David, and out of the town of Bethlehem where David was?" So there was a division among the people. This is crucial. John does not tell you that Jesus was actually born in Bethlehem and no one knows it. He just lets you, the reader, know that the Jewish people were expecting the Christ to come from Bethlehem, and Jesus isn't from there!

Chapter 8 opens with Jesus coming from the Mount of Olives to the temple to teach when the Pharisees and scribes bring unto Him a woman caught in adultery. Jesus basically shames everyone that wants to condemn her, and when they had departed, tells the woman: "Neither do I condemn thee, go and sin no more."

Jesus starts to teach again and the Pharisees begin to argue with Him. He explains that He is not of the world, but from the Father and because they won't accept Him, they are from the devil. During the argument, Jesus explains that they will lift Him up, signifying the crucifixion. Many believe on Him and are instructed that if they want to follow Him as His disciples, and continue in His words, as such they will know the truth and it will set them free.

The Jews that did not want to believe tried to justify themselves by claiming to be Abraham's seed and are under bondage to no one. Jesus explains that they are under bondage to sin and hence a servant to sin. The servant doesn't stay at home for ever, but the Son does, and the Son will be in the presence of God forever, as well as those that are made free, by the Son.

The argument goes full circle where Jesus is explaining that He is from the Father and they will not accept it. Finally Jesus tells them that they are from their father the devil, and won't listen to Him because they are not of God. They accuse Him of being a devil possessed Samaritan. With this, Jesus talks about honor, glory, and judgment; concluding with saying that whoever keeps His word will not see death.

This was the opening that the Jews were looking for. They ask if He is greater than Abraham or the rest of the prophets, because they had all died. Jesus explains that He is honored by God, and Abraham rejoiced to see His day and he saw it and was glad. The Jews question how this could be as He was not nearly old enough to have seen Abraham. Jesus states: "Verily, verily, I say unto you, Before Abraham was, I am." With this, the Jews pick up stones to stone Him, but he walks through them out of the temple.

Right after Jesus passed through the crowd that wanted to stone him, at the beginning of Chapter 9, Jesus sees a man who was born blind from birth. His disciples want to know who had sinned in this man's life to bring this on him from birth. Jesus explains that no one had, but he was born this way for this very miracle that He is about to perform.

He anoints the man's eyes and tells him to wash in to pool of Siloam. This is a shock to everyone that knows the blind man. When the Pharisees find out that someone has been healed on the Sabbath, they are outraged and insist that his parents tell them how he was healed. His parents are fearful and explain that he is of age, and that they need to ask him. The man that was born blind explains that he doesn't know who did it as he was blind. Later Jesus reveals himself to the man, and makes a teaching point to those that follow Him, that for judgment He had come into the world.

Chapter 10 is the parable of the good shepherd that protects and leads His sheep to pasture. Jesus explains why He is like a shepherd that will lay down His life for the sheep. Other sheep besides His own will follow Him. Then He states that no one could take His life, it is His to give, and the Father had given Him the power to take it again. This statement brings division among those that listen.

During the Feast of Dedication, in the winter, Jesus walks in the temple at Solomon's porch. Once again the Jews want Him to state whether He is the Christ. Jesus explains that they will never believe Him, after all, He has already done many miracles and they still don't believe. Jesus finally explains, "I and the Father are one." This brings an immediate response to stone Him, when He asks, "Which one of these works do you stone Me?"

They respond, we are not stoning you for the good works that you have done. We are stoning you because you have just blasphemed, making yourself God. Jesus then begins a debate where He reminds them what it says in the Psalms and the crowd is calmed, until He states that "the Father is in Me and I in Him." Jesus escapes the crowd and resorts back beyond the Jordan.

Chapter 11 starts with the death of Lazarus. Jesus knows that he is dead, but waits several extra days to ensure that everyone knows and understands that he is truly dead. When He makes His way back to Bethany, He is met on the way by Martha who states to Jesus, "Lord, if thou hadst been here, my brother had not died." She understands that whatever Jesus requests of God, God will give it to Him.

Jesus tells her that her brother will rise again. Martha is thinking He is talking about end-times and agrees, but doesn't understand that Jesus is talking about rising again today. Jesus states "I am the resurrection and the Life: he that believeth in Me, though he were dead yet shall he live: and whosoever liveth and believe in Me shall never die. Believest thou this?"

Martha agrees that Jesus is the Christ, and goes to find Mary. Mary rises quickly and goes to Jesus. Mary too tells the Lord: "Lord, if thou hadst been here, my brother had not died." Jesus is very sorrowful and cries. When they lead Him to the grave, Jesus asks to have the grave opened. Martha objects as her brother has been in the grave for four days and now would be stinking. Jesus assures her that if she will believe, she will now see the glory of God.

Jesus goes to the grave, has the people remove the stone that is securing it, looks to heaven and thanks God and then states: "Lazarus come forth." With this Lazarus comes bound forward and Jesus tells those there to take the dressings off of him. Many that are there believe on Him.

This causes a problem for the Pharisees. Jesus has brought back the dead and many are believing on Him. This may bring the power of the Roman government on them if they can't subdue the movement. The High Priest then proclaims that they must kill Him, and they begin in earnest to find a way. The chapter closes with Jesus living in the wilderness as the Passover was nearing and everyone wondering if He would show.

Chapter 12 opens some time later with Jesus coming again to Bethany where they made Him a supper. This is six days before the passover according to the chapter. Martha was serving, Lazarus was dining with Jesus, and Mary takes a valuable ointment and anoints Jesus' feet and wipes them with her hair. This is unappreciated by Judas and He is rebuked by Jesus and then tells them there that this anointing is against the day of His burial.

Many people know that Jesus is there and come not only to see Jesus, but to see Lazarus that was brought back from the dead. The following day, Jesus comes into Jerusalem and the people take branches of palm trees and meet Him in the way and cry: "Hosanna, Blessed is the King of Israel that cometh in the name of the Lord." Jesus, when He finds a young ass, sits on it. These things were not understood by the disciples but they recall this after His resurrection. The Pharisees are very troubled and explain: "Behold, the world is gone after Him."

What do we learn from these passages? It is funny that the more you compare these "two different gospel stories," the more you have to acknowledge the differences.

At the conclusion of the feeding of 5000, Jesus sends the disciples away by ship as in the Books of Matthew and Mark, but not noted in the Book of Luke. John too agrees that the disciples are sent away by ship. When Jesus walks-on-the-water in the Books of Matthew and Mark it appears that all things are normal when Jesus steps into the ship and then they land in the land of the Gennesaret.

The New Testament, the Facts and the Fiction

Here again, John tells a very different story. When Jesus steps into the boat, "and immediately the ship was at the land whither they went." So, the ship was miraculously transported to where they were going. This is the ever increasing miraculous power that is shown by John. First Jesus changed one thing into another; water into wine. He has cured disease. He has made something from nothing; feeding the 5000. Now, He has power to move mountains, if you will.

John takes five verses to make sure that his reader understands that His being on the other side, without a ship to take Him, is absolutely not understood by those that were there. The people are plainly confused how Jesus is on the other side of the sea.

But that isn't why I brought your attention to this story. Where does John say that they landed when they came ashore? It was in Capernaum. This is the town where Jesus was raised. His family was from here, and now, not before, Jesus is about to teach in the synagogue. Read John Chapter 6, verse 41 and 42. " The Jews then murmured at Him, because He said, I am the bread that came down from heaven. And they said, Is not this Jesus, the son of Joseph, whose father and mother we know? How is it then that He saith, I came down from heaven?"

The authors of Matthew, Mark and Luke have all told various stories that are from this one meeting with His "kinsmen." Stories that supposedly began to happen way back in His ministry. Stories, that if you added them up, you would have to ask yourself, why do they let Him in town? After all, they have already tried to throw him off a cliff in the author of Luke's account.

Jesus doesn't make any friends in this meeting, and actually looses many followers. You will see that He offends those, of this, His home town, just like in the other gospels, but for a very different reason. This is where you see the Bread of Life title given by Jesus in John's epistle. Do you see how it is seamlessly sown into the story line. It fits perfectly because the story develops around it.

Think of how Christians throw around that title. We understand it as a title of Jesus today, but what would you have thought, if someone just called themselves "the candle to lightness." It has no significance. But, Jesus has called Himself the "Bread of Life" for a reason. He is showing that the manna that came from heaven wasn't or isn't the real bread from heaven, it is He. He is the real bread sent from God the Father. Go back to the woman at the well in John Chapter 4. What did He call Himself? The Living Water! Most of our titles for Jesus come from the Apostle John's rendition of Jesus' life on earth.

But, if you reflect back on the other stories given by the authors of Matthew, Mark, and Luke you will note in their stories, Jesus cannot perform any miracles in His home town because of lack of faith on their part. Those stories were told way back in Matthew Chapter 13, Mark Chapter 6, and Luke Chapter 4. Here you find a huge inconsistency that you must discern. Not only does Jesus have this meeting way at the end of His ministry in the Book of John, you also learn that it is in Capernaum.

Jesus has done dozens of miracles in Capernaum in the Books of Matthew, Mark and Luke! But, if this town is His home town, the authors of Matthew, Mark and Luke tell you that he cannot do any miracles "save healing a few sick for their unbelief." Which brings back the question, whose faith does it require for God to do a miracle?

At the Feast of Dedication in John Chapter 7, you have a very interesting conversation about where Jesus is from. It is clear that Jesus is from Galilee, but the Jews believe that if He is the Christ, He must be from Bethlehem. This is a fact that all Jews believed, the Christ must come from Bethlehem. Just because they believed it, doesn't make it so. They also believed that when the Christ came, He would overthrow the empirical powers that ruled Israel.

Did Jesus come? When He came, did He throw off the Roman Empire? Yes He came, and no, He did not throw off the Roman rule. That is why the Jews had a hard time, and still have a hard time, with the whole Jesus thing in the first place.

This is very, very important to understand. The Jews wanted Jesus to be from Bethlehem. John makes it perfectly clear here that Jesus is not, or was not, from Bethlehem. There is no reassuring his readers that Jesus was "secretly" from Bethlehem, but that "no one knows it." No, John just leaves you understanding that this is one of the problems with Jesus' life. He is not from Bethlehem.

This story brings into question the whole Jesus in the manger at Bethlehem. After all, the two authors that brings you this manger story don't agree about the story either. Go back and read the chapter *Up to and Including the Baptism*. Not only does John tell you here that Jesus was not from Bethlehem, the two authors that do, can't agree on the facts. Then why did they tell the story if it wasn't true?

As I have not received a vision, I can only presume. All four gospel authors are trying to tell the story of Jesus as the Son of God, the Messiah, the Christ. Did the Jews believe that the Christ had to come from Bethlehem? Of course they did. Were these authors there to witness the birth? No, but they had to have an answer as to the Bethlehem problem. So, they wrote it!

Don't believe me, use some discernment and let the facts help you understand it. Remember, no author was there at the birth, and the only time an author (John) was present at a conversation about where Jesus was from, He was not from Bethlehem. Are you trying to learn the truth, or are you trying to make excuses for accepting everything in the Bible as the inerrant word of God? You can't have it both ways.

Just go back and read Micah. The entire book will only take you about 15 minutes. You will see that there is a savior that will appear at the beginning of Chapter 5. It will be in the middle of some very specific circumstances. There will be some very specific outcomes. This guy is from Bethlehem. Once you have read this, even if Jesus was born in Bethlehem, did Jesus fulfill this prophesy? It's not even close.

So that makes his birth in Bethlehem mute. The author of Matthew and Luke have told the birth in Bethlehem just to show that Jesus is fulfilling the prophecy, but He doesn't. But the birth or no birth in Bethlehem does not have anything to do with whether or not He is the Christ. It doesn't say in the scriptures that the Christ will come from Bethlehem, just that this coming savior will come from Bethlehem.

They had many saviors that throw off oppressors. They called them Judges. Go back and read the Book of the Judges. See what they did. If you note what they call this guy in Micah Chapter 5., he is a judge. His job in this prophesy is to throw off the Assyrian!

By this time I hope that you can reason outside of the box. Just because you always thought that the Bible was written and preserved by God, does that make it so? Who wrote the Books of Matthew, Mark and Luke? No one can tell for sure. When were they written? Same answer. Do they reinforce each other's account, or bring them into question? I would have to say that when read critically, the validity of each is brought into question.

In Chapter 8, Jesus has forgiven a woman caught in adultery and then begins teaching when He is questioned who He is. The Jews want to hear Him state plainly if He is the Christ. He ends the conversion with the "I Am" statement. This signifies that He is saying that He is at least the "Angel of God."

Many so-called Christians would like to say that Jesus has just claimed to be God, because they don't really understand authority and respect as it was given in days of old. If you came in the "Name" of that entity, you had the title of that entity. To help you understand that they did honor in that way, take a lesson from Steven.

Look at the stoning of Steven in Acts Chapter 6. Steven explains that the voice of the burning bush was the Angel of God. I would hope that you would listen to our first martyr, who is believed had been given the power of miracles. I would expect that he had a better explanation of the Old Testament than some guy in the pulpit that wants your money. As you will learn I do not give a lot of credence to the Book of Acts either, but at least the author believed the story.

At the beginning of Chapter 9 we see Jesus healing a blind man. He spits on some clay and makes an ointment that He puts on the man's eyes. Then, He tells the man to wash off at the pool of Siloam. This is the first time John has told you that the Lord restored vision to anyone. This is also near the end of His ministry. As stated earlier many times, this is a Jesus that is ever increasing the show of His miraculous power. Is this the real Jesus, or is it the other Jesus of the Books of Matthew, Mark and Luke, who has restored many people's vision by this time in His ministry.

Chapter 10 has the parable of the good shepherd. At the end of the parable, Jesus has once again been threatened with stoning, but instead of miraculously walking through the crowd, He debates the point. He has said, "I and the Father are One." This sentence is used by many so-called Christians to show that Jesus has said that He is God, as in the Trinity. The Jews believe the same and hence, want to stone Him.

But then they change their minds. Why? Jesus quotes from Psalm Chapter 82, verse 6, which, if you read the entire Psalm, it shows that He can still be a "god" in title as God called men "gods" in this verse. The Jews understand and now they don't have a legal reason to stone Him. A real Christian should look up this chapter in Psalms and realize that Jesus didn't elevate Himself to God the Father, just a Son of God.

The raising of Lazarus in Chapter 11 is crucial to understanding why the authors of Matthew, Mark and Luke are so wrong in their message. In their gospels, by now Jesus has already done every imaginable miracle that can be performed. He has given the same power(s) to His disciples. In their gospels, Jesus has used the same techniques to do the miracles that John explains, but their Jesus may take a couple of tries to get it right.

Take restoring the sight of a blind man. John shows Jesus make an ointment from spit and clay to cure the blind man. In the author of Mark's account of this miracle, Jesus needs two tries with the ointment for it to work. But Jesus doesn't usually use an ointment in their versions of the gospel, He just says the word. Here in John, it isn't like that. There isn't the endless miraculous powers where multitude after multitude are healed. Just a slow methodical increase in power. I don't care how hard-necked a people are, if you had the endless healing and feeding of the masses to include bringing back the dead as told by the authors of Matthew, Mark and Luke, the people would be sold. They would know that Jesus is the Christ. Did I forget to point out, in the Books of Matthew, Mark and Luke, Jesus and the disciples even cast out devils. This just doesn't happen in the Book of John.

But in John, that isn't how it is. Jesus has done miracles, but they are limited. He has power, but it isn't flaunted. But here in Chapter 11 we see John telling us that Jesus is about to bring back the dead, FOR THE FIRST TIME! How do we know that it is the first time?

Jesus loved Lazarus, Mary and Martha. They were three siblings. Even though the other authors don't know who Lazarus is, they do know who Mary and Martha are. They make reference to them, but they never reference Lazarus, whom Jesus loved. So what does this have to do with knowing that this is the first time that Jesus will bring back the dead?

Martha has an exchange with Jesus starting in John Chapter 11, verse 21. She states: "Lord, if thou hadst been here, my brother had not died." She is an intimate friend to Jesus. If you read the rest of the account, she has no clue that Jesus has the power to bring back the dead. Mary too states: "Lord, if thou hadst been here, my brother had not died." They know that Jesus can heal anything, but the power to bring back the dead has obviously not been seen.

If He had the power to bring back the dead, they would have just stated: "Well, it really is too bad that Lazarus has missed the party that we had for him. But, now that you are here, would you please bring him back to life as you did to Jairus's daughter and the man from Nain." That's right, if you go back to the other gospels, Jesus had brought back the dead, very early on. Jesus was an intimate friend to Lazarus, Martha and Mary. Don't you think that they would know if He had already displayed this power?

To accentuate this even more, when Jesus tells them to open the tomb, Martha warns Him: "Lord, by this time he stinketh." Even after all that Jesus has been saying to her, she really doesn't get it. That is because this has never been done before. Don't take my word for it, take it up with the Apostle John.

But, it gets worse, if you want to believe that the other gospel accounts are still OK. The Pharisees hear of the incident and know that there is a growing problem with Jesus. He is beginning to sway the people. They decide that they have to kill Him and they feel it is advisable to kill Lazarus also (found in Chapter 12). They can't have a man that was brought back to life by Jesus hanging around. They feel that Lazarus gives credibility to the thought that Jesus just might be the Christ. You don't see them saying we need to kill Jesus, Lazarus, Jairus' daughter and the man from Nain.

Chapter 12 is some time later, but six days before the Passover, Jesus is again back at Lazarus, Martha and Mary's home. It is obvious that it is at Lazarus' house as He is sitting at dinner, Martha is serving, and Mary is ministering to Jesus in a very different way. It was a normal greeting to have a servant wash the feet of those that were guests. Here, Mary is washing and or anointing Jesus' feet with spikenard and then wiping His feet with her hair. It is said to be worth 300 pence, and here, Judas is unhappy with this "waste" as he puts it.

Jesus rebukes him and tells everyone that this thing that Mary has done was for the day of His burial. We know that this Mary, is the Mary, sister to Lazarus and Martha, because John makes mention of this anointing back in Chapter 11, verse 2. How many times will you see a story like this where a woman will anoint Jesus?

Just ahead in Mark Chapter 14, we see that it is two days before the Passover and a woman with an alabaster box anoints Jesus' head with spikenard worth 300 pence. And this is said to be a waste of money by those there, but Jesus rebukes them and states that this is done "aforehand to anoint my body to the burying." So in John's account it was 6 days prior to the Passover and Mary anoints His feet and wipes them with her hair. Jesus has to rebuke His disciples and then four days later an identical amount of spikenard is used again to anoint Him on the head and now He has to rebuke His disciples again. Do you think they were that stupid to have to be rebuked twice within four days for the same thing?

But wait, it gets better. Look at the story starting at Luke Chapter 7, verse 36, where a Pharisee has asked Jesus to come and dine with Him. While there, a woman brought an Alabaster box of ointment, and stood at His feet and washed them with her tears and the hairs of her head. Then anointed them with ointment.

Could these similarities be a coincidence? This is where we have to get back to discernment. The story of the life and ministry of Jesus Christ is spread verbally throughout the region by those that wanted to believe. The author of Mark agrees with the context of John's account, but got the day wrong and missed the anointing of the feet. The author of Luke knew of the story, but did not know where it fit in, so he just added it in wherever, and then made a story to flow around it. This story of Mary anointing Jesus before His burial is one more example that it was a verbal tradition, that, when put to pen and paper, was already polluted.

According to John, the Triumphal Entry begins with the people coming to see Jesus, but they also want to see Lazarus because he was brought back to life. This reinforces the fact that this was the first time that they had seen this type of miracle, the actual bringing back of life. In John's account Jesus "finds" the young ass, and the disciples do not understand the significance of this day until after the resurrection. Did He send two disciples to take an ass from some stranger's house, or did Jesus find the colt of an ass, as John has just plainly told you happened? The people are excited because a "new" prophet with great powers has come to Israel.

Have you ever wondered why His disciples didn't understand the significance of this event? If you just read the gospels, trying to line them up to what is currently accepted in the Christian religion of today, Jesus has already explained all things to His disciples. This is why so many Christian believers today can't understand why the disciples all flee and leave Jesus all on His own in the garden. You feel they are weak.

But, in the Book of John we don't see that anywhere. Jesus has walked throughout the region, and slowly performed ever-increasing miracles. He has followers that have followed Him. But, have you ever read where John has told you that Jesus told His disciples that He was going to Jerusalem to be punished for our sins and then three days later will be resurrected? No, John doesn't ever give you that story, it is only found in the other gospel accounts.

There is only one time that John explains that Jesus tries to explain that He will be taken away, but that is just before He will be arrested. In fact, He doesn't tell them that He will be resurrected in that story. They have all kinds of reasons to be afraid. They are following someone who has done great things, but kept them in the dark as to what will happen in the future. They only know that Jesus will be with His Father and that is just shortly before Jesus is arrested.

This is where I have to ask you to answer honestly. Do you really believe that God could have "preserved" these gospels over all these years, and when you have a real good look at them, they are so different? Could these really be the work of God? Not that they were not written out of as much honesty and love that a man can have, but are they really telling the same story?

There are too many problems with the text to be "God sent." Does this mean that it is not true, that a Christian has nothing to believe in? No! But it means that you can't make doctrine on the words found in the Books of Matthew, Mark and Luke. They disagree with each other on most occasions, so why would you base doctrine on the times when only one of them tells you a certain story.

You have to grasp that fact before you read the *Stories of Luke*. This is where Christians receive much of the gospel that they try to form doctrine on. If Luke, who was a Gentile, has told you so much of his story wrong so far, why would you believe the stories where he is the only one that will tell the story? I can't fathom it! They are nice stories, but many of them don't make sense either.

This is why the *Stories of Luke* follow *Catching Up with John*. By this time, the Books of Matthew, Mark, Luke and John have come to the Triumphal Entry. But Luke has told a whole slew of additional stories that are held dear to many Christians. Do you really believe them to be 100% correct? Let's see what they are.

The Stories of Luke

As you have read through each chapter up until now, you have to be asking yourself, if each gospel is different, which one is correct? It is obvious by now that there are two different and distinct accounts of Jesus' life and ministry. You have the one told by the authors of Matthew, Mark and Luke; and you have the one told by John.

But, when you look at them more closely, you see that even the authors of Matthew, Mark and Luke tell different stories. Remember the opening to the Book of Luke? He states: "Forasmuch as many have taken in hand to set forth in order a declaration of those things which are most surely believed among us..." This statement tells you that this is not "vision" or revelation from God. It also tells you that the order of those things that he is about to write down are solid and it is "believed among us." Where is the "eyewitness." There isn't one. The Book of Luke is a story that the author believes to be true and he is very sure of the order of events as he is about to write them.

By now you should know that the Book of Luke is often at odds with The Books of Matthew and Mark, both in how and when the events happened. I want you to understand these facts before I explain what this chapter is all about. To get from the story of the Mountain of Transfiguration to the Triumphal Entry into Jerusalem, the author of Matthew will take just under four chapters. The author of Mark will take 2 chapters. They will do their usual trek. The author of Matthew will tell a very thorough account and the author of Mark will tell a Matthew "light" account. The author of Luke will tell a similar story, but here he adds a lot of stories that only the author will tell.

To me, it is bad enough that the Books of Matthew, Mark, and Luke tell a different story than the one that John tells, but here, the author of Luke tells stories that only he knows. Does this really make sense? If the author of the Book of Luke is really Luke the physician, he was definitely not there, as he was a Gentile. These stories are ones that are quoted more than the stories that are told by John in most churches! By the way, how many events has John told you about that the other gospel authors agree with so far?

They all agree that Jesus had a mother, but if you didn't have the Books of Matthew, Mark and Luke, you couldn't say that her name was Mary. Later in the Book of John you will see that Jesus' mother has a sister whose name is Mary! So you would have two sisters, both with the same first name, or John feels that Jesus' mother had a different name, but didn't care to share it with us.

They all agree that John the Baptist declared who Jesus was, but the Apostle John never tells you that Jesus was ever baptized. No, the first real event that they all agree on is that Jesus fed the 5000. But the circumstances surrounding the feeding of 5000 are totally different. Think about all the events that have happened so far and ask yourself, what are the chances that John could miss so many supernatural events in his account?

These stories in *The Stories of Luke* will begin in Luke Chapter 9 and follow through Chapter 19. If the story is told in this chapter it will not be told in in any form in the Books of Matthew, Mark, and John's accounts, over the same time period. Many of these are all wonderful stories that have a softer gentler love for others, that is emulated in churches today. My question to the reader is this: If the author of the Book of Luke retold many other stories that are told by the other gospels, and yet told a different account of the same story, why would you believe that the stories that only he told, found in this chapter, are correct?

Just because there isn't another story that shows that the author of Luke is wrong, yet again, why call the stories "gospel?" They are nice stories, but the author is continually at odds with the other authors. Luke was a Gentile. And, did you forget who the author was writing this letter to? It was to a Roman named Theophilus, not the church.

Let's start with Luke Chapter 9, verse 51 after the Mountain of Transfiguration. As they are leaving the area they come to a village that will not receive Jesus, since He is headed for Jerusalem. James and John want to personally rain fire down from heaven on the town, as the prophet Elijah had done. Jesus corrects them by saying that He has not come to destroy, but to save.

I like this story because it adds fuel to the fire, if you will, that the author of Luke has attributed great powers to James and John. The Books of Matthew, Mark and Luke have already told you that they can heal the sick, cast out spirits, and now they are sure that they can call down fire from heaven, even though Jesus rebukes them for the thought. But this has to bring to mind, that they are afraid of everyone, just a few chapters later, at the arrest. Besides, they have power that only works part-time. In the Books of Matthew, Mark and Luke, you just had disciples that could not cast out the spirit that was in the young boy, right after the Mountain of Transfiguration. So, they have sort-of-powers. Does God give out sort-of-powers? Contrast this to John' account where you don't see any powers given to the disciples, and hence, they have a reason to be afraid of the Jews in the future.

The author of Luke then tells a story of those that want to follow Jesus, that is similar to a story told in Matthew Chapter 8, where you see Jesus telling that if you want to follow Him, you must understand that He does not have a home. You should not be concerned about burying your dead as it is more important to follow Him, and He instructs them to let the dead bury the dead. But this is where they are different. In Luke's account Jesus adds a third part to the account: "No man, having put his hand to the plough, and looking back, is fit for the Kingdom of God." This implies that when you hear the call, you drop everything and forget about your past or present commitments, and follow Him blindly.

Once again, would Jesus request anything that is contrary to the Old Testament? Read the story of how Elisha was called by the Prophet Elijah starting in 1 Kings Chapter 19, verse 19. Here, Elijah has called Elisha, and Elisha first goes and tells his mother and father good-bye and then butchers the oxen that he has been plowing with, and holds a feast for those there, before he follows Elijah. It is a setting in order. One of God's Commandments is to honor your mother and father.

Chapter 10 opens with the sending forth of the 70 to heal the sick and cast out spirits. Remember, only the author of Luke tells this story. Look at the wording from Matthew Chapter 10 and Mark Chapter 6, where Jesus is sending out the 12 to heal the sick and cast out spirits. It is the very same verbiage. I mean that many of the sentences are verbatim! This includes the charge to those being sent and the warning to the cities that won't receive them.

But then, the author of Luke adds an upbraid to the cities of Chorazin and Bethsaida and others, as part of the charge to the 70. This same upbraid is found in Matthew Chapter 11, verse 21. Once again it is word-for-word with what is found in the Book of Matthew, but it is from an entirely different story. So, you have a story here in Luke, that is made up of two different events, and of course you have 70 new followers of Jesus Christ that have been given these supernatural powers. Don't forget that the author of Luke just told you that John and James have expressed that they have the power to call down fire from heaven.

When the 70 return, they are amazed at their power through His name and Jesus explains: "I beheld Satan as lightening fall from Heaven." He then explains that He has given them power to tread on serpents and scorpions, and over all the power of the enemy: and nothing by any means shall hurt you."

This is a major problem with the Book of Luke. In his account, Jesus is constantly giving powers to those that follow Him. Here, Jesus has explained that these 70 individuals have no reason to fear anything at all. This verse is held dearly by many Christians, but does it pass the discernment test. If it was a true and factual statement from Jesus, why would they fear so much, so soon? For that matter, this isn't the 12 disciples, they are held in higher regard to this group of 70. Do the 12 have even more power than this? After all, we know that the author of Luke has told you that James and John can call down fire from heaven.

So, you have the Apostle John who never makes mention of supernatural powers being given to anyone. You have the Books of Matthew, Mark and Luke testifying that Jesus gave the 12 disciples the power to heal the sick, and cast out spirits. And then you have Luke telling you that He gave this same power to 70 more followers along with the power over anything that is in anyway against them. And yes, the author of Luke tells you that James and John have the power to call down heavenly fire.

When Jesus is taken at the garden, what is the posture of His Apostles? If they had this great power, why would Peter use a sword? Why would they run in fear? Why not call down heavenly fire and burn them up? This is the problem with the story line. If I had these great powers I would be like Elisha. He sat on a hill in 2 Kings Chapter 1, and destroyed captain after captain with their men using heavenly fire. Finally he goes with a polite captain to visit the King of Israel after God sends him. If I have God's backing I have nothing to fear.

You take so many things for granted that you believe are scriptural when you are a Christian. I call it church baggage. It isn't really there, but we believe it to be true, so it is, at least until we do a little research. I wrote this far along in this book before I came to a startling revelation. I had to go back and correct the book to make it scriptural. What are the powers that Jesus has while He is on earth? What are the powers that He gave those that He sent out two by two? They were to heal the sick and the ability to cast out spirits and devils.

What is so strange about that? Take out your concordance and look up demon, devil, and spirits. There is only one documented account of anyone being demon, devil, or spirit possessed in the entire Bible except in the Books of Matthew, Mark, Luke and the Book of Acts. But in the Books of Matthew, Mark, Luke, and the Acts of the Apostles it happens all the time. There is no casting out of demons, devils, or spirits in the entire Bible, accept for in the Books of Matthew, Mark, Luke, and the Acts of the Apostles. Paul, the guy that gives you more doctrine than any other New Testament author tells you what the gifts of the Holy Spirit are, and there isn't a gift to cast out demons, devils, or spirits! It may be attributed to him in the Acts of the Apostles, but he didn't write that book, and it isn't in any of his letters.

There are only three types of events when an individual is controlled by a supernatural force. You will see many times across the Bible that God hardens a heart. If the Father wants to force an outcome, He will harden a heart. Look up "harden" in the concordance. The Spirit of God rests on several individuals in the Old Testament. Samson is a great example of this. The only other event is when Satan enters into Judas, in the Book of John. You will note that Jesus does not cast Him out. This is the only event in the entire Bible where a demon, devil, or spirit has entered into a human, other than in the Books of Matthew, Mark, Luke and Acts.

Don't you find it strange that devil possession and exorcism only happened from the birth of Jesus until shortly after His death? Paul, Peter, James, Jude and John never mention it. Did devils dwell in people when Jesus was here on earth and then decide they didn't enjoy it anymore?

Don't forget, in the Book of John, even Jesus doesn't cast out spirits or devils, he just heals the sick, blind and brings back one man to life later on! This super, supernatural power to cast out spirits and devils can only be found in the writings of the authors of Matthew, Mark, and Luke. As a side note, why not look at the powers that the Apostle Paul attributes as gifts of the Holy Spirit. The power over devils or casting out of spirits is not a gift listed!

At the conclusion of the return of the 70, Luke attributes: "In that hour, Jesus rejoiced in Spirit..." and goes on to thank God for reveling these things to the "babes" and not to the "wise and prudent." This carries on for several verses, and was to have happened after they had returned. This statement is again found in Matthew Chapter 11, but it is part of the upbraid that Jesus had made when He was sending out the 12. What is funny, is that the author of Luke used part of Matthew's story in the sending out of the 70 and the rest of it when they had returned.

The author of Luke follows this with the story about the lawyer asking what he must do to inherit eternal life. When Jesus asks what the scriptures say, he explains to love God and love thy neighbor. But then the man asks, who is my neighbor? Jesus tells the story of a man that is mugged by thieves and is left to die by those who passed him by. Those persons who passed by, were held in high regard to the Jews. Then a Samaritan comes along and saves his life. Remember, a Samaritan was considered an unclean person to the Jews. So the act of kindness by this unclean man showed that he was a better neighbor than those that were held in high regard in this story.

Chapter 10 closes with a story about Mary and Martha having Jesus over for supper in Martha's home. Mary is sitting at Jesus' feet while Martha is serving, and Martha asks Him to tell her sister to help with the serving. Jesus doesn't agree and tells Martha that Mary has chosen the right thing to do. Unfortunately, the author of Luke doesn't know that Mary and Martha live with their brother Lazarus, who Jesus will restore to life (bring back from the dead). He loved Lazarus, Martha, and Mary as we learn in the Book of John. As would have been the tradition of the day, the house would have been Lazarus', not Martha's.

Chapter 11 opens with the author of Luke telling you that this is where Jesus gave us the Lord's prayer. But the author of Matthew told you that the Lord's prayer was taught at the Sermon on the Mount. It is followed by a story of a man that is in need of some bread after bedtime. He visits his neighbor, but the neighbor will not heed to his request. For some reason the author of

Luke tells you that the neighbor does not rise to give him bread because he is a friend, but he then gives the bread to him because of his "importunity." That story leaves me wondering why Luke told the story, or what his point was.

The author of Luke then tells a couple of stories that are found in a different time period in the Books of Matthew and Mark and ends with Jesus explaining why His power cannot be from Beelzebub. He appears to explain this with a story about how a strong man keeps his possessions, but when a stronger man comes along, "he taketh from him all that he has." There are many stories located in this part of Luke Chapter 11, but there is no apparent cohesion between the stories and the reason to tell them here.

Chapter 12 starts with stories happening during Jesus' ministry that happened at other times according to the authors of Matthew and Mark. Then Jesus is met by a man that asks Him to have his brother split the inheritance left to them. Jesus responds "Man, who made me a judge or divider over you?" Then He warns of covetousness and told a parable about a rich man that had a plentiful harvest. Since there was too much harvest for the barns that he had, he tore them down and built bigger ones. That evening the man dies.

The author of Luke affirms that Jesus felt that the man had done an inappropriate thing, to store the bounty that God had provided. He had laid up treasure on earth, instead of laying up treasure in heaven. He then teaches His disciples not to plan on what you will need in the future. After all, the birds of the field don't store food. And as for what you wear, doesn't God dress the lily better than the finest garments?

So according to the author of Luke, Jesus is telling His followers not to worry about your future needs as God will take care of them. In fact, in verse 33, he tells you that you should sell what you have, and it appears that He is telling you to give it away. That way you have treasure in heaven and you have nothing on earth where it can be taken from you by thieves.

Remember, this story is only told by the author of Luke, who has been in contradiction to the Books of Matthew and Mark. This story actually teaches not to save at all! It's not about hoarding, it's about working hard and then putting it away for the future. What about when Joseph interpreted the vision for Pharaoh? There was 7 years of plenty followed by 7 years of famine in Genesis Chapter 21. Did Joseph save? Or all the rich men that were blessed in the Bible like Abraham, King David, or the ant in Proverbs Chapter 6? Isn't Boaz in the Book of Ruth a rich land owner? Doesn't he save? Isn't he blessed? Don't you consider him righteous?

The total teaching of the Bible makes it clear that we should not "worship" our wealth. We should not "trust" in our earthly riches. But we are expected to "work" for our wages and not be a sluggard. Paul will teach in II Thessalonians Chapter 3, verse 10, that "those who do not work, will not eat." We are also directed to share with those that are in need. So it isn't the having of wealth that is wrong, it is the hoarding of wealth that is wrong. It is selfishness.

In the Book of Luke, Jesus then continues by telling the disciples a story of how we should be like servants that are ready for their Lord when he returns from His wedding. When he returns you are ready to receive him. When he finds you ready for him, he will reward you by waiting on you. This is similar to a man that is ready to catch a thief. You must always be ready.

Peter then asks if this parable was directed to the disciples, or to all people? Jesus explains that the wise and faithful servant will be rewarded and made ruler over all that his Lord has. But, if the servant becomes slothful, thinking that the Lord will not come, the Lord will cut him to sunder and cast him out with the unbelievers. Additionally, the servant that knows the will of his lord, and was not prepared ,will be beaten with many stripes. But, if through ignorance you did things that were wrong, you will be beaten with a few stripes, but you will still be beaten! "To whom much is given, much will be required."

This teaches that we will all be accountable for the life that we have lived. Even if we have committed sin though ignorance, we will be held accountable for these sins. This mirrors Old Testament sacrifice policies where the High Priest sacrificed once a year with a sacrifice for those sins that had been committed by the Nation through ignorance. This is where you are all in, or all out, with the teachings of author of Luke. If you like some of the teachings that only he has recorded, then you have to keep this one also. Do you think that you have committed sins through ignorance? Then you will be given stripes (whippings).

The Book of Luke then tells of Jesus explaining that He came to create a division between mankind rather than peace on earth. If man can discern the weather, why can't he see the times that they are in? Why are we not using righteous judgment? This is followed by the story about the man that should make it right with someone that he has wronged before they get to court where the man may be put in jail.

Chapter 13 opens with a couple of stories that are told to Jesus about men slain by Pilate where their blood is mingled with a sacrifice and a tower that fell on 18 persons. Jesus explained that this is not proof that they were sinners, but we all need to repent or we will perish. He then taught a parable about a man and his fig tree.

A certain man planted a fig tree in his vineyard and it did not bare fruit for three years. When he was ready to have it pulled up, his servant asked him to leave it for one more year so he could fertilize it. If it doesn't produce after that, then cut it down. The author of Luke does not attribute what teaching lesson was to be learned from this parable.

On a Sabbath day, Jesus was in a synagogue when He met a woman that had an infirmity for 18 years, leaving her hunched over. He placed His hand upon her and she was immediately lifted upright. The ruler of the synagogue was upset that Jesus would do this on the Sabbath. Jesus called him a hypocrite because everyone will loose his ox or ass and lead them to water on the Sabbath, why shouldn't this woman be loosed from her infirmity? All those that opposed Him over this matter were ashamed when they heard His answer.

Luke Chapter 13 concludes with many stories that are told in the Books of Matthew and Mark, but he recorded them here having them happening at different times in Jesus' ministry.

Chapter 14 opens with a Pharisee asking Jesus to dine at his house on a Sabbath day. There was a man there that had, what was called dropsy. Jesus asked those there: "Is it lawful to heal on the Sabbath," but no one answered. Then He asked: "which one of you shall have an ox fall into a pit, and will not straightway pull him out on the Sabbath day," but they did not answer again. So He told a parable about a man that held a wedding feast.

When a certain man sat at a very important place at this feast, a more important man came and the first was asked to take a lesser position and he was ashamed. So, when you go to a wedding or a feast, take a lower position so that you may be honored and moved to a higher position. Then Jesus stated to the Pharisee that had asked Him to dinner, when you hold a dinner, don't invite those that can recompense you for this good tiding, but rather invite those that cannot ever repay you for this good time. Then your reward will be a blessing.

When someone said, blessed is he that shall eat bread in the Kingdom of God, Jesus replied with another parable about a man that had made a great supper, who invited those he knew. They all made up excuses why they could not attend. The master of the house was very angery and said to go out quickly and invite those who would normally never be invited. "For I say unto you, That none of those men which were bidden shall taste of my supper."

All this appears to have happened while Jesus was at the Pharisee's house for dinner. They are interesting stories, but they have a little problem flowing together. First you have the man with dropsy. While Jesus is contemplating the reasoning why one might want to heal on the Sabbath, He tells a parable.

If the parable was about Sabbath healing it would make sense, but it is about wanting the upper most position in a feast. This same parable is found in Matthew Chapter 23 and Mark Chapter

12, but told for a different reason. Then Jesus transitions into telling the Pharisee that invited Him, that he should invite those that cannot repay him for the invite. Finally, He tells a parable about a man that invites his friends to a feast, but none of them want to come and so He invites "unclean" people instead.

After these things, the author of Luke tells us that a great multitude was following Jesus and He turned to them and stated that if they wanted to follow Him, they first had to hate their father, mother, wife, children, brethren, and their own life, and then bear their cross and follow Him. This is because you have to calculate the cost first, before you begin. Examples sighted are the building of a tower, a king going to war, and salt loosing it's savory flavor.

I always marvel how we glide over lists that state who we should leave or "hate" for us to follow Jesus. The word wife can never be in the list. It is anti-scriptural. The two are entwined as one. Read Job. God allowed Satan to take everything from Job, even his health. But Job still had his wife! This is a bad translation. Look at this verse in the Greek and you will see that the word "wife" has been added.

One last thought about the salt loosing its savory favor. I had heard this explained several ways how the salt could loose its flavor. Salt is made up of sodium and chlorine. It will always have this flavor. It can't loose it. You can dissolve it and then dry it back out and it is just salt. Do you have salt in your cupboard? Do you ever throw it out because it has gone bad? It would make sense if it would have been about garlic powder or onion powder, but it is about an elemental compound that is made up of two types of molecules. It can't loose it's savory flavor, its salt!

In Chapter 15, Jesus is with a crowd when some Pharisees start murmuring that Jesus is receiving and eating with sinners. So He tells them a parable about a shepherd that leaves a flock of 99 sheep to look for one that is lost. Jesus explains that this parable tells of the joy that is felt in heaven when one sinner repents. This is emphasized by the story of the prodigal son. In this story, there is a man that has two sons. One wanted what was going to be his in advance, and his father gave it to him. He wastes the entire sum and finds himself eating the feed meant for pigs. He finally comes to his senses and returns home, where his father is ecstatic to receive him home.

Once home his father has a party for this "lost" son. The other son is upset that his father has never held a party for him. After all, he had not blown the father's wealth. The father explains that all that he has is the faithful son's now! The joy is knowing that the lost son or brother is now found.

The joy of understanding that a lost sheep or a lost son can be found, or come to their senses and repent is a wonderful story, and one that makes sense, but is it a story actually told by Jesus? The author of the Book of Luke tells you that He did, but then he follows with the story of the unjust steward. This is, according to the author of Luke at the same "story-time."

In the unjust steward, beginning in Chapter 16, a rich man had left all that he had in the control of an unjust steward, who he is now accusing of wasting his wealth. Knowing that his time was short, the unjust steward readjusted the books to show that many of the debtors owed less than they really did to the rich man. In this way, they would be debtors to the unjust steward. "And the lord commended the unjust steward, because he had done wisely: for the children of this world are in their generation wiser than the children of the light. And I say unto you, make to yourselves friends of the mammon of unrighteousness; that when ye fail, they may receive you in everlasting habitation. He that is faithful with least is also faithful with much."

It goes on for a couple of more verses, but it really doesn't make any sense. It's not Christian in any way! It starts with an unfaithful servant that "cooks" the books. Then the master praises the servant for this embezzlement. It then goes on to tell you to make friends with the world so that they can take care of you. This is one story told by the author of Luke that really bothers me.

I couldn't find any saving grace to the story, and there isn't one. It is totally opposed to any teaching that we know of God. But then, it is told by the author of Luke. It closes with "If therefore ye have not been faithful in the unrighteous mammon, who will commit to your trust true *riches*?" That is the problem with this story in a nutshell. The story tells you that the unjust steward was praised by his master for being untrustworthy!

During this same extended story-time, the Pharisees become unhappy with Jesus, and He accuses them of justifying themselves before men, but their actions are actually an abomination to God. Then, for some reason the author of Luke explains that Jesus states that the Law and the Prophets were until John the Baptist, but now the kingdom of God is preached and every man wants in. It is easier for heaven and earth to pass away, than to have one tittle of the Law to fail. Any man that divorces his wife and marries another is committing adultery, likewise if a man marries a divorced woman, he commits adultery.

I know that this chapter is supposed to be about the stories only told by the author of Luke, but these last three sentences (from the above paragraph) are stories that are told in just three verses during this time as one story. But, they are actually a very condensed version of three lengthy stories told in the Book of Matthew found in Chapter 11 (John the Baptist), Chapter 5 (Tittle), and Chapter 5 (divorce).

Luke Chapter 16 concludes with the story of the rich man and Lazarus. This is the only time in the Books of Matthew, Mark or Luke that the name Lazarus is used. It also happens to be the name of Mary and Martha's brother who is not mentioned, even as a brother, except in the Book of John. Jesus loved Lazarus according to John, and brought him back to life, so he was known to the author of Luke, he just didn't know why!

In this story, Lazarus is a poor man that lives and begs at the gate of a rich man's house. The day comes when Lazarus and the rich man both die. Lazarus is carried to Abraham's bosom, but the rich man goes to where he is tormented by flames. The rich man asks Lazarus to come and quench his thirst, but there is a gulf that they cannot pass through. Then the rich man asks Lazarus to go back and warn his brothers of their fate.

Abraham tells the rich man that they have the the Law and the Prophets that they can learn from, but the man explains that if one comes back from the dead to warn them, they will repent. Abraham states: "If they hear not Moses and the Prophets, neither will they be persuaded, though one rose from the dead."

You may say that the name Lazarus could have been a common name and Jesus just used it in this story. That may be true, but remember this story just followed the three mini-stories that were thrown into this chapter, and they followed the story of the unjust-steward story that doesn't have any saving grace. But it gets better. Talk about stories that are just thrown in, the very next words start Chapter 17.

These verses start with Jesus saying: "It is impossible but that offenses will come: but woe through whom they come! It is better for him that a millstone were hung about his neck, and he be cast into the sea, than that he should offend one of these little ones." It is true that these statements are spoken about this time in the Books of Matthew and Mark, but where do they fit into this story by the author of Luke? He explains that Jesus has just given several stories and is about to give a couple more, but out of nowhere He is ridiculing those that offend "these little ones." Where are "these little ones" in the story? This is one of the big problems with the Book of Luke, out of nowhere there is a smidgen from some story in the past just thrown between two other stories.

Then Jesus tells His disciples to rebuke a brother if he transgresses against you. If he repents, forgive him, even if he transgresses against you seven times in a day, and tells you he repents seven times, forgive him. Once again the author of Luke is affirming Jesus states that we "will" forgive a brother if he transgresses against us if he asks for it, no matter how many times he does the same transgression against us.

I find this hard to believe. What if the transgression is adultery, and your brother comes back again, and again. It is a great Christian act to forgive, but what is meant by repent? Repentance is the act of remorse for something that you know that you did wrong. If you really repent, you should be forgiven. But if you have remorse, will you really do the same transgression seven times to your brother in the same day? This shows that the one who actually told the story did not understand what is meant by repentance.

Then "the apostles said to the Lord, Increase our faith." And the Lord explained that if you had just a little faith you could do great things. But which of you having a servant that has worked all day, call the servant in and set food down before him? None of you would. You would say to that servant after his hard day, "make me supper." And after you had ate and drank, then he could eat.

After all, that servant had done what was expected of him, why should he be rewarded. Same for you. If you had done all that was expected of you, you are just an unprofitable servant and should expect nothing for your reward, you have done your duty.

Once again, in this last story, the author of Luke tells us something that is hard to understand if it is true. What ever happened to the words, "Well done, good and faithful servant." In Luke's account, there is no reward for being a good and faithful servant. No nice words, no pat on the back, just "make me dinner!" Try to hold on to these non-loving stories when you get to one that you want to hold dear to your heart. If you want to believe those stories that only the author of Luke tells you about, then you have to accept these stories that really don't sound very Christian.

As Jesus was going to Jerusalem, He entered into a town where ten lepers met Him and asked for mercy to cleanse them. Jesus sends them to see the priest, and as they went they were all cleansed, but only one came back to thank Him. This man was a Samaritan. Jesus sent Him on his way and told him that his faith had made him clean.

The point of this story was that one Samaritan had come back to thank Jesus. The other nine, inferring that they were Jews, did not come back. It is a nice story of how the Jews took for granted the healing, but the Samaritan was the only one truly thankful enough to come back to personally thank Jesus. Did you miss the problem with this story?

A Samaritan could not go into the temple to show himself in the first place. A priest would not talk with him if he did. He was considered unclean just because he was a Samaritan! Jews did not mix with anyone that was a Gentile, and the Samaritans were the worst. Why do you think that Peter is taken to the carpet when he visits with Gentiles in the Book of Acts, Chapters 10 and 11? But then, this is the Book of Luke, where the Jews were the bad characters and the outsiders are accepted. The author of Luke has again tried to label these Samaritans as a better people than the Jews.

The Pharisees again try to get Jesus to commit when the Kingdom of God should come. Jesus explains that it won't be by an identification of a time or observation, "for the Kingdom of God is within you." Then He said to His disciples that the day will come when they will want to see Him, but He will not be with them. Some will say He is here or there, but He warns "don't believe them." When He returns it will be like lightning from one end of the heavens to the other. But first, He needs to be rejected of this generation.

So the author of Luke is telling you that Jesus has explained that the Kingdom of God is within you. He will be taken away, but will return, but first He has to be rejected by "this generation." Most of this, I have to admit, I don't have a clue what he is talking about, but one thing is for sure, Jesus has now told them again that He is to be rejected.

Then Jesus explains how unexpected it will be. Just as no one was expecting anything different to happen in the times of Noah or Lot, when Jesus returns, it will be sudden and severe. When it happens don't turn back or you may be lost, just as Lot's wife. "He who shall seek to save his life shall loose it, but he that looses his life shall preserve it." One will be saved and one will be lost. "And the disciples answered and said unto Him, where, Lord? And He said unto them, Wheresoever the body is, thither will the eagles be gathered together."

Many of the same lines are used in Matthew Chapter 24, but the author of Matthew is telling a very different story with these same lines. The author of Luke is telling you that this is all brought about on the day that the Son of Man is revealed. In Matthew these examples are used to explain the Last days when the Anti-Christ begins to persecute the faithful followers of God, and we must flee for our lives. The author of Matthew's story is at least in agreement with the Book of Revelation. But Luke has told you that on the day that the Son of Man is revealed (comes), all these things will happen. The Anti-Christ comes earlier than Jesus' return in the Book of Revelation.

If you read the entire set of verses starting with the Pharisees demanding to know when the kingdom of God should come, until "the eagles be gathered together," you will have to agree that it has no flow. And what do the eagles have to do with anything? It isn't until you read later on in the Book of Matthew, that it makes more sense. In the Book of Luke the statement actually says "Wheresoever the body is, thither will the eagles be gathered together." In the Book of Matthew we learned that it isn't the "body" it is the "carcase." The eagles are there to eat the carrion left after the persecution of the great tribulation.

Luke Chapter 18 starts with Jesus teaching the parable of the unjust judge, who did not fear God or regard man. But, to get a woman off his back, he avenges her of her adversary, no matter if she was right or wrong. Jesus equates this judge to the way that God will judge when the Son of Man cometh. Once again, I don't see the parallel that the author of Luke is trying to make between God's righteous judgment and the judgment used by the unjust judge.

Then Jesus tells the parable of the Pharisee and the Publican, to those that trusted in their righteousness and despised others. Both men are praying before God and the Pharisee tells God that he thanks God that He is living a righteous life, but the publican humbly bows his head and asks God to be merciful to him for being a sinner. Jesus affirms that the publican was justified rather than the Pharisee.

I guess this parable, told only by author of the Book of Luke, falls right into the arms of the modern church. Let's say that the Pharisee was living a righteous life. Can it be done? Many people in the Bible were righteous. If he was thanking God for giving him this way of life, and he was willing to live it, what is wrong with that? Now, if the publican was a sinner, as alluded to in the parable, it is well that he asks for mercy, but why does this make him better than the guy that is living the life that God has asked us to live?

This story just gives modern Christians ammunition to live in sin, but ask for forgiveness for the sins that they are living and intend to do in the future. This story is melded with the one earlier where Jesus is telling us to forgive our brother, even if he has done the same sin seven times in the same day, if he asks for forgiveness. So you can sin as much as you like if you ask for forgiveness. This cannot be found in any book of the Bible but Matthew, Mark, Luke and Acts (Luke II).

Finally, Luke Chapter 19 has two more stories that only he credits to Jesus during this time frame. They are the dining with Zacchaeus and the parable about the pounds.

When Jesus enters into Jericho on His way to Jerusalem for the triumphal entry, He meets a very short man named Zacchaeus who is a rich publican (tax collector). Zacchaeus is so happy that Jesus decides to dine with him that he exclaims that he will give half of his wealth to the poor, and repay anyone that he has overcharged four times the amount.

Jesus is pleased and tells Zacchaeus that "this day has salvation come to this house." Once again this shows the inconsistency found within the author of Luke's account. Zacchaeus has obviously overcharged people in the past, but agrees to give half of what he has to the poor. Notice that it isn't all that he has to the poor. Why this is so inconsistent is that the rich young man, just a couple of pages back had never overcharged anyone and lived an honest life, but Jesus expected him to give all that he had to the poor. You can't have it both ways, is it half or all? Zacchaeus was obviously both covetous and a thief, why let him off so lightly?

Until now in the Book of Luke, you see the disciples never understanding what is going to happen to Jesus when He mentions the crucifixion. He has told them of it several times and the text always references their lack of understanding. But here in Chapter 19, verse 11, it is obvious in this author's account that all of the people here know that the Kingdom of God is about to appear. The people know who He is according to this text. Remember this, as it doesn't meld with how they feel just a few more chapters away. Why would they understand it here and then not have a clue so soon after.

With that, Jesus tells a parable about a nobleman that went to a far country to become their king. Before he left he gave ten servants money to work with while he was gone. Many citizens hated him and stated that he would never rule over them. When he returned he took account of the money that he left with the servants. One servant had made ten pounds from the pound that he had. One had made five pounds from the pound that he had received. Finally, one brought the pound that he had kept in a napkin because he feared what would happen if he had lost the pound in doing business.

The nobleman rewarded those that had done well, but punished the man that fearfully saved the pound in the napkin until he had arrived. This servant was called a wicked servant. Then the nobleman slayed those citizens that did not want him to rule over them.

I guess that you can make the point that God wants us to be happy to have Him rule over us, and if we are not, He will slay those that are not. But I really don't understand why you would punish someone that is too afraid to gamble with what has been given to you to take care of. This flies back in the face of giving all that you have to the poor. Are we to be greedy or giving? Is it a sin to be fearful of the unknown? This isn't the God of the Book of John.

So, what was the point of this chapter? By this time you have to understand that the Books of Matthew, Mark and Luke tell one gospel story, and John tells another. Within the Matthew, Mark, and Luke story line there are really two different stories. The author of Matthew tells a story that can be compared to a mathematical number line like this: 2,4,6,8,10,12,14,16.... It is all the even numbers in order.

The author of Mark tells a story that can be compared to this mathematical number line: 2,4,8,14, 18... It is what I call a "Matthew light." They are the same stories, but each event is simplified and he doesn't tell you about all of the events. It is like Mark's author has heard Matthew's story many times and then wrote what he remembered of it. It doesn't mean that this backs up the author of Matthew's account, it just means that they knew the same stories.

But then you have the author of Luke. Luke's order is all wrong to Matthew's. He tells you many stories that occurred with Matthew as a follower of Jesus, even though Matthew himself affirms that these stories happened before he was a disciple. He tells you many stories that should have been recorded in all the gospels, if they were true, but are only recorded by him. Many of these stories oppose what we know to be true of God and some were found in this chapter. I liken Luke's number line to this: 1, 2,6,3,4,14,8, 9,11,12,10,13,15,14,18...

So the two story lines are headed in the same general direction, but in the Book of Luke's, they are all out of order with the Book of Matthew and Mark, and there are a lot of stories that are only told in Luke. If the physician Luke was the author of the Book of Luke, he was a Gentile, and was never on the scene while Jesus was on this earth. If he is in constant conflict with the stories that he and Matthew tell that are the same, why would you believe the stories that only Luke tells you?

Early Events After the Triumphal Entry

Unfortunately, we must leave John again to discuss these events. Once again, the author of Matthew will tell a story of events and Mark will give a condensed version. The author of Luke will tell many of these same events and stories, but they will be in a different order. Jesus will have a lament over Jerusalem in the Book of Luke that will happen as He is entering just after the triumphal entry, but it won't be discussed in the Books of Matthew or Mark until later, and of course, John will not make mention of it at all.

Many things happen between the triumphal entry and the crucifixion according to the various gospel accounts. According to the two passages found in John Chapter 12, verse 1 and verse 12 we know that the triumphal entry happened on the 9th day of Abib (Hebrew calendar).

This is going to be hard for some of you to take, but Jesus did not eat His passover with His disciples, He ate the last supper with His disciples. What is the difference and does it matter? Here is where a Christian will have to decide, do I believe John's account or the Books of Matthew, Mark and Luke?

The Last Supper will be covered in depth, in a couple of chapters from now, but in John Chapter 18, verse 28 you learn that after Jesus has had His Last Supper with His disciples and been arrested, it is still not the Passover. Read it yourself. " Then led they Jesus from Caiaphas unto the hall of judgment: and it was early, and they themselves went not into the judgment hall, lest they should be defiled; but that they might eat of the Passover." So it is obvious that the Jews would not enter the judgment hall or they would be defiled and not able to partake of this great feast.

The story from the Books of Matthew, Mark and Luke would have you believe that He ate the Passover. Did He? John tells you most definitely that He did not. I have given these texts to show the time frame that has to transpire between the triumphal entry and the arrest. Passover is the evening of the 14th day of Abib. Jesus is in the judgment hall in the morning of some day prior to Passover. If he was arrested on the evening of the day prior to the Passover it had to be the 13th day of Abib. So at the most, the next several chapters occur in only four days.

As I stated above, none of what you will read in this and the next chapter is collaborated by John. John shows that time was short and very few events happened between the triumphal entry and the arrest. Let's look at what the Books of Matthew, Mark and Luke have to say.

The New Testament, the Facts and the Fiction

Matthew Chapter 21, verse 12, through Chapter 23, verse 39 According to the Book of Matthew, directly after Jesus enters the city, He goes to the temple and casts out all the vendors stating: "it is written, My house shall be called the house of prayer, but ye have made it a den of thieves." Then He healed the blind and lame. The people rejoice, which was displeasing to the chief priests and scribes. Jesus explains to them that out of the less educated, comes perfect praise.

He rests that evening in Bethany and in the following morning sees a fig tree, which, when He approaches, finds no figs. He curses the tree and it withers immediately. He uses this miracle as an example of what you can do if you have enough faith. He ends this example with a statement: "All things, whatsoever ye shall ask in prayer, believing, ye shall receive."

When He is teaching in the temple, the Jewish leadership come to Him and demand that He explain what authority He has for the things He is doing, and who gave Him that authority. Jesus agrees to give them the answer to their question if they will first answer one of His questions. He asks: "the baptism of John, was it from heaven or from man?

With this question they realize that Jesus has set a trap for them. If they say from heaven, then Jesus will ask, why didn't they believe him. But, if they say man, then they feared what the people would do to them as the people held John to be a prophet. So, they told Jesus, that they could not tell. Jesus then tells them that He too would not tell them what He had been asked.

With this, Jesus tells the parable of the man with two sons. He asked both to go out and work in the vineyard. One said no, but went. One said yes, but didn't. Jesus asks, which one did the will of his father? They replied, the first. Jesus replied that those considered the "losers" of their society will go into the Kingdom of God before those of the Jewish leadership, because John came in the way of righteousness and the leadership believed him not, but the commoner believed. What's worse, after the leadership had seen, they still would not believe.

This parable was followed by another about some wicked vineyard men who were caretakers of a vineyard for a man that prepared it before traveling to a far land. When the man sent back for some fruits for his labors, the wicked vineyard men beat or kill those that were sent. Finally, the man sent his son, feeling surely that they would respect him, but they killed him. When Jesus asked what the crowd felt the man would do when he returned, the multitude said that the man would miserably destroy those wicked men.

Then Jesus reminded them what was stated in the scriptures, how the stone that the builders rejected became the head of the corner. Therefore, the vineyard will be taken away from those that it was given to and given to those that will bring forth fruit. The chief priests and Pharisees that heard were sure that He spoke this parable about them and would have taken Him, but were too afraid of the crowd.

Chapter 22 opens with Jesus telling another parable explaining that the Kingdom of Heaven is like a King that made a wedding feast for his son. He called all the regulars to the feast, but they did not want to come, even beating some of his servants that came to ask. The king was very mad and sent out his army and destroyed those that didn't want to come. Then he sent out his servants and called everyone that would come, to come. But one man came that was not in a wedding garment and the king asked him why he had not dressed appropriately? The King told his servants to tie him up and throw him out into outer darkness.

The Pharisees thought they might be able to entangle Jesus with His words, so they sent their disciples with some Herodians asking: Do you think it is lawful to pay tribute unto Caesar? Jesus understood the trap, if He said do not pay tribute He would be in violation of the local law. But, if He said pay tribute, then the Jewish leadership would say He was honoring Caesar by not paying His tithe to God. He asks for them to bring Him a penny, and asks them whose image is on it? They say to Him that it is Caesar's. Then Jesus says: "Give unto Caesar what is Caesar's, give unto God what is God's," they marveled and went on their way.

The Sadducees, who believe that there is no resurrection, ask Him about a woman who has married seven brothers in succession upon each of their deaths. In the life after, whose husband will she be since she has been the wife of each of them? Jesus explains that they do not understand their scriptures, and that none of us will have wives but will be as the angels of Heaven. As for the resurrection of the dead, God does not see us as dead, He is the God of the living, our souls never die.

Then a lawyer asks: "which is the great Commandment in the law?" Jesus replies to love God as the first Commandment and to love thy neighbor as thyself as the second. "On these two Commandments hang all the law and the prophets."

The author of Matthew closes Chapter 22 with a question, Jesus asks the Pharisees, how can Christ be the son of David, when David calls Him Lord? "If David then called Him Lord, how is He then his son?" No one can answer this question and from this moment on no one dared ask Him anymore questions. Chapter 23 is an address by Jesus to His disciples and the multitude. It is warning them about the practices of the Jewish leadership. They give burdensome religious requirements which might be good practices to perform, but they won't do them themselves.

Jesus then begins to upbraid the leadership about continually looking good rather than following God's desires. They want positions of importance and being greeted by the commoner and yet they are taking the position of God. They have missed the mark, to be great in God's eyes, you must be a servant. Then Jesus began to criticize them by saying: "Woe unto you, Scribes and Pharisees, Hypocrites!" He then gives many examples of their foolishness and lack of understanding.

He ends this chapter with a lament over Jerusalem where he had often wanted to call them together as a hen gathers her chicks. But now their house is left desolate. "For I say unto you, Ye shall not see me henceforth till ye shall say, Blessed is He that cometh in the name of the Lord."

Mark Chapter 11, verse 11 through Chapter 12 verse 44 The last time we read from the author of Mark, he tells us that Jesus had just entered Jerusalem in what Christians call the triumphal entry. The author of Mark assures the reader that Jesus then goes directly to the temple where He looks around and then goes to Bethany for the evening with the twelve.

The next morning Jesus is hungry and sees a fig tree and approaches it. When He sees that it has no figs, He curses the tree and then heads on to Jerusalem where He goes straight into the temple and begins to cast out all those that sold sacrifices. While there, He taught saying: "Is it not written, My house shall be called of all nations the house of prayer? But ye have made it a den of thieves." The Jewish leadership wondered how they might destroy Him but fear the crowd. In the evening Jesus leaves the city.

The next morning when they were passing the fig tree, Peter makes note that it had dried up to the roots. Peter asks Jesus about this and Jesus comments that if you have faith in God, and shall not doubt in your heart, you shall have whatsoever you shall ask for. But, if you are looking for forgiveness, first you must forgive those that require it from you.

As they enter into the temple, the leadership comes to Him and asks by who's authority is He doing all that He is doing? Jesus tells them that He will tell them what they want to know if they first tell Him whether the baptism of John the Baptist was from heaven or of man. The leadership understands that if they answer in any way, they will either look unrighteous, or be mobbed by the crowd. So they tell Him that they cannot tell, and with that, Jesus replies that He will not tell them what they want to know either.

Jesus then tells a parable of the wicked vineyardmen that starts in Chapter 12. A man builds a vineyard and rents it out to some people. After the harvest, he sent a servant for a portion of the crop, but they beat him. The master sent many servants, but they beat some and kill others. Finally he sent his beloved son and they killed him hoping that now that the heir was dead, they might own the vineyard. Then Jesus tells them that the man will come and destroy the renters and rent the vineyard out to others.

Have you not read in the scriptures where the stone that was rejected by the builders became the cornerstone, declares Jesus? The leadership wants to punish Him for this parable, because they know that He has told it about them. So they send some followers to try to trap Him in His words.

First the Pharisees and Herodians come and ask Him if it is lawful to pay taxes to Caesar. Knowing that it is a trick, He asks them for a penny and then asks, "whose image is on the coin?" They say that it is Caesar's. He then tells them to give to Caesar what is Caesar's. They marvel at how He had out-foxed them.

Next the Sadducees, who do not believe in life after death, approach Him. They tell a story of a woman who had seven husbands under the Mosaic law, then they ask Him: "after she dies and in her resurrected body, whose wife will she be as all seven husbands were lawfully hers." Jesus tells them that they do not know their scriptures. We will be as the angels in our resurrected bodies where we will not be given in marriage.

Then a scribe comes to Him and asks: "Which is the first commandment of all?" Jesus explains that it is to love God with no reservations and to love your neighbor as much as you love yourself. The scribe notes the wisdom which Jesus had displayed with this answer. Jesus explains to the scribe that by understanding His logic, he is close to the kingdom of God. With this, no one asks Jesus any more questions.

Jesus then poses a question to those in the temple. "How say the scribes that Christ is the son of David?" After all, David is calling Him Lord when he, David, is in vision. So how can the son of David be his Lord? With this He begins to warn them of the doctrine of the religious leadership. They want to be recognized for their position, and cover their sins with long prayers, but secretly they are taking the last savings from widows, which will be their damnation.

Chapter 12 closes with Jesus sitting by the treasury and notes that a poor woman cast in all that she had, even though it was very little. He explains that this woman had given more to God than those that had given much more, because they had given out of their abundance but she had given all that she had.

Luke Chapter 19, verse 41 through Chapter 21, verse 4. After the triumphal entry, as Jesus is coming near, He begins to lament over the city, saying: "If thou hadst known, even thou, at least in this thy day, the things unto thy peace! But now they are hid from thy eyes." Jesus then explains that the time will come when the city will be laid siege and not one stone will be left, one on top of another, because they didn't recognize this day, that He has arrived.

Then He enters the temple and casts out those that are buying and selling sacrifices saying "Is it not written, My house is the house of prayer: but ye have made it a den of thieves." After this, Jesus teaches daily at the temple, but the leadership seek a way to destroy Him.

Chapter 20 begins with Jesus teaching in the temple and the Jewish leadership coming to, and asking Him, by what and who's authority is He doing these things. Jesus asks them a question to answer first: was the baptism of John the Baptist from man or from God? Fearing for their lives if they say from man, and knowing they will be drilled as to why they didn't believe him if they say it was from God, they tell Jesus that they can't discern. Then Jesus tells them that He too will not answer their question and begins to teach a parable about them.

It is the parable of the wicked vineyardmen that rented out a vineyard and refused to pay their rent when the man that owned the vineyard asked for it. Each servant that he sent for the rent was beaten. Finally, he sent his only son to ask for the rent and the wicked vineyardmen killed him hoping to keep the vineyard as they know there was no one to receive the inheritance. Jesus explains that the man will come and destroy these vineyardmen and shall rent it out to others. Then He adds that the cornerstone that the builders had rejected will crush them when it falls on them.

The Jewish leadership understand that they are the wicked vineyardmen in the parable and that Jesus is telling them that He is the cornerstone that they have rejected and that He will crush them. They want to physically harm Him for this, but fear the people as the multitude hold Jesus as a prophet.

Discretely these leaders try to catch Jesus in His words. First they send one to ask if it is lawful to pay your taxes to Caesar. Jesus understanding their intent asks them to bring Him a penny and asks, who's image is on the coin? They explain Caesar's. Then Jesus tells them to give those things unto Caesar that are Caesar's and those things unto God that are God's.

Next, the Sadducees ask Him about whose wife a woman will be after the resurrection if she had lawfully been the wife to seven different men. Jesus explains that they don't have a good understanding of the scriptures as we will not be married in our resurrected bodies. Then He adds that God is the God of the living, for all live unto Him.

Then Jesus asked them a question. "How say they that Christ is David's son?" After all, in the Psalms, David called Him Lord. How can your Lord be your son? Then Jesus openly rebukes the scribes by saying that they are always looking for the praise from man and yet they will be condemned for taking advantage of widows.

As He looked up, at the beginning of Chapter 21, He sees a widow casting in a meager offering into the treasury. Jesus explains to all there that she has given more than all the others that may have given great offerings, because she has given all that she had, while they had given out of their abundance.

What can we take away from these passages? They all start with Jesus entering Jerusalem, which is what most Christians refer to as the triumphal entry. The people celebrate in all four gospel accounts. Remember, except for the triumphal entry, John does not tell you of any of these events found in this chapter. What is more bizarre, John will tell you of other events that these three writers will not record.

In the Book of Luke, you have a discourse before Jesus enters the temple where the author of Luke asserts that this is the time when Jesus laments over Jerusalem. It is just part of a much bigger lament found in the Books of Matthew and Mark that happens later.

In the Books of Matthew and Luke, either directly after the triumphal entry, or soon after, Jesus enters the temple and throws out the venders that are there to make a profit on those visiting the temple. The author of Mark also agrees that Jesus enters the temple on the day of the triumphal entry, but He does nothing but takes a look around. In the Book of Mark, it is the next day, after Jesus has cursed the fig tree, when He enters into the temple to throw out the venders.

John also talked about Jesus throwing out these venders, but it was at the beginning of His ministry in John Chapter 2, once more showing how different these gospels really are. Was it in the early stages of Jesus' ministry as in John's account? Was it on the day of the triumphal entry as told in the Books of Matthew and Luke? Or was it on the second day after the triumphal entry as affirmed by the author of Mark? I guess that if you still believe that the entire Bible is written by the Holy Spirit, through these author's hands, Jesus may have entered the temple three different times and thrown out the vendors! If that is the case, you would think that they would have been ready for Him by now!

You will note that either the wording from Jesus was different in all four accounts of Jesus throwing out the venders, or the circumstances are different when He is recorded to use these statements. In the Books of Matthew and Mark it looks to be the same..."Is it not written, My house shall be called of all nations the house of prayer? But ye have made it a den of thieves"... In the Book of Matthew, Jesus is yelling it while He is casting out the venders, but in the Book of Mark, Jesus states this while He is teaching the crowd after He has thrown out the venders.

The following day, which is the second day after the triumphal entry, the authors of Matthew and Mark explain that Jesus approaches a fig tree that has no figs on it. Jesus is displeased and curses the tree. In the author of Matthew's story, the fig tree immediately wilts. In Mark's version, Peter notices how the fig tree had wilted the following day. In both accounts, Jesus adds a caveat to the teaching. Basically, it is an open ended guarantee that whatever you pray for, if you believe you will receive it, you will! That is a very misleading statement. The truth is, you will receive what you are praying for, if it is within the Father's will.

But did this fig tree event happen? It would be a very supernatural ability to curse a tree and immediately have the tree wilt. Remember the 12 were with Jesus, and John, who writes more about the happenings after the triumphal entry than any other, never records this story. More importantly many Christians use the verse in Mark, Chapter 11, verse 13 to prove that Jesus was crucified in early spring (Easter) as "the time of figs was not yet." But, if you look at the text you will see that the word "yet" is italicized. That means that the statement actually states that "the time of figs was not." In other words, it wasn't time for ripe figs on this tree. Why would Jesus curse a tree for not having fruit if it was not time for the tree to have fruit? Use some discernment. Where is the Glory to God in this "Miracle?"

So if this story is true it is telling you that it could have been fall, winter or early spring as figs are a summer fruit. Passover is the evening of the 14th day of Abib, which happens to be late September. Jesus did not die in the Spring, He died on Passover, as our Lamb and that places it late in September as commanded by God in Leviticus 23, no matter what tradition of man has been substituted for a commandment of God by modern day Jews or Christians.

In the parable of the wicked vineyardmen, it is a story given to show that the Jewish leadership had been given a great prize, but showed no respect to the One that had given it to them. It is told in the Books of Matthew, Mark and Luke. When the question is put forth as to what will happen to those wicked men, who answers? In the Book of Matthew, the crowd answers, but in the Books of Mark and Luke it is Jesus who pronounces the sentence on the Jewish leadership. Does it matter? Only that it is inconsistent, but did you notice that the author of Matthew tells you that Jesus first had told another parable, about the vineyardman with two sons, before this parable, to bring home the message?

At this point I would like to digress. For those of you that have a red- letter Bible, what do those red letters represent? They are the "words" of Jesus Christ! Are they really? Go back and read the last parable of the wicked vineyardmen. It is a story told by Jesus Christ and the red lettered words show you His very words! Are they the same words by Him in these three accounts of the same story? No, so are they really His words? No. You will note that besides what I have already pointed out, the amount of servants, and what was done to each of them, is different in these accounts. In the Book of Luke, no one is killed until the beloved son's death, but in the others, servants are killed. Which story is really the words of Jesus? I would have to say none of them!

The author of Matthew tells another parable right after the last one that is only told by him. It is about a king and a wedding feast. Basically, if you don't want to come and dine as the king has asked, then you will be destroyed. Then, those that thought that they were not worthy are invited. But, if you come, you had better be prepared, or you will be thrown into outer darkness.

This isn't a soft and gentle Christian thought. It is really teaching that God has a plan, and you need to abide by it. Those that feel they can do it their way, will be destroyed. As much as I believe in John's account of the gospels, I do believe this doctrine to be true. God doesn't care what you think is the correct life for you to live, He is looking for you to live as He has directed, and that just isn't taught in Christian churches today.

In Matthew Chapter 22, the author has told several stories, some of which are told in the Books of Mark and Luke. When Jesus is questioned by the lawyer in Matthew, He is asked: "which is the great Commandment in the Law?" In the Book of Mark it is, "Which is the first Commandment of all?" In the Book of Mark the lawyer comments after Jesus' answer about the wisdom with which Jesus had spoken.

In the Book of Matthew, the author affirms that Jesus states: "On these two Commandments hang all the Law and the prophets." Once again you have to ask yourself, do I believe the stories found in the Books of Matthew, Mark and Luke? If you do, then you have to accept this profound statement, to mean only one thing: All of the Old Testament is summed up into loving God thoroughly, and loving humans as you love yourself. By definition this passage has told you the only way you can have this kind of love is to follow the Law and the prophets, completely.

The author of Matthew teaches the woes of the Pharisees in Chapter 23, and he ends this chapter with a lament from Jesus saying: "Oh Jerusalem, Jerusalem thou that killest the prophets." This very same lament is recorded in Luke Chapter 13. But in the Book of Luke, it is given before the triumphal entry, at the close to a message that Jesus wants to send to Herod, whom He is calling a "fox."

During this reading the author of Matthew has again stated that much of the ministry of Jesus is foretold as prophesy from the Old Testament. Lets see how he did. When Jesus cast out those that were selling in the temple in Chapter 21, He makes a comment: "it is written, my house shall be called the house of prayer, but ye have made it a den of thieves."

There is no Old Testament scripture passage that states this. It can be made up by using two separate passages that if you add them together they sound similar to this statement. These are found in Isaiah Chapter 56, verse 7, and Jeremiah Chapter 7, verse 11. Remember that John records a similar event in John Chapter 2, but it was just Jesus' zeal, and whip, that is commented as to why and how he was driving them out of the temple, no reference to it being prophetic.

Again in Matthew Chapter 21, in verse 16, Jesus quotes the scriptures when he states that "Out of the mouth of babes and sucklings thou hast perfected praise." This is supposed to be a quote from Psalm Chapter 8, verse 2: "Out of the mouth of babes and sucklings hast thou ordained strength because of thy enemy..." It's not a scriptural reference as the author of Matthew has testified.

And yet again in Matthew Chapter 21, verse 42 through 44, Jesus is supposedly referencing scripture when He states: "Did ye never read in the scriptures, 'The stone which the builders rejected, the same has become the head of the corner: this is the Lord's doing and it is marvelous in our eyes.'" There are several texts that Christians try to credit this to as it is about a cornerstone, but the operative word in this passage is "rejected." This passage can only be Psalm Chapter 118, verse 22.

Many denominations, if not all, try to link this to Jesus being the head of the cornerstone in this passage, but that is way out of context. In the Book of Matthew it is delivered just after the the parable of the wicked vineyardmen, where the king (father) kills the wicked vineyardmen and gives the valuable vineyard to others. It is the "others" that are the head of the cornerstone in this story. Read the next few verses, the Jewish leadership understand this message. They are the wicked vineyardmen!

But Psalm 118 has no foretelling of the messiah to come or giving the "vineyard" to another group of more deserving fellows. It is about Israel living forever, even though they are compassed about, they will not fear. It is about the Lord sending them prosperity.

In Matthew Chapter 21, if you read through verse 44 you will see that this prophesy calls for the stone to fall on those and for them to be ground into powder. This is just not part of the message in Psalm Chapter 118. To this point in the Book of Matthew, I see very little, if any, that a scholar of the Old Testament could conclude that would lead someone to believe that the life that Jesus Christ was living would be a fulfillment of scriptures. If you are honest with yourself, you would have to agree.

Oh, there was one more Old Testament prophetic reference found in Matthew Chapter 22, verses 29 and 30. This is the conclusion of the trap set by the Sadducees about a woman who had seven husbands. This story is also found in Mark Chapter 12, and Luke Chapter 20. The verse goes like this: "Jesus answered and said unto them, Ye do err, not knowing the scriptures, nor the power of God in heaven. For in the resurrection they neither marry, nor are given in marriage, but are as the angels of God in heaven."

Only, if you use the reference in the middle of your pages you will see that it does not reference you back to the Old Testament. It can't. There is no Old Testament passage that even remotely tells you that we will be like the angels in heaven after the resurrection. There is definitely no reference to humans having no family interactions once we have left this world of sin. Think of the significance of this thought. All three authors of Matthew, Mark and Luke have told you that this story is true and yet, it is impossible. That is the importance of the Septuagint (the Greek translation of the Old Testament completed hundreds of years before this time). The Old Testament is/was thoroughly documented so we know that these authors have added a story that is totally unsubstantiated. Now lets get back to the conclusion of this chapter.

At the end of your reading in Matthew Jesus states "O Jerusalem, Jerusalem that killest the prophets and stonest them that are sent unto thee, how often would have I gathered thy children together, even as a hen gatherest her chickens under her wing, and ye would not." Where have we seen these very words before?

Back about half way into Jesus Christ's ministry in the Book of Luke Chapter 13, verse 34 you will see that Jesus delivered the same discourse. What are the odds of Jesus stating the very same words over a very different situation?

How close are the passages we have covered in the Books of Matthew, Mark, and Luke, which supposedly occurred in just a couple of days after the triumphal entry? Given the fact that none of this is recorded by the Apostle John, and the fact that most of it is in contradiction between themselves, how can you say that any of these stories are gospel? Sure, some of it might have been told, but was it told during this time period? The author of Luke tells you much of it was not.

Do I think that you should discard it because it is so contradictory? No, but you should understand that it is obviously not a single message system sent by God to you. There is no story or teaching that is found in the Books of Matthew, Mark, Luke or The Acts of the Apostles, that I will hang my hat on. They are good loving stories, but I will never take one of these and use it as a life model that I believe God has directed me to live by. How can it be? It contradicts itself!

This is proof positive that it isn't a single integrated message system sent by God to You and me to live by!

When these books are in agreement with the Old Testament, then I will accept their teaching, but when they appear to be in disagreement with the Old Testament, or appear to teach that the Old Testament is no longer applicable to a Christian's life, then I have to discard the teaching. After all, you have seen example after example of each of them disagreeing between themselves.

Did you forget that none of them are signed? None of them say they are from God. There is no declaration of spiritual inspiration. You can't say that about the Old Testament.

The Betrayal and Last Supper

The Books of Matthew, Mark and Luke will cover a couple of chapters each during this time frame. They will either state out right, or infer, that the Last Supper is the Passover meal. Once again, this will bring them into direct conflict with the Apostle John. Before I explain what to focus on in these chapters, let me digress a little.

John is the only gospel account that eludes to who has written one of the four gospels. None of the other three gospels gives you even the tiniest clue who wrote them. In John Chapter 21, verse 24, the author of the Book of John tells you that it is "he" that sat next to Jesus at the last supper and asked who would betray Jesus, that wrote the Book of John. You may want to argue if it was John, but you would have to agree that the author of the Book of John was a disciple. There is no passage in the Books of Matthew, Mark, Luke or the Book of Acts that any authorship can be established. It's just fable. Well maybe not fable, more like tradition, that these books were written by early church members, let alone another disciple!

So, if there is a direct conflict between the message that is found in the Books of Matthew, Mark, and Luke, with the one found in John, who will you believe? You have to take one side or the other. They are directly opposed! John will provide many facts that are counter to the other gospels as well as many beliefs that are taught in all churches today found in the Books of Matthew, Mark and Luke. These are called traditions of man.

We will take you back to the triumphal entry when we begin to cover John, because his story is so different to the other gospels that it wouldn't serve any purpose to teach it with the others. You will notice that John will call the Last Supper, just the "Last Supper." In the next chapter of this book, during the arrest you will learn that Jesus is arrested "before" the Passover. It will be mentioned twice. You will also learn that Jesus has to be removed from the cross because that evening is the beginning of a High Sabbath!

Does that mean that John is telling you that Jesus was crucified on a Friday? Of course not. There are weekly Sabbaths and then there are High Sabbaths. They are all listed in Leviticus Chapter 23. John tells you that Jesus is crucified before a High Sabbath. We will cover all this in the next couple of chapters. Keep a good eye on what John is telling you has happened. Most of the traditions that are followed in church about the Lord's Day worship, Friday crucifixion, and eating the Passover with His disciples will be destroyed by John. Who do you believe?

Matthew Chapter 24 verse 1 through Chapter 26 verse 30.

As Jesus is leaving the temple with His disciples at the beginning of Chapter 24, they comment to Him about the buildings. Jesus explains to them that not one stone will be left upon another. Later, when they are at the Mount of Olives the disciples come to Him and ask, when shall these things be, and what shall be the signs of thy coming, and the end of the world? Jesus' response will take the rest of this chapter as well as all of Chapter 25. Jesus begins His response by telling these disciples to be careful not to be deceived. Jesus explains of many deceptions or troubles that will happen, such as, false Christs, wars, famine, pestilence, and these are just the beginning.

You will be delivered up for My Name's sake, and many shall betray one another, and they will kill you. There will be many false prophets and the love will die in many. "But he that shall endure to the end, the same shall be saved." The end shall come when the gospel shall be preached as a witness to all nations. At this time an abomination of desolation will occur in the Holy place.

The trouble will come so quickly that we must flee to the mountains, not looking back or worrying about taking anything. "But pray ye that your flight be not in the winter, neither on the Sabbath day," for this is the great tribulation, the likes of which has never happened since the beginning of the world. If it wasn't for the sake of "those saved" all mankind would destroy itself. Don't be deceived by false Christs and false prophets that can show great signs and wonders for they can deceive even the most religious people. When the Son of Man returns, it will be like lightening shining from one side of the sky to the other.

Immediately after the tribulation, the sun will darken, the moon will have no light, and the stars shall fall from heaven. The Son of Man will appear and the people of the earth will mourn when they see the Son of Man coming in His glory. The angels with a great sound of a trumpet will gather the "saved."

Jesus then tells a parable of a fig tree, how when it starts to have leaves, summer is near. Just as the fig tree's leaves are a sign of summer, so are all of the things I have told you a sign that the end is near. No one knows of that time but my Father. And He gave a couple of examples: Two will be in a field and one will be taken, two will be grinding at the mill and one will be taken. Just as in the time of Noah, no one will be expecting what is about to happen.

So be ready, because the Lord will reward those that are ready. If you think that you can do what you want, and that the time won't come shortly, if He then comes, He will cut you asunder like an evil serpent.

Chapter 25 starts with the parable of the ten virgins, five of which had planned ahead, five had not. The five that were not ready were not allowed in to the feast.

The next parable was about a man that gave money to several of his servants and then went away to a far country. When he returned home he took an accounting of how these servants prospered with the money. The ones that made a profit he rewarded and said "Well done, good and faithful servant." But one of them was scared to invest the money and was afraid of his master, so he hid the coinage. When he gave his master back the single talent that his master had given him, his master was angry, calling him an unprofitable servant and punished him.

When the Son of Man comes, He will sit on His throne of glory, separating the sheep to His right and the goats to His left. Those on His right will be blessed because they cared for Jesus Christ's brethren when they were in need, but those on the left did not. Those on the left shall go away into everlasting punishment.

Chapter 26 occurs after all these parables, with Jesus noting to His disciples that it is only two days until the Passover when the Son of Man is to be betrayed and crucified. Then the Jewish leadership consisting of the elders, scribes, chief priests and high priest gather together and conspire how they can take Jesus and kill Him. But they knew not to do it on the feast day or there would be an uproar.

Jesus' head is anointed by a woman with an alabaster box of ointment while at Simon the Leper's house. The disciples are filled with indignation at the waste of this precious ointment. Jesus rebukes them and states that this was done for His burial. With this, Judas Iscariot leaves and meets with the chief priests and asks what they will give him to betray Jesus. They agree to give him 30 pieces of silver.

The author of the Book of Matthew then tells you that it is the first day of the feast of Unleavened Bread and the disciples come to Jesus to ask where they are to prepare the Passover. Jesus sends them into the city to a certain man, and the Passover is made ready. During dinner, Jesus predicts who will betray Him, and then warns: "but woe unto that man by whom the Son of Man is betrayed," and Jesus affirms to Judas that he will betray Him.

As they were eating Jesus took bread and wine and blessed it and calls it a New Testament, which is shed for the remission of sins. And after a hymn, they went out to the Mount of Olives.

Mark Chapter 13, verse 1 through Chapter 14 verse 26 As Jesus leaves the temple, one of the disciples makes comments about the construction of the temple. Jesus explains that the temple will be utterly destroyed. Peter, James, and John come to Jesus when they were at the Mount of Olives and ask Him two questions. When will this occur, and what is the sign that these will happen shortly?

Jesus takes the rest of Chapter 13 to answer these questions, and begins by warning them not to be deceived. There will be false Christs, wars, nations against nations, earthquakes and famines, but these are just the beginning.

He then warns them to be ready to be beaten and brought before rulers for "My Name's sake." But before the end can come the gospel needs to be told throughout the world. If you are caught and brought before authorities, don't worry about what you will say, as the Holy ghost will speak through you.

Brother will betray brother, family member against family member, even to deliver them unto death. You shall be hated for My Name's sake, "But he that shall endure unto the end, the same shall be saved." But when you see the same type of abomination that is written in the Book of Daniel, it is time to flee.

Don't look back. Leave everything. I pity those that have breast feeding babies. Pray that it is not in the winter. There has never been an affliction as there will be during this time. Only for the reason that God wants to save His elect, and shortens this time, all life would be destroyed. Even at this time there will be false Christs!

After this tribulation the sun will be darkened, the moon will not glow, and the stars will fall from heaven. At this time will they see the Son of Man coming in His Glory. Then He will send His angels to gather up His elect.

These signs are given to show you when the time will be near. It is just like the time when you see the leaves of the fig tree beginning to emerge, you know that summer is near. This generation will not pass before all these things have happened. But, only God the Father knows the time when all this will happen.

So be ready. Just as a man that left for journey and left all that he had in his servants hands. Be ready for the time when the master returns, because you don't know when it will happen.

Chapter 14 opens two days before the Passover. The chief priests want to somehow kill Jesus. "But they say, not on the feast, lest there be an uproar of the people."

While dining at Bethany in the house of Simon the Leper, Jesus is anointed on the head by a lady with an alabaster box filled with spikenard. Some were unhappy with this act, but Jesus rebuked them and tells them that she has done a good work, and it is done beforehand for His burial.

Judas then goes out to meet with the chief priests to see what they will give him to betray Jesus. They are pleased and promise him money.

On the first day of the Feast of Unleavened Bread, Jesus' disciples ask Him where they will eat the Passover. Jesus sends them into the city and explains who to look for. They follow His instructions and make the room ready as they were directed. At evening, Jesus arrives and they eat. During the dinner, Jesus explains that one of them will betray Him. They all become sorrowful and ask: "Is it I?" Jesus explains that it is one of the twelve. Jesus then gives a warning to the one that will betray Him.

As they ate, Jesus began to break bread and pray over the wine as He passed it around and tells them that this is My blood of the New Testament which is shed for many. And after they had sung a hymn, they went to the Mount of Olives.

Luke Chapter 21, verse 5 through Chapter 22 verse 38 Some with Jesus make comments about the beauty of the temple. Jesus explains that the days will come when all this will be destroyed. And they ask Him: Master, when shall these things be, and what sign will there be when these things will happen? Jesus warns them not to be deceived.

There will be many that come in my name, but do not follow them. Don't worry when you hear of wars, or when nations will fight nations, there will be earthquakes, famines, pestilence, and great signs from heaven. But before this happens, you will be persecuted for My Name's sake. You have no need to worry about what you will say, because I will put the words in your mouth. I will give you the wisdom you will need so that your words cannot be resisted.

You will be betrayed by all family members and friends, putting some to death. You will be hated for My Name's sake. "But there shall not an hair of your head perish." when you see Jerusalem surrounded by armies, then you know that the time of the end is near. Quickly flee from Jerusalem and it's countryside. "For these are the days of vengeance..." Hopefully you won't have babies. Jerusalem will be destroyed and the people will be led away into captivity by the Gentiles.

All things that we think of as nature will be perplexed. Men's hearts will be in fear, and then shall they see the Son of Man coming in His glory. It is like the fig tree. When the leaves begin to come forth, we know that summer is near. So, when you see these signs, know that the Kingdom of God is at hand. This generation will not pass away until all this is fulfilled. Be ready. Don't let the cares of this life become too important that you become unaware. And He taught in the day time and spent the evenings at the Mount of Olives.

Chapter 22 opens with the Passover being close. The chief priests are still looking for a way to kill Him. Satan enters into Judas and he went to talk with them on how he might betray Jesus. They were glad and offered him money. He agreed to try to deliver Jesus into their hands away from the multitude.

"Then came the day of unleavened bread when the Passover was to be killed." Jesus sends Peter and John to make ready for the Passover meal. He and the twelve disciples ate the Passover and then Jesus broke bread and had the disciples share the glass of wine, telling them: "This cup is the New Testament in My blood, which is shed for you." He then explains that the one that would betray Him was at the table with Him at that moment.

He then cursed that person with: "woe unto that man by whom He is betrayed." The disciples all wondered who it was. At the same time, they began to argue among themselves who should be accounted for being the greatest. Jesus explained that this is not how His followers should feel, for it is the servant to all that is the greatest of all. You have endured with Me and will eat and drink at My table and you will judge the twelve tribes of Israel.

Then Jesus told Peter that Satan desired to have him, but He had prayed for him, that when Peter was converted, he would strengthen the brethren. Peter states that he is ready to suffer or die for Jesus. Jesus explains to Peter that before the rooster crows in the morning, Peter will have denied knowing Him three times.

Jesus begins to remind them of when they had been sent out with the power to heal, did they lack anything? They reply no. But now Jesus wants them to keep their money and buy a sword if they don't have one. The disciples explain that they have two swords, and Jesus states that, that is enough. Then they depart for the Mount of Olives.

John Chapter 12, verse 20 through Chapter 17 verse 26 The last we read from John, Jesus was entering Jerusalem in the Triumphal entry. All of the events recorded in the Books of Matthew, Mark, and Luke from the last chapter will not be noted by John, nor most of what is recorded in this chapter. John told you in Chapter 12, verse 12, that the Triumphal entry happened just five days before Passover.

John explains that many want to see Jesus. Jesus knows that His hour is come, and explains that a seed needs to die in the ground, if it is to bring forth fruit. He explains that those that love Him will want to be with Him more than here on earth, and they will be honored by God the Father. Jesus is troubled over the coming events and really doesn't look forward to what will happen, but knows that this is why He is here and states: "Father, glorify Thy Name." Then a voice from heaven spake: "I have both glorified it, and will glorify it again." Jesus explains to those there that the voice was for their benefit, not His, and then states that it is about time for Satan to be cast down.

Jesus then explains that when the Son of Man is lifted up, signifying the crucifixion, that it will draw men to Him. The people do not understand because they believe that the Christ will live forever, then ask, "who is the Son of Man?" Then Jesus explains in a riddle about walking in the light. And, even though He had done so many miracles, they still didn't believe that He was the Christ. This was foretold by Isaiah. Even still, many believed, but would not openly profess this belief for fear of being put out of the synagogue.

Jesus then cries out "he that believeth on Me, believeth not on Me, but on Him that sent Me. And He that seeth Me, seeth Him that sent Me." If you believe on Me you won't abide in the darkness. If you don't believe Me, I will not judge you, as I came to save the world. But if you don't believe Me or My words, these words will judge you in the last days. I didn't make up these things that I am telling you, the Father sent me to say what I have spoken. I know that what He has told Me to speak will lead to everlasting life.

Chapter 13 opens with Jesus finishing His Last Supper with the disciples and He knows that His time is near when He will return to the Father, for it is almost Passover. At the end of the meal, the devil puts into the heart of Judas to betray Jesus.

After dinner, Jesus rises and begins to wash the feet of the disciples to show them that we should serve others. When He comes to Peter, he doesn't want his Lord to perform it. Jesus explains that if Peter will not allow it, then he will have no part in Him. Peter agrees and then asks if He should wash his hands and head. Jesus takes this time to explain that even though He has washed them all, they are all not clean, eluding to Judas.

Then He asks if they understand what He had done. He explains that He had given them an example of how they should act among themselves. After all, He is Lord and Master and performed this lowly service to them.

Then Jesus explains that the scriptures foretell that one that has eaten with Him would betray Him, and this He was sharing with them, so when it happened, they would know that He had predicted it. Then He becomes very depressed and cries: "Verily, verily, I say unto you, that one of you shall betray me." The disciples looked at each other.

Peter asks the author of the Book of John (I believe it to be the Apostle John), to ask Jesus who it will be. Jesus explains that it is the one that He shall dip the sop with. When He had dipped it, then He gives the sop to Judas. With this, Satan enters into Judas Iscariot. Jesus then tells Judas:

"That thou doest, do quickly." No one understands what has happened, but Judas leaves, and it is night. Jesus then states: "Now is the Son of Man glorified, and God is glorified in Him."

Jesus then explains that He will not be with them for long, and where He will be going, they cannot come. He tells them that He is giving them a new commandment to love one another as He had loved them. Peter then asks why he cannot go with Him now, as He would lay down his life for Him. Jesus explains that Peter will deny Jesus three times before the rooster crows the following morning.

Jesus delivers the farewell prayer in Chapter 17. It is an affirmation that He is from God and God has sent Him. He affirms that He has glorified God while He was on earth, and has finished the work that He was sent to do. He has kept those safe that God had given Him, and now He prayed for them, that God should keep them from evil. And not only did He pray for His disciples, but He also prayed for those that believed on Him. Jesus professes that He had been with God from the beginning and the love that God had loved Him would be in them and He in them.

At the conclusion of this prayer, at the beginning of Chapter 18, Jesus leads His disciples over the Brook Cedron to a garden.

So, what comparisons have we found in these chapters?
Just after the triumphal entry, John tells you that Jesus had many people that desired to see Him. During this exchange, a voice from heaven spoke to Jesus and said: "I have both glorified it, and will glorify it again." This is not recorded in the other gospels. This is the only recorded voice from heaven in the Book of John. Why this is so odd, is that John was supposed to be there at other times when a voice is recorded in other gospels, but this is the only voice from heaven, according to John!

In Matthew Chapter 24, Jesus delivers the signs of the second coming. This is also recorded in Mark Chapter 13, and Luke Chapter 21. Once again, the authors of Matthew and Mark tell a very similar story about how those that love Jesus are persecuted. Mark tells a condensed version. Two very important verses are found in Matthew Chapter 24. Verse 13 is talking about a time after the persecution that these people have just endured, and states: "but he that shall endure to the end, the same shall be saved." The same statement is found in Mark Chapter 13, verse 13.

Think carefully what this statement has just told you. Many who think they are saved, who pretend to love God and man more than themselves, who have walked down that sawdust path and said those canned lines, really aren't saved. This persecution refines those that are truly saved, and the rest will <u>fall away</u>, hence, they are not saved!

Also found in this story in Matthew Chapter 24, verse 20, is the sentence: "but pray ye that your flight not be in winter, neither on the Sabbath day." Out of the three gospel writers that give you this story, who do you believe most? If the author of the Book of Matthew was the Apostle Matthew, he was supposed to be there, and Jesus is supposed to have told this story. If you are going to believe that Matthew's gospel even happened, why wouldn't you believe this part? It is telling you that Jesus is warning you to "pray that this does not happen on the Sabbath (paraphrased)." Why don't Christian's believe in the Sabbath? It's Friday sundown to Saturday sundown. I can't fathom it.

Just today, I was leaving the Medical Lake detention facility where I was visiting with a friend. It happened to be Superbowl Sunday. There were a couple of Christian volunteers that were there for a Sunday meeting with the inmates. One stated that he was not going to watch the Superbowl, but was recording it because it was Sabbath. He told the person that he was talking to, that he was going to watch it at midnight to see how it turned out.

What's wrong with this picture? Christians have substituted a sundown to sundown commandment with a different day and a different time for days to begin and end. Face it, it isn't convenient to follow God's commandments, so Christians have substituted man made traditions as they suit themselves.

Now take a close look at the story found in Luke Chapter 21. Even though the author of Luke's story sounds similar to the one found in the Books of Matthew and Mark, who is being persecuted, and by whom? In the Books of Matthew and Mark, it is those who love Jesus who are being persecuted by those who do not. In the author of Luke's rendition, it is the Jewish people, or at least those who are living in Jerusalem, that are being surrounded by other nations. Is it Jesus' followers who are being persecuted, or the Jewish people as the Book of Luke is trying to tell you? Once again this shows a problem with the story found in Luke.

What makes the author of Luke's story even worse, is that he has told much of this story in Luke Chapter 17 before the triumphal entry, although it is told in full here in the Books of Matthew and Mark. So this single story told by Jesus, recorded in Matthew and Mark, is told as two different stories recorded in Luke Chapters 17 and 21. Can you really trust the author of Luke?

In the middle of these stories is a time when the people will be persecuted for His (Jesus') name's sake. You are instructed not to meditate on what you will say when questioned before kings and rulers. Who will put the words in your mouth for what you are to say? In the Books of Matthew and Mark it is the Holy Ghost, but in the Book of Luke it is Jesus that will put the words in your mouth.

A little further on in this same story found in Luke Chapter 21, verse 16, you see that some will be put to death. It's pretty straight forward, there will be persecution where family members will be betrayed by family members and some will be put to death. But then, two verses later is the sentence: "But there shall not an hair of your head perish." It doesn't compute. If some are put to death, then I believe that is a bit more drastic than loosing a few hairs. Which verse in Luke is the correct one? Some will die, or, you won't be harmed?

As I am sure you already know, in the Book of John this entire telling of the end-times tribulation is not mentioned. What amplifies this problem more is that if you turn back to Mark Chapter 13, verse 3, the author tells you that it is Peter, James, John and Andrew that have come to Jesus to ask of this foretelling. Doesn't it seem odd that if you look back at all these awesome stories found in Matthew, Mark, and Luke that most times it is just Jesus with Peter, James, and John, and yet none of this is recorded by John. I guess that John felt that none of this was important.

In Matthew Chapter 25, Jesus tells the parable of the man who gave talents (money) to several of his servants. Compare that to the story that the author of Luke tells in Chapter 19 verse 12 through verse 26. The stories are eerily the same especially the servant that hid his one coinage, the punishment was the same. Once again, only the author of Luke tells this story and the author of Matthew tells the one found in Matthew, but in the author of Luke's story it happens before the triumphal entry and in the author of Matthew's story it happens after the triumphal entry. One more thing to note in both of these stories, the master punishes the servant because of his fear of failure. That is one of my problems with this story found in both accounts. The God of the Old Testament doesn't punish us when we fear, we just don't reap the rewards.

In the second verse of Matthew Chapter 26, we see Jesus again telling His disciples that He is to be crucified. He even tells them how many days it will be before it happens. Although only told by the author of Matthew in this instance, how many times would you need to be briefed about a foretold happening before you understood what was to happen? But in all the Books of Matthew, Mark, Luke and John, the disciples scatter like frightened sheep when it happens.

This is where you have to use discernment. So far, Jesus has never told the disciples about this coming event in the Book of John. But if you review, it has occurred many times in the Books of Matthew, Mark and Luke. There is no reason for the disciples to be in unbelief in their accounts. You would think that they would have gathered together in prayer awaiting Him to be resurrected, but they don't. Here in the Book of Matthew, Jesus has told them again about His coming crucifixion. This is why I say you have to believe in either John's account, as it is a totally different and logical gospel, or you have to believe the one told by the authors of Matthew, Mark and Luke, which many times, makes no sense at all!

The Betrayal and Last Supper

In Matthew Chapter 26 and Mark Chapter 14, we see Jesus at Simon the Leper's house, <u>two days</u> before Passover, where a woman anoints His head with a precious oil. In the Book of Mark it is called spikenard. The disciples are filled with indignation over the waste. Jesus explains that this was done for His burial. Once again, Jesus is foretelling of His death shortly to come.

This story does have a strange twist. In John Chapter 12, we have Jesus in the same town sitting at dinner <u>six days</u> before Passover, that's four days prior to the account in the Books of Matthew and Mark. Mary takes a pound of spikenard and anoints His feet and wipes them with her hair. Judas Iscariot questions the waste of this ointment and Jesus rebukes him and tells him that this was kept for the day of His burying. This is the first hint in the Book of John that Jesus is to die!

So wait, Jesus has His feet anointed with spikenard six days prior to the Passover and then has to rebuke His disciples for bothering the woman that did it. Then four days later He has to rebuke His disciples again when He is again anointed with spikenard. This is what makes the comparing of the gospels so revealing. Do you really believe that it happened twice? Do you believe that if it did, he had chosen disciples that were so dense that He had to rebuke them again for the same error within four days?

But wait, the story becomes more bizarre when you go way back to Luke Chapter 7, starting at verse 36, and read about Jesus dining at a Pharisees house. During dinner, a woman anoints Jesus' feet with an ointment, from an alabaster box, and then wipes them with her hair. So, the author of Luke does not have a burial anointing as recorded by the other gospel writers, but he finds a way to weave the alabaster box, ointment, and a woman wiping Jesus' feet with her hair to an event that no other gospel author records.

In the Books of Matthew and Mark, after Jesus has been anointed on the head, Judas leaves Jesus to meet with the chief priests to see what they will give him to betray Jesus. This story kills me, I mean it totally kills me. Think of it, Judas is mad because Jesus has rebuked him over the anointing with ointment by the woman, so he goes out and betrays Jesus for 30 pieces of silver. Think about what the authors of Matthew, Mark, and Luke have already shared with you, the reader, in the powers given to him, Judas, by Jesus.

If you are to believe that the authors of Matthew, Mark and Luke's stories are gospel, Jesus has given Judas the power to cast out devils, to heal the sick and blind, and yet, he will trade all this for 30 pieces of silver? Jesus has brought back life, created something from nothing in the feeding of 4000 and 5000, and has demonstrated that He knows what others are thinking. Do you really want me to believe that Judas was that stupid that he felt that it was a good investment in his future to betray Jesus? This is the problem with the gospels of Matthew, Mark and Luke.

They obviously stem from one story, and it is always telling stories that supposedly are foretold in Old Testament scripture. And yet, when you read the Old Testament, although many of the points sound similar, the story really doesn't apply. By this time, if you have been following along in your Bible, you will have to agree that there was one story told by someone that all three authors of Matthew, Mark, and Luke have retold. One of these authors could have been the original author. But if these are truly inspired by the Holy Spirit, they would not disagree so much. Is this message from God or just presumed as Moses has prophesied? Let's look a little more closely at the 30 pieces of silver and the differences between John's account.

In the Book of John, the disciples are not given these great powers that have been supposedly given to Judas and the other disciples. Jesus has not been walking to and fro healing the sick and blind or bringing back people from death. In the Book of John you could make the case that Judas might want to try to make a profit from Jesus. After all, Jesus has not been so "powerful" in John's account, nor has Jesus given Judas any supernatural powers. But in John, it is never mentioned that Judas has any preconceived betrayal thoughts. In John Chapter 13, verse 2, you see that Satan had put the betrayal into Judas' heart, and in verse 27 it states: "And after the sop, Satan entered into him."

Who can resist God? That is a pretty obvious answer. But, who can resist Satan entering into one's self? For Satan to enter into Judas, it would have to have been with the permission of God the Father. Read the Book of Job and see the relationship between God the Father and Satan when he wants to try to get someone to denounce God.

So was the betrayal actually Judas, or Satan? John tells you that Satan had entered into him. Do we see Satan in Judas' body going to the chief priests asking for money? Satan just wants to help mankind to kill Jesus. He has no need for money. Judas is a tool that unwittingly Satan uses to fulfill God the Father's original purpose. There is no further condemnation of Judas in the Book of John, nor should there be if He was a tool of God.

But Luke was a little more coy. He has blended both the stories found in Matthew and Mark with the one found in John. The author of the Book of Luke tells you at the beginning of Chapter 22, that Satan entered into Judas and then went to commune with the chief priests about betraying Jesus. They were happy and agreed to give him money. Once again this brings up the issue, if Satan had entered into Judas, why would he care about money? Who is in charge if you are devil possessed? If you are to believe the author of Luke's story, then you have to believe all of his stories. Remember each of the devil possessed men in the Book of Luke? Once the devils are cast out, the people can properly reason. But, until then, they are being controlled by the devil that is possessing them.

Not that I believe in devil possession, as I stated earlier in this book, devil possession is only found in the Books of Matthew, Mark, Luke and the Acts of the Apostles. It isn't anywhere else in the Bible, New or Old Testament. There isn't a gift of the spirit recorded by Paul that gives the power to cast out devils. That is probably because they can't possess people. If they could, we do not have free choice. We would not be at fault when we sin. Use some discernment and you will see that this act of devil possession is not true!

In the Book of John, there are no devil possessed men and women ever mentioned. There is no casting out of devils. There is only this one occasion when Satan enters into Judas. The only other people that are possessed or controlled by spiritual entities in the entire Bible, are those people where God had hardened their hearts or are indwelt by the Spirit of God, such as Samson..

If you believe the stories of devils possessing people in the time of Jesus, why doesn't it happen today? I used to wonder if some of the chronically sick people I knew were actually devil possessed. That was because I thought it was common throughout the Bible that people had been devil possessed. That was an unfortunate lack of knowledge and use of discernment on my part. It's just not so. The only authors that bring you this devil possession, are the authors that wrote the Books of Matthew, Mark, and Luke (who also wrote Acts). The author of the Book of John, who has to be a disciple as stated in John Chapter 21, verse 24 (most probably the Apostle John), did not make mention of this Satanic power. This is one more reason why the Book of John appears to be the real gospel.

But what about the thirty pieces of silver? Where does this fit in. In Matthew Chapter 27, verse 9 you learn that the 30 pieces of silver are foretold in Jeremiah, only it isn't in Jeremiah. The only 30 pieces of silver mentioned in the Bible is found in Zechariah Chapter 11. Read the story. The 30 pieces of silver are used to pay a price, and then it is cast to the potter, but does the story fit?

In Zechariah it is a story of God breaking his covenant with Israel. In the middle of the story "someone" in the story is speaking and asks, "If ye think good, give my price; and if not, forbear. So they weighed for my price thirty of silver. And the Lord said unto me, cast it unto the potter: a goodly price that I was priced at of them. And I took the thirty of silver, and cast it unto the potter in the house of the Lord."

So, in the prophesy someone is asking what I am worth, and they agree that it is 30 pieces of silver. They pay him his price and God tells him to cast it to the potter. Is that what happens in the Book of Matthew?

The Book of Matthew does explain why there are 30 pieces of silver and a potter's field mentioned, but does his rendition apply to the prophecy? Go back and read the Book of

Zechariah. Jesus isn't paid the price and then He gives it to the potter. The Jewish leadership offers Judas 30 pieces of silver to betray the "someone" in the story. Then Judas casts it back to the leadership who buys a potter's field. Is it cast by the "someone" in Zechariah's prophesy to the potter? It's not even close!

Even though we will discuss this again in the Book of the Acts of the Apostles later in this book, read Acts Chapter 1, verses 16 through 20. In these verses written by the author of the Book of Luke you will see a totally different story about the 30 pieces of silver. In this story, Judas buys the Potter's field. So who bought the field? You can't have it both ways, either Judas bought it, or the Jewish leadership bought it! Either way, neither version agrees with the prophesy in Zechariah.

There are 4 different prophesies that you will find in Zechariah that the authors of Matthew, Mark, and Luke will use to tell the story of Jesus Christ. Even John will reference it once. It will take about 30 minutes to read. When you come to one of the familiar stories, ask yourself, does it really apply? And, as I stated before, the reference to prophecy came from the author of Matthew who tells you it is Jeremiah, not Zechariah that prophesied this prophesy!

One more bizarre thought, who was there to record this transaction? The only way that the author of Matthew, Mark or Luke could record this transaction or list of events is if it was vision or presumed. Moses has told you it is presumed.

Matthew Chapter 26, verse 17; Mark Chapter 14, verse 12; and Luke Chapter 22, verse 7, all tell you that it is the <u>first day</u> of the Feast of Unleavened Bread, and the day of Passover. The disciples are wanting to prepare for the meal that is about to take place. This is a crucial error in the text that is easily disproved if anyone has a <u>basic</u> understanding of the Old Testament. You have to believe in this one-day celebration if you are to fit the Friday crucifixion and the Sunday resurrection into modern Christian beliefs, only, it isn't correct!

First, you just didn't eat any old lamb on the 14th day of Abib. There was a ceremony. The Lamb was to live with you for four days. So, you would choose a lamb without blemish, bring it into your home and it lived with you for four days. The Passover celebration and feast can be referenced in Exodus Chapter 12; Leviticus Chapter 23; Numbers Chapters 9, 28 and 33; and Deuteronomy Chapter 16. All these chapters agree with each other exactly. They explain the event, and how this event is celebrated in relationship to a separate, yet concurrent celebration, The Feast of Unleavened Bread.

Look back at Matthew Chapter 26, verses 3-5 and Mark Chapter 14, verse 1 and 2. If you want to believe that the story of Jesus eating the Passover as told by the authors of Matthew, Mark, and

Luke is the "true" gospel, then test it. The authors of Matthew and Mark tell you that the Jewish Leadership did not want to take or kill Jesus on the feast day or there would be an uproar of the people. First ask yourself, do I really know what the feast days are? In the first three gospels, it is pretty clear that Jesus ate the Passover and then was arrested that night by a Jewish mob. He was held and sentenced in the court of the Jews that evening and the following morning by midday was hung on the cross. Before evening, He was dead and was removed before the Sabbath. But remember, the leadership would not take or kill Him on a feast day, as these authors have written.

Do you see any problems with that order of events? When is Passover, and what is the next day? Read Leviticus Chapter 23. Passover is in the evening of the 14th day of Abib. It is followed by a week long ceremony called the Feast of Unleavened Bread. These two feasts are symbolic of the first Passover and the exodus from Egypt the next morning. The first day of the Feast of Unleavened Bread is identified in Leviticus Chapter 23, as the 15th day of Abib. Both the first and last day of this week are feasts and Holy convocations, or better stated, High Sabbaths.

Remember, Leviticus Chapter 23 is identifying the feasts, and the 14th and 15th day of Abib are both feasts. These dates are the day of Passover, and the day after Passover, or more correctly stated, the first day of the Feast of Unleavened Bread! This is a major problem with the Books of Matthew, Mark, and Luke. Leviticus Chapter 23 specifically states that Passover isn't the first day of the Feast of Unleavened Bread, it is the day that precedes it.

The Book of Luke is really off the mark with these dates. He also has a problem with his understanding of the celebrations when He states in Chapter 22, verse 1, "Now the Feast of Unleavened Bread drew nigh (near), which is called the Passover." Once again, the Passover isn't the Feast of Unleavened Bread, nor is it the first day of the Feast of Unleavened Bread. It is the day that precedes the first day of the Feast of Unleavened Bread. It is perfectly clear in Leviticus Chapter 23, and Numbers Chapter 28, as to what the feasts are, and on what day they are to be celebrated. Both references show that Passover is the day before the Feast of Unleavened Bread.

So, if you want to state that Jesus ate the Passover with the disciples, He would have been held in court, sentenced, hung and died on the first day of the Feast of Unleavened Bread, which is a Holy Convocation or a High Sabbath, and oh yes, it is a feast. In Leviticus Chapter 23, and Numbers Chapter 28, you have learned that they could do no work on a holy convocation day! So, the stories found in the Books of Matthew, Mark and Luke do not hold water. The one thing the Jewish leadership did not do, was break with tradition. As stated in Matthew Chapter 26, verse 5, they knew better than to do this on a feast day. The authors telling the stories of Matthew, Mark and Luke were either not Jews, or it had been so much time after the event when it was recorded, that the story was heavily polluted.

We know that if Luke wrote the Book of Luke, he was a Gentile, so we would not expect him to see these subtleties. But who really wrote the Books of Matthew and Mark? I don't know and neither can any other living person, truly prove who really wrote these books. But anyone with half a brain at this point, should be able to use their God-given gift of discernment to understand that the time frame and events recorded by the authors of Matthew, Mark and Luke have problems between their story of the events, and Jewish customs and the Law.

But let's just say that there stories are correct and Jesus ate His passover meal with the disciples. Did Jesus break the Law? Where in the Books of Matthew, Mark, and Luke have you noted that Jesus broke the Mosaic Law? He hasn't. Jesus has made a distinction between the commandments of men, called the traditions of the elders, and the commandments of God, found in the Law. He has had no problems breaking the commandments of men, but has never broken a commandment of God, found in the Law. Why would He break the Law here in the eating of the Passover?

What did the Passover consist of? Exodus Chapter 12 explains that it was a roasted lamb that you had kept in your home since the 10th day of Abib. You were to be wearing your shoes and have your staff in your hand. What remained of the lamb that was not finished, including bones, by the morning was to be burnt in the coals. This was a tradition that was to be passed down and celebrated for all generations.

In Numbers Chapter 9 you learn that the meal consisted of a roasted Lamb, bitter herbs, and unleavened bread. Do you see anything about a roasted lamb or bitter herbs anywhere in the stories of Matthew, Mark and Luke? Do you see the cleansing of the remains?

Finally in Deuteronomy Chapter 16 you learn the name of this first month of the Hebrew Calendar was Abib. You also learn that this celebration or feast was to be held <u>all night</u>. Deuteronomy Chapter 16, starting in verse 4, and continuing through verse 7, you learn that you are to celebrate all evening until the morning and then you are to turn into your tents in the morning.

So this was the celebration or Feast of the Passover. How much of the Passover celebration do you see in the Books of Matthew, Mark and Luke? If this was the Passover, where would have Judas found a mob to bring back and arrest Jesus. After all, it was an all night celebration where you were not to leave until the morning, and then you were to turn into your tents. So, to believe the Books of Matthew, Mark and Luke, Jesus was leading His disciples astray (from a commandment of God) by taking them out into the night to go to the garden and the mob was also leaving their celebration to arrest Him. Who would leave the celebration feast?

The Apostle John does not tell you that it is the Passover, and expressly tells you that it isn't. All four stories tells you that Jesus took bread and blessed it. The stories in Matthew, Mark, and Luke were either written without any knowledge of what transpired, or they have become heavily polluted over the years. Either way, this proves that you cannot take lines from them to live your Christian life by. They are too polluted, for whatever reason.

We don't have any of these problems with the Book of John. In it, the author clearly tells you that the last supper was only called the last supper because it was the last supper that Jesus ate with His disciples before His trial and crucifixion. Just read the first two verses of John Chapter 13. It is clear that the Passover is almost here in verse one, and that the last supper has ended in verse two. So after the last supper we were getting close to the Passover, but it wasn't here yet.

I know that we are not there yet, but the author tells you clearly in John Chapter 18, verse 28, that Jesus is going into Pilate's judgment hall after the Jewish trial, before the Passover will take place. The Jews will not enter, "lest they should be defiled; but that they might eat of the Passover." So what do you do with this verse? It gets worse in the next chapter, but this verse alone tells you that you have to choose between gospel accounts. Is it the one that is given by the authors of Matthew, Mark and Luke, that states that Jesus ate the Passover, or is it the gospel account that makes total sense given to you by John? You can't have it both ways. You have to accept that only one can be right. I guess that you can, once again, stick your head in the sand and say: "I don't want to know!"

Please note what Jesus calls the taking of the bread and drinking of the wine at the Last Supper in Matthew Chapter 26, Mark Chapter 14, and Luke Chapter 22. Many Christian churches like to say that this is the end of the old "Mosaic" covenant and the beginning of a new one. Is that what it states? A covenant is a deal, like making a promise. You keep your word, and I will keep mine. This was not a covenant, it states clearly that it is a new testament. A testament is a statement from one who has something notable to say, as in a testimony. Is there anything here that states what we call today the Old Testament, as being replaced? No, in fact the Old Testament was not called a testament at all, it was the scriptures. Jesus does not say this is the new scriptures, just that it is His testimony.

Did you notice when Jesus foretells that Peter would deny Him before the morning? It is affirmed by two gospel authors in this chapter that it happened during the last supper, and it will be told by the remaining two that it happens in the garden in the next chapter. Did it happen at the dinner, or in the garden? Better yet, does Peter deny Jesus three times before the rooster crows once or three times before the rooster crows twice? You may ask yourself, does it matter? That is the point of this book. If it was God sent, it would be accurate.

At the close of the meal in Luke Chapter 22, verses 35 through 38 it is clearly a call for these disciples to have the means to take care of themselves and to defend themselves if needed. It states that they should sell their clothing if that is what it takes to purchase a sword. Also, did you note that after Jesus explains that someone will betray Him, Judas is never mentioned, nor does he appear to ever leave the dinner.

Have you ever taken the time to compare what is happening at the last supper? In the Books of Matthew, Mark, and Luke you have the Passover meal followed by Judas taking the sop and leaving, then they sing a hymn and go out to the Mount of Olives. Short and simple.

In John we have a meal with the disciples that happens before the event of the Passover. After the meal, but before they leave for the garden beyond the Brook Cedron, John tells you that Jesus washes the disciples feet, gives them a new commandment, foretells Peter would deny Him, delivers the farewell discourse, tells of the comforter to come, and delivers the farewell prayer. Then they leave the building! Where were they headed? It was the garden, beyond the Brook Cedron.

Do these two different gospel accounts have anything in common? Not really, but Jesus and the disciples were there! Other than that, they are entirely different.

But let's not forget to see how the author of the Book of Matthew is doing with his Old testament references to the ministry of Jesus Christ. In this chapter he has referenced the Old Testament two times. How do you think he will do?

This first one really bothers me. In Chapter 24, verse 15, we see Jesus talking about the end times. This reference is used by all denominations as a sign of the last coming. "When ye therefore shall see the abomination of desolation, spoken of by Daniel the prophet, standing in the Holy place (whoso readeth let him understand) then let them which be in Judea flee to the mountains."

Think about what is written here. Most Christians believe, because of this passage, that the abomination of desolation must occur before the end of time and the return of Jesus. Earlier in my Christian walk I felt the same way, but through constant study I have begun to doubt. Here is the first problem. Does it say "like in the Book of Daniel?" No, it is the abomination of desolation <u>spoken of in the Book of Daniel</u>. For those that are not aware of the story, it is a vision found in Daniel Chapter 11 and 12.

It is a vision telling the coming history of Greece. Once Alexander the Great dies, his empire is broken into four empires with the kings of the North and South in constant battle. Near the end of this conflict we have one of the kings desecrating the temple. This is commonly known history, but it was in the future during the time of Daniel.

So the abomination of desolation had already occurred. It was several hundred years before Jesus Christ was born! The second problem with this foretelling of history through Daniel's vision by the author of the Book of Matthew is that it applies to the people of Judea. So do the rest of us have to flee to the mountains?

That is the problem with much of the Book of Matthew, the scope is all wrong. He isn't concerned about those that believe living in the rest of the world, it is a focused study for those converted Jews in Judea. If this story or vision in Matthew was really told by Jesus, do you believe that He would know that Christianity would grow larger than just Judea?

In Matthew Chapter 26, verse 24, Jesus is to have said "the Son of Man goeth as it is written of Him: but woe unto the that man whom the Son of Man is betrayed!" Here is the problem with referencing that sentence. You will find many prophets in the Old Testament being called the Son of Man. In the Book of Ezekiel alone you will see Ezekiel being called the Son of Man ninety-two times. So this is an untraceable reference.

How has the author of the Book of Matthew been doing? Not so good in my calculations. This isn't to say that Jesus Christ is not referenced in the Old Testament. I am just saying that if you were a Jew at about 50 AD who knew his scriptures well, the author of Matthew would not be making the point that the Jews should have recognized Jesus.

One last comparison between the stories of the Apostle John and the other three authors. We see that John does not talk of demonic possession and casting out of devils. You have noted beginning in this chapter that the Passover was not the Last Supper. If you look back in John Chapter 15 you will read the farewell discourse. Read John Chapter 15, verse 24 again.

This verse states that only Jesus is able to do the works that He has been doing. The text is referring to miracles, and here in John Chapter 15, He is telling you that He is the is only one that can do them. There isn't a note that Jesus has given this power to the disciples, just that He is the only one that can do them. This again is forcing a decision between the trustworthiness of the other gospels that has told you over and over that His 12 were given this great power, then another 70 were given the power and finally that even the Jews had much of this power. John is writing plainly that Jesus, or God the Father, has not given this power to anyone except Jesus.

If you turn back to John Chapter 14, starting in verse 5 you have Jesus talking with several of His disciples explaining that He will be leaving shortly. By the time you read to verse 12 you will see that Jesus has again explained His proof that He is from God, displayed through His works. He concludes that if you believe on Him that you to will have this power to do these works. What good would it be to believe on Jesus to have these works if you already had these powers to do these works?

In the Garden, the Arrest, and the Trial

This chapter could have two different starting points. The Books of Matthew, Mark, and Luke tell you that Jesus led His disciples to the Mount of Olives. Two of these accounts tell you that they go to a garden called Gethsemane. John tells you that Jesus leads them over the Brook Cedron to a garden. Is it the same starting point? As the Brook Cedron is only mentioned one time in the entire Bible, and that is here, you really can't be sure, but the author of the Book of John knows where the Mount of Olives is, and makes no mention of it. There is a Brook Kidron in the vicinity of Jerusalem, but is it the same brook?

Gethsemane is only mentioned twice in the Bible and it is here in two of the gospels. So there is really no Biblical documentation to show the relationship between the Brook Cedron, the Mount of Olives, or Gethsemane. The only way that you can make the case that they are all starting at the same point is to presume! If you take the time to research these names and find that I have given you the correct facts, can you really say that the garden that is beyond the Brook Cedron is the garden called Gethsemane?

What is the purpose of true study? It is to learn. What you should be learning is to shed those ridiculous thoughts that the Bible is totally from God and is error free. Once again, you have to look at what each of these writers portrays as truth. Either the mob that arrests Jesus has the power to control Jesus, or they don't. They are either fearful of His powers, or they are not. The mob either tries to restrain Jesus' followers as the author of Mark will assert, with the young man in the linen cloth, or they have a reason to let them all leave in piece as told by the Apostle John. You have to decide if you want to learn, or just live your life with your head in the sand. Most Christians will choose the later.

You will note from the last chapter that Jesus spent a long time with the disciples at the Last Supper in John's account. The other gospel writers give the supper little time, but with a lot of time spent in the garden. John on the other hand, has Jesus arrive about the same time that He is arrested.

Note the escalating power that is still apparent in the Book of John during the arrest. With a word from Jesus, those that are there to arrest Him fall over. This would be a good reason for the arresting crowd to heed Jesus' request to leave the disciples alone. Doesn't it seem odd that if Peter had taken a swing with a sword at one of those that were arresting Jesus, that they wouldn't have arrested him also? But they don't. Why? They truly had to fear something that happened, and it only happens in the account by the author of the Book of John.

Matthew Chapter 26, verse 31 through Chapter 27 verse 26

At the Mount of Olives, Jesus explains that all of them (His disciples) will leave Him this evening in fear, but when He rises from the dead, He will go before them into Galilee. Peter states that he will never be offended by Jesus. But Jesus predicts that before the rooster will crow, Peter will have denied Him three times this night. Peter tells Him that it is not so, and so do all the other disciples.

As they enter Gethsemane, Jesus takes Peter, James, and John and leaves the rest of the disciples while He goes to pray. Jesus was very sorrowful and heavy hearted, and went a little farther alone and began to pray. Jesus asks the Father if He will remove the burden of the coming event.

When He returns back to Peter, James, and John, He finds them asleep and wakes them for moral support, and then goes away to pray again. After praying, once again when He returns, He finds them asleep, and leaves them to go and pray again. On the third return He finds them still asleep and tells them to sleep on. But then states, "rise, let us be going, and the Son of Man is betrayed into the hands of sinners."

Just then, Judas comes with a great armed multitude along with many of the Jewish leadership, and he kisses Jesus. They take Jesus, but just then a disciple draws his sword and strikes off the ear of one from the multitude. Jesus tells him to put the sword back in the scabbard. Jesus explains to him that He could be rescued by twelve legions of angels if He wanted. But this arrest is done to fulfill the scriptures.

Jesus asks the multitude why they came out armed to take Him. After all, He taught daily in the temple, why not come and peaceably arrest Him there? With this the disciples flee. Those that arrest Jesus lead Him away to the High Priest Caiaphas.

Peter follows to the High Priest's palace to see what will happen to Jesus, and sits with the servants. In the Palace, many false witnesses come before the council but there was no charge that could convict Jesus to death. Jesus does not answer any of the false accusations. The High Priest asks for Jesus to just say bluntly whether He is the Christ, the Son of God.

Jesus explains that those are his words, but soon you will see the Son of Man coming in His glory! With this, the High Priest rips His clothes and states that they have no more need of witnesses as Jesus has just spoken blasphemy. The people agree that He is guilty of death. Those there abuse Jesus, and taunt Him by saying: Prophesy to us who has struck you.

While Peter is sitting and watching, a young lady comes up to him and says: "Thou also wast with Jesus of Galilee." Peter denies it and goes out to the porch where another says: "This was also with Jesus of Nazareth." Again he denies the accusation. After some time, they that stood by came and said unto him: "Surely thou art of them; for your speech bewrayeth thee." Then Peter began to curse and swear: "I know not this man!" And immediately the rooster crowed, and Peter remembered how Jesus predicted his actions. Peter went out and wept bitterly.

At the beginning of Chapter 27 it is morning and the Jewish leadership have decided to put Jesus to death, and they bring Him to Pontius Pilate. In the mean time, Judas has a change in heart when He sees that Jesus is condemned. He gives back the money and hangs himself. The leadership takes this money and buys a potter's field to fulfill a prophecy by Jeremiah.

Pilate asks Him: "Art thou King of the Jews? Jesus responded: "Thou sayest." After being accused of many things by the Jewish leadership, Jesus said nothing. Pilate has the opportunity to release one person to the people at the feast and he puts it to the people, should I release a very bad man named Barabbas or Jesus. He was sure that the people would take Jesus because it looked like Jesus was not a guilty of anything.

In the mean time, Pilate's wife sent word to him that she had suffered greatly in a dream over the matter with Jesus, who she called a just man. But the Chief Priests whip the crowd up into a frenzy and call to have Jesus crucified. Then Pilate washed his hands with water and told the crowd that his hands were clean and the blood of this just person would be on their heads. The people answered that the blood of this person is on them and their children. After releasing Barabbas, he had Jesus scourged and delivered for crucifixion.

Mark Chapter 14, verse 27 through Chapter 15, verse 15. After leaving, Jesus tells them they will all scatter this evening when He is smitten. Peter tells Jesus that all the others may leave Him, but he won't. Jesus foretells that Peter will deny Him this evening three times before the rooster crows twice the next morning.

As they arrive at Gethsemane, Jesus leaves the disciples and removes Himself from them to pray, taking only Peter, James and John. He walks a little further alone and prays that this hour could be taken from Him by the Father. When He returns to them, He finds them sleeping and wakes them up. Then He again goes a little ways and prays, only to find them sleeping when He returns. So Jesus went away to pray a third time. When He comes back he tells them "Sleep on now and take thy rest." Then states: "Rise up, let us go, lo, he that betrayeth me is at hand."

Immediately as He was speaking, Judas arrives with an armed multitude sent by the Jewish leadership. Judas kisses Jesus, as a sign of who they are to take, and the multitude took Jesus. Then one of the disciples took a sword and cut off the ear of a servant of the high priest. Jesus asks why they came out as an armed mob to take Him when they could have come peacefully when He was teaching each day in the temple. Then the disciples flee.

They led Him to the High Priest where the Jewish leadership were waiting. Peter followed and entered in where the servants were, by a fire. The leadership were looking for any witness that could say something worthy of death, but none could agree. When questioned by the High Priest, Jesus said nothing. Then the High Priest asked: "Art thou the Christ, the Son of the Blessed?" Jesus answers: "I am: and ye shall see the Son of Man sitting on the right hand of power, and coming in the clouds of heaven."

Then the High Priest asked why they needed any more witnesses, as Jesus had just committed blasphemy and those there agreed, and they abused Jesus after this. Peter is approached by a maid and asked whether he was a follower of Jesus and he denies it. Then a rooster crows. Two more times he is approached and both times he again denies that he knows Jesus. After the third total denial, a rooster crows again. Peter remembers the words of Jesus, and wept.

At the beginning of Chapter 15, Jesus is taken to Pilate. Pilate asks Him if He is the King of the Jews. Jesus answers him: "Thou sayest." then the chief priests accuse Him of many things, but Jesus responds to none of them, and Pilate marvels.

Pilate asks the crowd, who would you rather that I release today, Jesus or Barabbas. Barabbas had been convicted of insurrection and murder. The chief priests worked the crowd and they asked for Barabbas. When Pilate asks the crowd what they want him to do with Jesus, the crowd answers Crucify Him! So, Pilate delivered the sentence and scourged Him.

Luke Chapter 22, verse 39 through Chapter 23, verse 25 Jesus led His disciples to the Mount of Olives. He asked them to pray that they did not fall into temptation, and then went a short distance from them to pray by Himself. In prayer He asked the Father, if it was possible, to take this coming event from Him. Jesus is in agony to the point of crying tears of blood. While there, He is strengthened by an angel. When He came back to the disciples, He found them asleep.

Just then, Judas appears with a mob and gives Jesus a kiss. Jesus asks him if he is to betray the "Son of Man with a kiss?" The other disciples ask if they are to fight, as one strikes off the ear of the servant of the High Priest with a sword. Jesus stops them and heals the ear. Jesus asks the Jewish leadership why they came armed to arrest Him, as He was in the temple each day.

They then take Jesus to the High Priest's house, with Peter following from a distance. When Peter enters, he sits by the fire and a maid sees him and accuses Peter of being with Jesus. Peter denies knowing Jesus. After a while another comes to Peter and inquires if Peter is of them. Peter denies the charge. Finally, about an hour later someone else affirms that Peter is of them as he is a Galilean. Peter denies it again and immediately the rooster crows and Jesus turns and looks directly at Peter. Peter remembers the prediction of Jesus. Peter leaves and weeps bitterly.

Jesus is then abused badly by those that are holding Him. In the morning He is led before the council where they ask Him if He is the Christ. Jesus responds with: "If I tell you, ye will not believe: And if I ask, ye will not answer me, nor let go. Hereafter shall the Son of Man sit on the right hand of the power of God." Then they ask: "Art thou then the Son of God?" Jesus responds: "Ye say that I am." With this they feel that they need no other witness as He had stated it out of His own mouth.

Chapter 23 begins with the entire multitude taking Him to Pilate. They accuse Jesus of many things and of calling Himself, Christ a King. Pilate asks if He is king of the Jews. Jesus replies: "Thou sayest." Pilate explains to the Jews that he can find no fault in Him, but the people explain that He is stirring up all the people from Galilee to Jerusalem.

When Pilate hears that Jesus is from Galilee, he sends Him to Herod who just happens to be in Jerusalem. Herod was glad to see Jesus as he had wanted to see Him for some time, hoping to see a miracle. Jesus did not answer any of his questions.

Herod and his men mock Jesus and put gorgeous robes on Him and returned Him to Pilate. This sending of Jesus back and forth forged a friendship between Herod and Pilate. Then Pilate called the Jewish leadership together and told them that he and Herod had found nothing worthy of death and would chastise Him and then release Him.

Pilate intended on releasing Jesus as it was the custom to release one person that had been accused, at the feast. The crowd cried, away with this man, and release Barabbas. Barabbas had been arrested for sedition and murder. When Herod again tried to convince the crowd, they cried: "crucify, crucify Him." Pilate asked them why? The cries of the people and the chief priests won out in the end and Pilate released Barabbas and delivered Jesus into their will.

John Chapter 18, verse 1 through Chapter 19 verse 16 After all that was spoken in the Last Supper, Jesus leads His disciples over the Brook Cedron to a garden. Judas leads a Jewish leadership sponsored armed mob to where he knows Jesus will be resting. As they approach, Jesus asks them: "Whom seek ye?" The mob states that they are looking for Jesus of Nazareth. Jesus states: "I am." With this reply the mob falls over backward to the ground. Jesus asks again: "Whom seek ye?" They answer Jesus of Nazareth. Jesus answered: "I have told you that I am: if therefore ye seek me, let these go their way."

With this, Peter takes his sword and cuts off the High Priest's servant's ear. Jesus then tells Peter to bolster his sword, as these are "works" that the Father had given Him. Then the mob bound Jesus and led Him away to Annas.

Peter follows a short distance back with another disciple that was known to the High Priest. Peter stood at the door while the other disciple goes in with Jesus, and then returns to retrieve Peter from the damsel that controlled entry at the door. The damsel asks Peter if he is one of "this man's disciples." Peter denies the charge, and went to warm himself by the fire.

Jesus is asked about His disciples and His doctrine by the High Priest. Jesus explains that He has openly taught in the temple to all that wanted to listen, why not ask them? Jesus is struck for speaking in this way to the High Priest. Jesus asks the man that struck Him, why He struck Him if He had answered honestly?

As Peter is warming himself, someone asks Him if he is one of Jesus' disciples, and Peter denies it. Then, another comes to Peter and states that he thought that he saw Peter in the garden with Jesus. Peter denies the charge, and immediately the rooster crows.

The next morning they lead Jesus from the High Priest's Palace to Pilate's Hall of Judgment. Chapter 18, verse 28 states: "and they themselves went not into the judgment hall, lest they might eat the Passover." Pilate goes out to meet them and asks why they came? They explain that Jesus is a malefactor. Pilate tells them to judge Him under their Law. They explain that He needs to be put to death, which they are not allowed to do under Roman Law.

Pilate calls Jesus forward and asks Him if He is the King of the Jews? Jesus responds: "Sayest thou this thing of thyself, or did others tell it thee of me?" Pilate wants Jesus to explain why the religious leadership had delivered Jesus to him for the sentence of death. Jesus explains that His kingdom is not of this world, for if it were, His servants would fight for Him, but now is not the time. Pilate asks Jesus if He is indeed a king? Jesus explains that He was born for this position and all that hear the truth will understand His message.

Pilate doesn't understand and goes out to the people and proclaims that he finds no fault in Jesus. He then reminds the crowd that there is a custom that he should release one convicted man at Passover and asks: "Will ye therefore that I release to you the King of the Jews?" The crowd disagrees and asks for Barabbas, who is a robber.

At the beginning of Chapter 19, Pilate instructs His men to scourge Jesus. The solders made a crown of thorns for His head and dressed Him in a purple robe, then mocked and beat Him. Pilate then presented Jesus to those there and explains that he finds no fault in Jesus and says:

"Behold the man!" The chief priests and officers cry to crucify Him. Pilate tells them to do it themselves, but the Jews answer that they have a law that says that He must die as He has made Himself the Son of God.

This truly troubles Pilate, and He returns to the hall to question Jesus. But, He would not answer. Pilate then tells Jesus that He must speak to him, as he had the power to release or crucify Him. Jesus responds that Pilate only has the power that is given to him from above. Pilate really wants to release Jesus at this point, but the Jews warn that if he releases Jesus, he is letting someone go who calls himself a king, which speaks against Caesar.

When this final threat is delivered, Pilate sits down in the judgment seat and says to the Jews: "Behold your King!" You will note in the same verse, Chapter 19, Verse 14 it states: "And it was the preparation for the Passover..." Then the crowd calls for them to take Jesus away and crucify Him. Pilate asks if they really want to crucify their King? The chief priests exclaim that they have no king, Caesar is our king. Then Pilate delivered Jesus into their hands to be crucified.

What did we learn? The author of Matthew and Mark tell you that after Jesus and the disciples had left for Gethsemane, He told them that they would flee from Him that evening. Peter tells the Lord that it isn't so, that he would rather die for Him. Jesus foretells that Peter will deny Him three times before a rooster will crow once in the morning. But in the Book of Mark, the Lord predicts that Peter will deny Him three times before the rooster will crow twice the next morning.

According to the author of Matthew, Peter denies Jesus three times and then the rooster crows. In the author of Mark's account, Peter denies knowing Jesus once, then the rooster crows. Then, Peter denies Jesus two more times and the rooster crows one more time, for a total of three denials and the rooster crowing twice. So, did the rooster crow once or twice? Better yet, did Jesus predict it here in the Garden of Gethsemane or was it during the meal as told be the authors of Luke and John in the last chapter?

Adding another twist to these stories is that in the Books of Matthew, Mark, and John, Peter denies Jesus after Jesus has been sentenced, just before His removal to Pilate's palace. In the Book of Luke, Peter denies Jesus before the questioning begins.

Over and over the gospels tell us stories that we think we know what they say, only to find if, you line them up with each other they tell totally different stories. Do I believe that this incident with a rooster happened? I do, but was the prediction during the Last Supper, was it in the garden, did the rooster crow once or twice? You can make the case that Jesus gave a prediction that Peter would deny Him that evening and used a rooster in the prediction.

This is true, but was the message that we read in the pages really sent by God, and written by a man's hand for us to read today? I don't believe so. If God wanted to send such a message, it would have been preserved. So that only leaves you to understand that these four books that we call the gospels are four versions of the story of Jesus Christ while He was on the earth. Three of which follow similar paths, but yet disagreeing about the facts constantly. Then there is the one recorded in the Book of John. It has some similarities with the other three authors, but is very, very different.

When Jesus made this prediction in the Books of Matthew and Mark, you see that He also tells them that He will be smitten and will rise again. He tells them that He will go before them into Galilee. If this story is true, when He is crucified, why don't they go directly to Galilee to meet Him after He is risen? This is one more time when Jesus has foretold to them exactly what will happen, and yet they are all in fear and will not heed what He has instructed them.

This is even stranger, because in the Book of Matthew, after they learn that He has risen, they eventually meet with Him in Galilee. After Jesus is crucified and risen, the eleven remaining disciples leave for Galilee where Jesus appears to them. Even in the Book of John, Jesus will meet with some of His first (seven) disciples at the Sea of Tiberias (thought to be Galilee). My problem is that Jesus has supposedly told these disciples exactly what will happen in the Books of Matthew, Mark and Luke, over and over, and yet they have no faith.

Once at the garden, Jesus takes Peter, James, and John with Him to pray. This account is found in the Books of Matthew and Mark. The author of Luke tells you that Jesus leaves all the disciples and prays separately a short distance away. Jesus is troubled by what is about to transpire and asks the Father if it was possible, to remove this load that He is about to carry.

This last paragraph is in great contrast to the Jesus found in the Book of John. Even in the farewell prayer at the Last Supper, you never see Jesus wanting to have this burden, the payment of our sins on the cross, removed from Him. In the Book of Luke it is to the point of crying with tears of blood. What a difference these two versions of the story show.

If you are looking at it through the eyes of the average loving christian person, this display of remorse about the coming painful infliction is understandable, but John helps you understand that Jesus is more than a man. In John's account, Jesus knows what is about to transpire and was more troubled by the fact that one that He had eaten with was about to betray Him. In John, there does not seem to be a concern over the pain He is about to endure as it is the "works" of the Father.

In Matthew Chapter 26 in verse 31 you see that it is to be prophetic that "the shepherd will be smitten and the sheep will scatter" and then in verse 56 it is again told to be prophecy when it happens. This is supposedly referenced in Zechariah Chapter 13 verse 7. Read the entire chapter. It does not follow that this prophesy has anything to do with the disciples leaving Jesus. In the prophesy it states: "Awake, O sword, against my shepherd, and against the man that is my fellow, saith the Lord of Hosts: smite the shepherd, and the sheep shall be scattered: and I will turn my hand upon the little ones."

What happened to the little ones in the prophesy? Who are the sheep? Who are the little ones? In Zechariah, only a third of them are saved? Is this a prophecy of Jesus' disciples? Which of them are the third that are saved and which of them are the two thirds that are not saved? I believe that again the author of the Book of Matthew has tried to force circumstances surrounding the story he is trying to tell of Jesus into Old Testament prophecy.

I was completely done with this book and had put it down waiting to proof read it. While I was in that time frame, I was, of course, still reading my bible through, from front to back. At that time I came to the lesser prophets, Hosea through Malachi. One morning I was reading Zechariah and came upon this very story. Please read with me the entire chapter of Zachariah, Chapter 13. The entire point of my book can be summed up if you would reference Matthew to Zechariah.

Matthew has asserted here that Jesus in the garden is foretold in Zechariah Chapter 13. How preposterous! Zechariah Chapter 13 opens with God cutting off the names of the idols in the land along with casting out of false prophets and unclean spirits. Verse 3 shows that parents will kill their sons for prophesying lies. Verses 4 and 5 shows that a false prophet will admit that he is nothing more than a shepherd. Is this guy a good guy or a bad guy that is ashamed of his past? This same guy is discussed in verses 6, 7, and 8 so I will quote these passages. Remember he was a false prophet!

Zechariah Chapter 13, verses 6 through 8: "And one shall say unto him, What are these wounds in thine hands? Then he shall answer, Those with which I was wounded in the house of my friends. Awake, O sword, against my shepherd, and against the man that is my fellow, saith the Lord of Host: smite the shepherd and the sheep will be scattered: and I will turn my hand upon the little ones. And it shall come to pass, in all the land, saith the Lord, two parts therein shall be cut off and die; but a third shall be left therein."

Can this prophesy of Zechariah have anything to do with Jesus in the garden and the disciples running for their lives? Go back and read Zechariah 13 again. The shepherd in Zechariah's prophesy is a false prophet who is ashamed of his past. The author of the Book of Matthew is pulling at straws to try to squeeze Jesus into Old Testament prophesy, but is failing miserably. Once again, Jesus is in the Old Testament, but you may prefer to use the references of the Apostle John or Paul. The author of Matthew will use Zechariah over and over, but if you read Zechariah in it's entirety, instead of the odd verse here and there, you will see that the Book of Matthew cannot be inspired!

Did you ever think about who recorded the supposed words that Jesus prayed when He was in the garden? Who was there? We know that in the authors of Matthew, and Mark's account, Peter, James and John were asleep, and Jesus had left the others back a ways. In fact, Peter, James and John slept through a time when Jesus tried to wake them, and then He returned to pray again. In the author of Luke's account, Jesus leaves all of them and goes a stone's throw distance away. All the disciples are asleep during Luke's account and an angel appears with Jesus in agony and crying with tears of blood. Who recorded this? If you saw an angel appear, do you think that you would just nod off?

The words in each account are different, let alone Jesus coming back twice to wake up the disciples in two of the accounts, and then there was the angel and tears of blood. Are they really a single integrated message system sent to us? Look, go back and read what Moses has to say about these authors accounts.

Deuteronomy Chapter 18, verses 21-22: "And if thou say in thine heart, How shall we know the word which the Lord hath not spoken? When a prophet speaketh in the name of the Lord, if the thing follow not, nor come to pass, that is the thing which the Lord hath not spoken, but the prophet hath spoken it presumptuously: thou shalt not be afraid of him."

Moses has just told you that since all three accounts are different, only a maximum of one of them can be from a vision from God. The rest are presumed! In other words, only one can be from God, if that, making the rest just stories!

When Jesus comes back from prayer to the disciples for the final time there is the strangest set of words found in all three of these accounts. First Jesus tells them to "sleep on now and take your rest" and then states "rise, let us be going." Which one is it, rest, or rise? This entire event of praying for having this load lifted and the disciples sleeping through the entire thing can easily be explained. Read the Book of John. It doesn't happen! In John, as Jesus and the disciples arrive at the garden, beyond the Brook Cedron, they appear to arrive at the same time as Judas and the mob!

Before I cover the arrest, do you see a common thread about the armament that Jesus' disciples where wearing? In Matthew Chapter 26, Mark Chapter 14, and Luke Chapter 22 it is recorded that one of the disciples had a sword and cut off the ear of the chief priest's servant. Jesus doesn't say to throw away the sword. No, He tells him to put it back in it's place. That would be a scabbard. Remember in the Book of Luke during the last supper, Jesus tells them to sell their garments if they do not already have a sword and buy one. In John Chapter 18, you learn that the disciple that used the sword on the High Priest's servant's ear was Peter!

Why I bring this up is the notion that Christians should be all about love. We are not supposed to have firearms or think about killing people in self defense. What was a sword used for in the time of Jesus? It was not a self defense weapon for animals. That would have been a staff or a spear, maybe a sling. A sword is a close order killing machine. I equate it to a fully automatic weapon of today. There was only one reason to have a sword and Peter is showing you what they did with it.

The arrest has, as usual, two different accounts. One in the Books of Matthew, Mark and Luke and a different one found in John. In the accounts by the authors of Matthew, Mark, and Luke, Jesus has been praying in the garden and then the mob shows up to arrest Jesus. Judas betrays Jesus with a kiss. There is a minor scuffle and then they take Jesus away. Peter actually follows, but is not arrested.

In John, they arrive at the garden about the time that the mob arrives. Jesus does not spend any time bemoaning the events that are about to unfold. When Jesus asks what they want, the mob says that they are looking for Jesus of Nazareth. When Jesus states: "I am," the mob falls over backward. Judas does not betray Jesus with a kiss. The mob asks for Jesus, and He plainly lets them know who He is. Then Jesus explains that they came for Him and to leave the others alone. This explanation explains why they didn't arrest the others, especially Peter, who had used a sword on one of them! Think of how the mob must have felt. They were sent out by the Jewish Government and they wanted to bring back Jesus.

If you had run into a man with powers to knock you over with only His "word," would you be fearful? I would have been terrified! Hence, when He stated that He would go with them, but they had to leave His followers alone, I would have been happy to leave them in peace. And, this is how it is recorded in the Book of John.

Either you believe John's account that gives you a reason why the mob did not arrest the rest of Jesus' followers or you believe the other three. Either Jesus told them who He was, or Judas betrayed Jesus with a kiss. But if you side against the Apostle John, why didn't they arrest Peter? It is clear that he cuts off the High Priest's servant's ear. Very shortly thereafter Peter is in the High Priest's palace. If there was nothing for the mob to fear when they arrested Jesus, you would think that the mob would have focused on Peter, but they ignore him.

After the arrest, starting in Matthew Chapter 26, verse 58 it is clear that Peter follows and walks into the High Priest's palace and sits down. While Peter was sitting and watching, a young lady came up to him and said: "Thou also wast with Jesus of Galilee." Peter denied it and went out to the porch where another said: "This was also with Jesus of Nazareth." Again he denied the accusation. After some time came some others that state: "Surely thou art of them; for your speech bewrayeth thee." Then Peter began to curse and swear: "I know not this man!" And immediately the rooster crowed, and Peter remembered how Jesus predicted his actions. Peter went out and wept bitterly.

Mark Chapter 14 tells you a very similar story to the one told by Matthew, but the first verbal exchange with the maid is a little different. After the first denial, a rooster crows. Then a second maid sees Peter and the verbal exchange is again different to what is recorded in Matthew. Finally, Peter denies knowing Jesus a third time and the rooster crows the second time.

In Luke Chapter 22, Peter has followed the arrested Jesus to the High Priest's house where he is warming himself. He has three similar encounters with people as told by the authors of Matthew, and Mark, but in the Book of Luke, besides the verbal discourse between all the gospels being a little different, there is additional drama. When the rooster crows, Jesus immediately turns His head and looks at Peter!

So, the Books of Matthew, Mark and Luke have all told a similar story, and yet the words spoken by Peter, the maid, and others are different, yet similar. The author of Matthew and Luke told you that Jesus explicitly told Peter that the rooster will not crow until Peter had denied Him three times. Although most people read across this statement, the author of Mark tells you that after Peter had denied Jesus the first time that the rooster crows! So did the rooster first crow after Peter's first denial or after the third?

John Chapter 18 will make the entire story a little bit more strange when you learn that there was another disciple with Peter. In John's account the first maid that talks with Peter is the maid that kept the door. Do you see any significance to someone keeping the door? The High Priest was the Highest Jewish ruler of the State of Israel. Although Rome ruled all the known world, the High Priest carried clout. Do you think that you could just walk into the house of, say, a state governor without assistance? John tells you that there is someone else with Peter that first goes in and then comes out to vouch for Peter to get him through the door.

Even non-important people had protective doorways back them. In Acts Chapter 12, starting at verse 11, you find Peter again at the door of a gate. This is the house of Mary, the mother of John Mark, where he is knocking, trying to get in. Doesn't it seem odd that in the author of Matthew,

Mark, and Luke's account, that Peter has unfettered access to the High Priest's house? Isn't he, or wouldn't he, be considered a troublemaker of the day? Those accounts really don't make sense.

Peter's second denial in the Book of John was to a group that had gathered around at the fire. Finally, a kinsmen of the man who's ear Peter had cut off at the garden asks Peter if he was in the garden with Jesus? Peter then denied for the third time, and immediately the rooster crows. This account from John is very different from the other three. Which one is correct?

So what really was the question that is railed at Jesus in Caiaphas' palace, and what was His answer? There isn't any correlation between John's account and the other gospel accounts. For that matter, the Books of Matthew, Mark and Luke, do not line up either. What is it that condemns Jesus? In the Book of Matthew they are at Caiaphas' palace and many witnesses are brought before the counsel to testify against Jesus. None of this appears to be working for a sentence of death, so the High Priest asks, "I adjure thee by the living God, that thou tell us whether thou be the Christ, the Son of God." Jesus answers, "Thou hast said: nevertheless I say unto you, Hereafter shall ye see the Son of man sitting on the right hand of Power, and coming in the clouds of heaven."

Think about the answer that Jesus has given in this account. He still hasn't stated in this answer that He is the Son of God, just that the accusation has been levied, but that they will see the Son of Man doing great things!

In Mark Chapter 14 it is the High Priest that asks, "Art thou the Christ, the Son of the Blessed?" Jesus answers: "I am: and ye shall see the Son of Man sitting on the right hand of power, and coming in the clouds of heaven." So here in the Book of Mark the verbal discourse is similar, but Jesus is stating plainly that He is the Christ and the Son of the Blessed!

In the Book of Luke it isn't the High Priest that asks of Him, it is the elders of the people, the chief priests, and scribes that ask: "Art thou the Christ, tell us." Jesus' response was: "If I tell you, ye will not believe: And if I also ask, ye will not answer me, nor let me go. Hereafter shall the Son of Man sit on the right hand of the power of God." Here again, Jesus has not stated that He is anything in relationship to God, only that the Son of Man will have this power. But in the Books of Matthew and Mark they have brought witnesses to testify against Jesus before the High Priest asks the question of deity, here in the Book of Luke, it is the first question!

Remember, if you believe that the Bible is the inerrant word of God, then which of these direct quotes from the High Priest, or council is the question that they used to try to condemn Jesus? Which one of the answers given by Jesus is the response that condemns Him? Let's look at John's account.

Reread John Chapters 18 and 19. It starts with the arrest and Peter cutting off Malchus' ear (there is no mention of Jesus healing the ear as found in the Book of Luke). They bind Jesus and take Him first to Annas and then to Caiaphas' Palace. The High Priest asks Him of His doctrine and Jesus explains that he might want to ask those that had listened to Him. Jesus is struck in the face for this answer. Then Peter denies Jesus three times and the rooster crows. There is no asking if He is the Christ or Son of God and no renting of the High Priest's clothes.

After this they lead Jesus to Pilate's judgment hall, but the Jews would not enter. The Jews explain that they want Pilate to put Him to death. To this point you have not heard Jesus asked if He is the Christ, or any other supernatural title for that matter. It is Pilate that brings up the subject for the first time in John Chapter 18, verse 33, and he doesn't ask Him a supernatural deity question, it is: "Art thou the King of the Jews?" It is obvious that this is the charge that is brought to Pilate.

Think back, or maybe reread the last several chapters in all four gospels and see why the leadership wanted to put Jesus to death. They have wanted to kill Him for months if not years, but not because He has blasphemed. It is because He has been showing the obvious faults that the leadership has demonstrated by substituting traditions of man over commandments of God. They have shown <u>NOT</u> to have righteous judgment. They are delighting in the praise given to them by man. Jesus has been showing everyone that will listen that they are not concerned of the things of God, they are only concerned about their own selfish desires. They hate Him for it, and are looking for any reason to "earn" the sentence of death.

In John, they have no idea how they can make any charge stick. First the High Priest asks of His disciples, then he asks of Jesus' doctrine. They still have nothing, so they lead Him to Pilate, hoping to get a sentence, just because they are asking for it. It isn't until the next chapter in the Book of John that Pilate finds out that they have thrown in the extra charge by accusing Jesus of calling Himself the Son of God and this is troubling to Pilate.

According to John, the Jewish leadership had nothing and Pilate understood this. That is why Pilate argues to release Him. But, in the end, he gave into the desires of the Jewish leadership and sentenced Jesus to the cross.

But, what was the real order of events in the trial of Jesus? In the Book of Matthew it is the arrest by the mob, they led Jesus to Caiaphas the high priest, in the morning they take Him to Pilate where He is sentenced to death. The author of Mark agrees with Matthew's series of events.

In the Garden, the Arrest, and the Trial

John tells you that after the arrest, the mob first takes Jesus to Annas. He is the Father-in-law to Caiaphas. Then they go to Caiaphas' palace. In the morning they go to Pilate's hall of Judgment, where Jesus is sentenced to death. It is very similar to the authors' of Matthew and Mark's accounts with the addition of an early stop at the High Priest's Father-in-law's place.

As usual, there is one gospel with extra drama. The author of Luke affirms that they led Jesus away to the High Priest's house at night. In the morning the council met and sentenced Him, and led Him to Pilate. Pilate sends Jesus to Herod for sentencing. Herod sends Jesus back to Pilate, where Pilate finally sentences Jesus. In the midst of Pilate sending Jesus to Herod and back, Pilate and Herod become good friends, as before they were not. Was Jesus really brought before Herod? Only if you want to say that the Book of Luke is the real gospel story, and I am certain that there has been enough issues brought up so far that the Book of Luke cannot be the true gospel.

During John's account, the Jews led Jesus from Caiaphas' Palace to Pilate's Judgment hall? Why wouldn't the Jews enter? John Chapter 18, verse 28. "Then led they Jesus from Caiaphas unto the hall of judgment; and it was early; and they themselves went not into the judgment hall, lest they should be defiled; but that they might eat the <u>Passover</u>. Once more you are at a decision point in your Biblical quest for knowledge. Do you trust the authors of Matthew, Mark and Luke, who told you that Jesus ate the Passover at the Last Supper, or do you trust the Apostle John who also wrote 1st, 2nd, and 3rd John and the Book of Revelation? At this point John is telling you that the Passover has not yet happened, but it's close!

One more problem that the author of Luke has created. In his account Herod's men have mocked Jesus, dressed Him in robes and made Him a crown of thorns. The author of Matthew, Mark and John affirms that it is Pilate's men that have done this act. Only one account can be right. One of these two stories is incorrect.

You can see by the way that the author of Matthew ended these reading passages, why many Christians in history past have been able to feel justified about the way that they have treated the Jews. If you believe the Book of Matthew's account, the Jews that were in the crowd called for Jesus to be crucified unjustly. They accepted that the blood of this just man shall be on them and their children. It was a sentence of death on your own head if you had accepted the responsibility of the wrongful death of another.

This is one more reason why I have a hard time with the authors of the gospels of Matthew, Mark and Luke's rendition of the events of the life of Jesus Christ. They have forgotten the promise made to Abraham by God: "I will bless those that bless you and I will curse those that curse you." There is no time limit on that promise. The Book of Matthew has called for a curse on all Jews and their offspring by saying that they accept the responsibility of Jesus' wrongful death on them and their children.

The Apostle John does not make this condemnation. Yes, the crowd is calling for Jesus to be crucified, but they do not accept the "blood of this just man" to be on them or their children. You do not know who is in this crowd. Remember the threat that is put to Pilate, "we will tell Caesar that you let a man go that claims to be a king!" All that had to be making this accusation was the council and or the High Priest. The entire Jewish nation, or Jerusalem, is not condemning Jesus in John's account, and yet, Jews have been murdered, and that action justified through the years because of the words found in the Books of Matthew, Mark and Luke!

One huge difference between these four gospels is the role that Herod has in all of this. The authors of Matthew, Mark and John all show a time line with what happens after Jesus is presented to Pilate. Pilate actually tries to release Jesus. But then sends Him to be crucified.

Remember, the Passover is in the fall. It is the 14th day of Abib. Even though the Jewish calendar moves a little each year to ours, it places it somewhere around the end of September. Jesus is taken over to Pilate's palace in the morning after the council had tried Him. He is crucified in the third hour according to Mark Chapter 15, verse 25.

That means three hours after sunrise, Jesus is hanging on the cross. The author of the Book of Luke is trying to persuade you that Jesus has been tried by the Jews, walked to Pilate's palace, been interrogated, sent on foot to Herod's place, been interrogated, dressed in gorgeous robes, returned on foot to Pilate's palace, interrogated again and sentenced. All this is in time for Jesus to be walked to Calvary, nailed to a cross and then raised within 3 hours! There is too much distance, things that must happen, and too little time. Besides, the Book of Luke is the only one that has recorded this extra drama, and if Luke the physician has written this, he wasn't there!

One more little thing, but each contradiction should help solidify my point that these books, at least three of them, are not inspired writing from God. Notice, I will not say what three are not, as you have to line them up for yourself. What was the charge against Barabbas?

It doesn't say in the Book of Matthew, other than he was notable, but the authors of Mark and Luke tell you that he is a murderer. I can't fathom a custom that will allow anyone to go free from jail, especially a murderer. In John you learn that Barabbas was a thief. I can sort of understand the Roman ruler allowing a thief go to show pity to the people, but a murderer? Either way, was Barabbas a thief or a murderer? At least one of the stories is wrong.

Have you ever taken a good look at what happens to Judas and the money? I have a hard time congealing all the stories about the betrayal by Judas, if you want to accept anything more than what was presented by John. In John and Luke, Judas is possessed by Satan. Is there any reason for someone who is possessed by Satan to have remorse or have a change in heart? In Matthew Chapter 27, verse 5, you learn that Judas hangs himself after a change of heart and the Jewish leadership buys a field with the money. None of the other gospels talk about how Judas died, but the Book of Acts does. As mentioned in the *Authors of the History Books,* it is commonly accepted that the author of the Book of Luke also wrote The Book of the Acts of the Apostles. Who wrote the Book of Acts is irrelevant for this discussion, only, it is also in question as to if it was inspired.

Remember what Moses states about someone supposedly writing inspired words, they must be 100% accurate if they are to be from God. Deuteronomy Chapter 18, verses 21-22: "And if thou say in thine heart, How shall we know the word which the Lord hath not spoken? When a prophet speaketh in the name of the Lord, if the thing follow not, nor come to pass, that is the thing which the Lord hath not spoken, but the prophet hath spoken it presumptuously: thou shalt not be afraid of him."

Turn with me to Acts Chapter 1, verses 15–19. Here you see the author of the Book of Acts explaining that Peter is telling the story about the death of Judas. In this rendition, Peter explains that Judas bought the field with the money, and then fell head long into it and burst asunder. So, did the Jewish leadership buy the field, or did Judas. Secondly, did he hang himself or did he "fall headlong and burst asunder in the midst, and all his bowels gushed out?" Once again, you can't have it both ways.

What is worse to me is the fact that anyone would try to convince you that Judas would have betrayed Jesus for money at all. The story by John about Satan entering into him is understandable, but to think that he would sell out Jesus to buy a field is inconceivable. What about the great powers that Jesus had given him? If it was one of greed as told by the authors of Matthew, Mark, and Luke, then you have to question it's validity when understanding what he would have lost without Jesus. How much is the power of miracles worth? It's very easy for me to say that I understand and believe the story told by John. That makes the other stories false.

Let's look a little more closely at the author of Matthew's version as he tells you that it is prophetic. When the author of Matthew asserts that Judas made a deal with the Chief Priests to betray the Lord, it was for 30 pieces of silver. When he gives it back, the Jewish leadership buys a potter's field with the money. He tells you in Matthew Chapter 27, verse 9 that this was to fulfill the prophecy of Jeremy (Jeremiah). The only thing remotely close to this, found in Jeremiah, is located in Jeremiah Chapter 32, verse 9. Sounds good and most Christians would just hold that for "gospel." But when you read the prophesy in Jeremiah, it was for "Jeremiah to buy his nephew's field for 17 shekels of silver."

This is where you have to dig deep and ask yourself, do I really want to know? Would I be better off just sitting in church and keeping my head in the sand like an ostrich, or, do I really want to know what parts of the Bible are trustworthy, and what parts are not?

Here is the strange twist, there is a place where it shows a prophecy where someone is betrayed for 30 pieces of silver. It is found in Zechariah Chapter 11, verse 12. But, that is the rub. If the Book of Matthew is written by the Holy Spirit, through a man's hand, why wouldn't the Holy Spirit tell us the right prophet? You have to say that either the Holy Spirit got it right, but the book has become polluted through the years, or the author of the Book of Matthew got it wrong. Either way, when we agree that one of these two events happened, it brings into question what is trustworthy and what isn't.

All the gospels tell a very general order of events. Jesus eats the Last supper, goes out to some garden where He is arrested, and is brought before the "people to be judged" that night and the following morning. It is the specifics that makes these stories fall apart.

In the Books of Matthew, Mark, and Luke the arrest, trial, and crucifixion are all happening on a feast day. If Jesus ate the Passover with His disciples, it is Passover evening and the first day of the Feast of Unleavened Bread when all these events happened. According to Leviticus Chapter 23 both these days are specifically dictated to be a feast, and a Holy Convocation where no work will be performed. Just a couple of days earlier, the author to the Book of Matthew, in Chapter 26, verses 3-5 has already told you that the entire Jewish leadership agreed not to take or kill Him on a feast day.

I've heard it over and over while I sat in under-informed churches, the guy in the pulpit would try to explain that the Jewish Leadership broke multiple laws and traditions during this time period as they "did away" with Jesus. Why not just use a little discernment and choose the better answer to this contradiction.

Don't you see a problem with the authors of Matthew, Mark and Luke's recollection as to the specifics surrounding this event? Once again, this is where the author to the Book of John can help. It makes sense that the leadership would not take or kill Jesus on a feast day as that would be breaking the Jewish Law and traditions.

John tells you that they did not take, try, or kill Him on a feast day, it is the day of preparation for the Passover! This is stated boldly in John Chapter 18, verse 28: "Then led they Jesus from

Caiaphas unto the hall of judgment: and it was early; and they themselves went not into the judgment hall, lest they should be defiled; but that they might eat of the Passover." Chapter 19, verse 14: "And it was the preparation of the Passover, and about the sixth hour..."

Finally in our next chapter you will read in John Chapter 19, verse 31: "The Jews therefore, because it was the preparation, that the body should not remain upon the cross on the Sabbath day(for that Sabbath day was an <u>High Day</u>) besought Pilate that their legs might be broken, and that they might be taken away." This verse shows that the day that Jesus was laid in the tomb was a day prior to a High Sabbath! A High Sabbath is a feast day.

Before I cover that following High Sabbath day, and how you know it was the Passover, understand how easy it is to fit all of what the authors of Matthew, Mark, and Luke have told you about the events by changing one fact that they have affirmed. If you understood that the Last Supper was not the Passover, but just the last supper that Jesus was to have with His disciples, it all fits. Look, at this point you have to choose once again between the Apostle John's account and the one recorded by the authors that wrote Matthew, Mark and Luke. John has told you that the Last Supper was not the Passover, and the other authors have affirmed that the Last Supper was the Passover. It can't be both ways. Either it was the Passover or it wasn't. Either way, you have to say that John is correct and the others incorrect, or the other authors are correct. And John is incorrect.

The Crucifixion, and Burial

In our last chapter there was very little actual Bible reading, but a whole lot of contradiction. It doesn't get any better here at the crucifixion and burial. Does Jesus carry His own cross or does Simon of Cyrene? Who is at the cross to hear Jesus' words? What did He say? Are there thieves on each side of Jesus or not? If they are there, do they mock Jesus or does one ask for forgiveness? Who buries Jesus and is His body anointed? If it is, is there any reason for Mary to do it again? When Jesus died, did saints come back to life? If so, was Jesus the first risen?

Remember, there has been plenty of times when the author of Matthew and Mark disagree with Luke, many times when the author of Luke and Mark disagree with Matthew, and of course many times when the author of Mark disagrees with either Matthew and Luke. There is no reason to even wonder if the Apostle John tells even a similar story to any of the three. Does this matter? Of course it does. Moses told you in Deuteronomy Chapter 18, verse 21-22 that if the vision wasn't 100% accurate, then it wasn't from God, it was presumed. So, if you haven't gathered by now that at least three of these gospels are not from God, you just don't want to know. You might as well believe in Santa Clause and the tooth fairy. But remember, they don't say that they are vision or inspired, that is only a modern Christian idea.

Many miraculous things just happened in the last chapter and now many more will happen in this chapter that would have to been either from vision or an eye witness, or just presumed. Who would have been inside the temple at the time of the crucifixion to witness the veil being torn from top to bottom? You had to be at least a priest to be in the outer chamber to witness it. In the Books of Matthew, Mark, and Luke they don't even know that the Apostle John is at the cross with others. Since their rendition states plainly that their only witnesses are "standing afar," how do they have a clue what is stated by the people at the cross?

But then you have the Apostle John's account. It is simple. No great miraculous things happening or recorded, just Jesus dieing in His humble humanity with those He loved most with Him. Let's open our Bible and read the four accounts of His death and use a little discernment about what really transpired.

Matthew Chapter 27 verse 27 through Chapter 27, verse 60   Then the soldiers took Jesus and stripped Him and gave Him a scarlet robe to wear and a crown of thorns, and put a reed in His hand and mocked Him as if He was their king. Then they abused Him, and when they were done, they took back the robe and gave Him back His clothes.

The Crucifixion, and Burial

Once out of the palace, the soldiers compel a man named Simon of Cyrene to carry Jesus' cross. When they come to Golgotha, they give Jesus some vinegar mixed with gall, but Jesus will not drink it. They crucify Him and part His garments. Then they sit down to watch Him, with the accusation above His head reading: This is Jesus, the King of the Jews.

There are two others crucified, one on each side of Jesus. Passers by and the Jewish Leadership insult Him, mocking that if He is who He says He is, that He should save Himself. Even the thieves on the other crosses mock Him. Suddenly from the sixth hour until the ninth hour there is darkness on the land.

Just then Jesus cries out: "My God, My God, why hast thou forsaken Me?" Some there think that He has called for Elijah and want to see if he will come to save Him. Then Jesus yelled one more time and gave up the ghost. Just then the veil in the temple was torn from top to bottom, the earth quaked and graves were opened of the saints and many arose.

There is a centurion watching as Jesus died, and he saw all that happened and proclaimed "Truly, this was the Son of God." There were many woman looking from afar off. They were Mary Magdalene, Mary the Mother of James and Joses, and the mother of Zebedee's children.

In the evening, Joseph of Arimathea went to Pilate to ask for the body. Pilate commanded the body to be delivered to him, and he took it and wrapped it in linen and laid Him in his own tomb and rolled a great stone to the door of the sepulchre and departed.

Mark Chapter 15, verse 16 through verse 47 The solders lead Jesus away and stripped Him and gave Him a purple robe to wear and a crown of thorns, and put a reed in His hand and mocked Him as if He was their king. Then they abused Him, and when they were done, they took back the robe and gave Him back His clothes.

The soldiers compel a man named Simon of Cyrene to carry Jesus' cross. When they come to Golgotha, they give Jesus some wine mingled with myrrh, but Jesus will not drink it. They crucify Him and part his garments in the third hour, and put a superscription over Him reading: The King of the Jews. There are two thieves crucified with Jesus.

Onlookers and the Jewish Leadership insult Him, mocking that if He is who He says He is, that He should save Himself. From the sixth hour until the ninth hour there is darkness on the land. Then, Jesus cries out: "My God, My God, why hast thou forsaken me?" Some there think that He has called for Elijah and want to see if he will come to save Him. Then Jesus yelled one more time and gave up the ghost. Just then the veil in the temple was torn from top to bottom.

A centurion watching notes how Jesus cried out and gave up the ghost and declares: "Truly this man was the Son of God." There are women looking on from a distance away. They are Mary Magdalene, Mary the Mother of James and Joses, Salome, and many others. And because it was the Preparation, the day before the Sabbath, Joseph of Arimathea went to Pilate to ask for the body.

Pilate marvels that Jesus had died so quickly, so he called the centurion to see if he knew if Jesus was dead. When Pilate understood that Jesus was indeed dead, he gave the body to Joseph. And he took linen and wrapped the body and laid it in a sepulchre and rolled a stone into the door. And Mary Magdalene and Mary of Jose beheld where He was laid.

Luke Chapter 23, verse 26 through verse 56 They placed the cross on Simon of Cyrene to carry it for Jesus to Calvary. There was a multitude that was following Jesus and He turned to them and told them not to weep for Him, but rather weep for themselves and their children because the time will come when they would wish that they had had no children. It will be so bad that you will wish that the mountains and hills would cover you.

Jesus was crucified at Calvary with two others crucified along side Him. Jesus prays to the Father not to hold this against the people because they do not understand what they are doing, then they parted His clothes. Everyone from the rulers, soldiers, to the common people mocked Him. They placed a superscription above His head that read: This is the King of the Jews.

One malefactor on an adjoining cross rebuffs Jesus and explains that if He was really the Christ, He should save Himself and them too. The other rebuked the first saying that they had deserved what they were getting, but Jesus had done nothing wrong. Then He said to Jesus: "Lord, remember me when thou comest into thy kingdom." Jesus explains that he will be with Him in paradise. There was darkness in all the land until the ninth hour.

The sun was darkened and the veil was torn from top to bottom, and Jesus cried: "Father, into thy hands I commend My Spirit." Then He gave up the ghost. When the centurion saw what was done he commented: "Certainly this was a righteous man." Those there smote their chest and returned. The women that followed Him, stood a distance off and beheld these things.

A man named Joseph of Arimathea went to Pilate to beg for the body of Jesus. He took the body down and wrapped it in linen and laid it in a sepulchre. That day was a preparation day for the Sabbath. The women who had followed, noted where He had been laid and returned to prepare spices.

John Chapter 19, verse 17 through verse 42 And Jesus went forth carrying His cross and came to the place of the skull, Golgotha. He is crucified between two others. Pilate wrote a title and put it on the cross that said: Jesus of Nazareth, The King of the Jews. It was written in Hebrew, Greek and Latin. The chief priests want Pilate to change the title, but Pilate won't. Then the soldiers part His garments, but cast lots for His coat as it was seamless.

Attending Jesus at the cross is His mother, His mother's sister, Mary the wife of Cleophas, and Mary Magdalene, and the disciple that Jesus loved. Then Jesus looked upon His disciple and said: "Behold thy mother," and to His mother He said: "Behold thy son." Jesus knowing that all things were accomplished said: "I thirst." They offered Him some vinegar. After receiving it, He said: "It is finished," and gave up the ghost.

John Chapter 19, verse 31: "The Jews therefore, because it was the preparation, that the body should not remain upon the cross on the Sabbath day (for that Sabbath day was an High Day) besought Pilate that their legs might be broken, and that they might be taken away."

Then the soldiers came to break the legs of those being crucified. But Jesus was already dead, so they did not break His legs, but a soldier pierced His side and out flowed blood and water. Joseph of Arimathea comes to Pilate to ask for the body, and Pilate gave it to him. Nicodemus came and joined Joseph with a hundred pounds of myrrh and aloes. They wound the body in linen and spices as the manner of the Jews for a burial. They laid Jesus in a very close sepulchre in a garden as the Sabbath was about to begin.

What did we learn? In the Books of Matthew and Mark at the beginning of this reading, after Jesus was given over to be crucified and already sentenced by Pilate, Jesus is robed in scarlet, and mocked by Pilate's soldiers, before He is led away to be crucified. But do you recall when this happened in the last chapter?

John tells you that this happened while still under the control of Pilate, before Jesus was sentenced. Pilate even brought Him out to the people in the purple robe with a crown of thorns (John Chapter 19, verse 2), and presented Him as their King. In the Book of Luke, Chapter 23, verse 11, Jesus is mocked and robed by Herod and his men, not by Pilate's men. These are three contradictory stories.

Also note that the color of the robe is different. You may think that purple and scarlet are similar enough, but then that shows that you don't understand the importance of color back then. Each color signified the different power that an individual had.

The authors of Matthew, Mark, and Luke tell you that the soldiers force a man named Simon of Cyrene to carry Jesus' cross to Golgotha. He isn't so fortunate in the gospel as told by the Apostle John. Jesus is laden with the cross that He will be crucified with. Have you ever wondered why the Roman government would sentence a man to death and then have someone else carry this weighty object for the convicted? John didn't think so either.

The Book of Luke, of course, will have another dramatic event before the crucifixion that the other gospel authors will not record. Jesus turns to the women that are following and tells them not to weep over Him, but to weep for yourselves and your children. The days are coming when you will feel blessed if you never had children, because it will be so bad that you will call for the mountains to fall on you.

At the Cross there is a superscription over Jesus. Each of the gospel authors tells you it is different. A maximum of only one can be right. In the Book of Matthew it reads: This is Jesus the King of the Jews. In Mark it reads: The King of the Jews. In Luke it is written in Greek, Latin and Hebrew to read: This is the King of the Jews. And last, in the Book of John it is also written in Greek, Latin, and Hebrew and it states: Jesus of Nazareth, The King of the Jews. Which sign was over Jesus Christ's head?

Here at the cross we find the events that unfold as prophesied in Psalm Chapter 22. The author of the Book of Matthew finally hits a home run with this prophesy. Jesus is on the cross and several things transpire that are foretold. But you will find that in John Chapter 19, verses 23 and 24 you have a much better detailed explanation of what transpired.

Did you note that the author of the Book of Matthew has referenced Old Testament prophesy dozens of times. He has only been correct three times. Once with John the Baptist, once that was a so, so reference to Jesus and here at the cross. The Apostle John has told you the same three events from scripture without all the off-base references to the Old Testament. Doesn't it appear that the author of Matthew had heard the story by John but thought that he needed additional references, all be it, wrong references to tell his story?

At the cross, Jesus is offered a primitive sedative. The author of Matthew tells you it was vinegar mixed with gall. The author of Mark tells you it is wine mingled with myrrh. According to their gospels, Jesus will have nothing to do with it. How could Jesus, after all He had stated at the last supper, in their accounts, that He would have no fruit of the vine any longer while He was on earth. But in John Chapter 19, starting in verse 28, Jesus tells those there that He thirsts, and they bring to Him a sponge filled with vinegar and he drinks of it. Which one is it? Does he have the fruit of the vine or not? It doesn't matter if He drinks it according to the Apostle John, as Jesus has not made this vow to them in the Book of John.

Next to Jesus, there are two thieves on their own crosses according to the Books of Matthew, Mark, Luke, and John. In Matthew, they mock Jesus. But in Luke, for just a little more drama, one of the thieves asks for forgiveness and Jesus gives it to him. Nothing other than the fact that these other two are crucified is mentioned in the Books of Mark and John.

At the cross between the sixth and ninth hour, the authors of Matthew, Mark, and Luke record that there is darkness in all the land. The author of Luke records that at the end of this time frame, the sun goes dark and the veil in the temple is torn from top to bottom. Then Jesus cries out: "Father, into thy hands I commend my spirit." In the Books of Matthew and Mark Jesus cries out: "My God, My God, why hast thou forsaken me?" Some there think that He has called for Elijah and want to see if he will come to save Him. Then Jesus yelled one more time and gave up the ghost.

So the last words recorded by these authors are different in all accounts. Who knew what He really said? After all, the authors of Matthew, Mark and Luke have all told you that His followers are all off at a distance. But then there is John's account. John tells you that he and several women are there at the foot of the cross.

The first three gospels record that just then the veil in the temple was torn from top to bottom. In the Book of Matthew, the earth quakes and saints from the past are risen. If saints were risen during the earthquake, then Jesus isn't the first risen. Once again, if this happened, why wouldn't John record of this supernatural event?

So was the veil torn before or after Jesus gave up the ghost? The story is different in all three accounts of the author's of Matthew, Mark and Luke. Who was there, of these three authors, to see this event? If it was torn and nobody was there to see it, how would you know that it was torn from top to bottom, let alone at all? We know that since there are so many errors, it can't be vision from God. This story is obviously presumed, and of course John doesn't record it.

And what were His final words? Although the Books of Matthew, Mark and Luke all follow the same trajectory, they are not telling the same story. As usual, they all tell something much more supernatural than the story given to you by John. Remember, John is the only author that told you that Jesus carried His own cross to Calvary.

John tells you why they cast lots for His clothes. It wasn't exactly for His clothes, it was for His seamless coat. It was valuable. John explains who was there at the cross to record this event. John never refers to himself by name, only as the one who Jesus loved. And yes, the one who Jesus loved was there at the cross along with some women. John tells you that Jesus accepted the vinegar on a sponge before He died, while the other gospel accounts explain that He would not have anything to do with it (vinegar). Remember, at the Last Supper, in the accounts by the authors of Matthew, Mark and Luke, they all tell you that Jesus said He would not have any fruit of the vine until He had it with them in heaven. John never makes that claim.

Finally, Jesus gives up the ghost rather quietly in John's account after He has first given the Apostle John instructions to take care of His mother. Many, many, many ridiculous Christian fables can be destroyed by John Chapter 19, verses 25 through 30. First, is the notion that Jesus' mother was always a virgin, even after the birth. Some want to believe that Jesus' siblings were from Joseph's first wife. The fact that Jesus was in a position to give His mother to someone for care after His death shows that He was the oldest son.

Next, we see that Jesus' mother was at the cross. John never tells you her name in the entire Book of John. But if you take a look at the sentence found in verse 25, you will note that it is Jesus' mother, her sister "Mary the wife of Cleophas," and Mary Magdalene. That is a total of three women. To make it gel with the other gospels, Christians like to say that it is four women: the mother of Jesus, her sister, and two other ladies named Mary. That is because you wouldn't name two siblings both Mary. I believe that this verse shows that Jesus' mother's name may not have been Mary in the first place. Think of all the other facts that the other three gospels have gotten wrong so far. What is one more?

Once again, in John's account in these six verses, you see a Jesus and heavenly powers, that are not doing any supernatural events during His death. Jesus does not cry out. Jesus does not forgive a thief. The earth does not quake. The sun doesn't darken for three hours. The veil does not tear. Jesus does not refuse the fruit of the vine. No one is casting insults. Jesus does not ask God why He has forsaken Him. He just humbly declares that it is finished, while those who truly love Him stand by Him in His passing. Can you honestly say that the story told by John is anything like the story told in the Books of Matthew, Mark and Luke?

You will note that there is a very wide spread opinion of who was there at the crucifixion and where they were located with relationship to the cross. John has told you that he, Jesus' mother, her sister "Mary the wife of Cleophas," and Mary Magdalene, were all at the cross in Jesus' final hour. The authors of Matthew, Mark and Luke tell you that those who followed Jesus were standing afar. They were Mary Magdalene, Mary the Mother of James and Joses, and the mother of the Zebedee's children according to the Book of Matthew. But the author of Mark leaves out the Mother of the Zebedee children and throws in a Salome with others. The author of Luke just tells you that those that followed stood a far off. If the authors of Matthew, Mark and Luke were correct, who was standing by the cross to hear what was said by Jesus and others?

In the Account of Matthew, Mark and Luke the Centurion is amazed when Jesus dies. In Matthew and Mark he expresses that Jesus must have been the Son of God, but in Luke he figures that Jesus was a righteous man. After this, according to the authors of Matthew, Mark and Luke, Joseph of Arimathea comes to Pilate to ask for the body. Pilate is surprised that Jesus has died so quickly, but once he has checked it out, he gives the body to him. Joseph wraps the body in linen and places it in a tomb. Some say that it was his tomb. Mary, and or others, watch where Jesus is laid.

John on the other hand has another version that is not very close to the other three gospel writers at all. Since it is almost a <u>High Sabbath,</u> the Jews request to Pilate to have the legs broken to kill those on the cross more quickly. This is because if someone that is crucified cannot stand, you will suffocate under your own weight. Pilate gives the order. When the soldiers come to break Jesus' legs, He is already dead. This would have been done on a High Sabbath or a weekly Sabbath. They would not let someone die and left to hang across the Sabbath. This is only recorded by the Apostle John.

Joseph of Arimathea asks for the body of Jesus. When Pilate gives Jesus to him, Nicodemus joins Joseph with the spices and ointments to perform a proper burial for Jesus. This is a point that is missed by the other gospels, and most Christians. If Jesus was to be in the tomb for three days and three nights then His body would have already begun to decay, and would have stunk. This point is made with the death of Lazarus. Here in the Book of John, the body of Jesus is already anointed and will not need to be anointed again, as some gospels will try to do again with Mary in the next chapter.

The authors of Matthew, Mark, and Luke tell you that the day of the crucifixion is the preparation day for a Sabbath. What Sabbath? John Chapter 19, verse 31 is critical if you are to understand what Sabbath this is. Go back and read Leviticus Chapter 23 if you need a refresh. Remember, there are weekly Sabbaths and then there are High Sabbaths. They are Holy Convocations which are both feasts and no work is to be performed on them, such as crucifixions, removing bodies, burials. John is telling you specifically that the next day, a Sabbath, is one of these High Sabbaths that is coming quickly with sundown.

John has already told you twice (Chapter 18, verse 28; Chapter 19, verse 14) that it is the day of preparation for the Passover. It is the first of two High Sabbaths. They fall on the 14th and 15th day of Abib. John Chapter 19, verse 31: "The Jews therefore, because it was the preparation, that the body should not remain upon the cross on the Sabbath day (f<u>or that Sabbath day was an High Day</u>) besought Pilate that their legs might be broken, and that they might be taken away." This verse shows that the day that Jesus was laid in the tomb was a day prior to a High Sabbath, not a weekly Sabbath!

The other gospels tell you that it is a preparation day for a Sabbath, which it is, but not a weekly Sabbath, it is a day of preparation for a High Sabbath, the Passover! Why do Christians make such a big deal about "not one bone was to be broken" and how when the soldiers came to break Jesus' legs, He was already dead, so they didn't. That entire thought process was in direct relationship to the celebration of the Passover Lamb. The Lamb was not supposed to have one bone broken. Jesus was our Lamb, and if so, He had to die on the evening of Passover! Do you see how John has shown you what day Jesus was to die, and how He could not have eaten the Passover with the disciples if He was to be "OUR" Passover Lamb?

In the Grave, the Resurrection and After

For those of you that have been reading your Bibles along as we passed through these chapters you will note that we are at the end. The Books of Matthew, Mark and Luke all have about one page of reading left, John has about three. But in this short amount of print, you will see big differences in their stories. This is where all four gospel writers will tell a totally different story as to who found Jesus missing from the tomb, why they went in the first place, when first Jesus appeared and how He ascended.

This, coupled with the fact that the translation of two words changes the entire meaning of the scriptures, should leave you spinning and wondering why this has never been shown to you before. The entire crucifixion on Friday, with the resurrection on Sunday hang on your ability to translate Greek to English. Why have you read this far in this book? It should be for your quest to understand what is truly gospel, and what is not.

Up until now, every time the New Testament has stated that something happened on the Sabbath, it was the Greek word Sabbaton. Greek is a very specific language that is much more specific than English. In English, we have one word for the word "love." We love puppies, friends, family, God, and we even "love" to do things. The Greek language gives you three different words, along with their variants, for the English word love, to break it into proper categories. They are Agapao and Agape which are the Love God has for others and we for Him. There is Phileo and Philadelphia which is to have an affection in very high order or brotherly love. And only once do we see the Greek word thelo. It means to will, to decide or to want. I show you this to make the point that if you look at the Greek, it is very specific as to what the author was trying to tell you.

There is a Greek word for the English word "day," it is hemera. There is a Greek word for the English word "first," it is proton or protos. There is also a Greek word for the English word "one," it is heis. All of these words are used many many times in the gospels. Use your concordance to look them up.

This translation ability is key to understand if what is in print in your Bible is correct, or just man's tradition, that for some reason has not been challenged. You will read seven times in the New Testament, five times in this chapter that we will be covering, the phrase "first day of the week." It is presumed to be Sunday. It is the "time" that Mary goes to the tomb. You will note that in your Bible it will look like this: first *day of the* week. That means that the words "day + of + the" are all added to the text. They are not there in any Greek compilation. The word that is translated into the English word "first" isn't from the Greek word protos or proton, it is the Greek word "heis." This translation of the Greek word heis into the English word "first" is only done seven times and it is always in the phrase "first day of the week." But what is the word that they translated to mean the English word "week?"

It is the Greek word Sabbaton. So, if you look at the seven times that the modern church would like to refer to Sunday, by using the "first day of the week" phrase, it is the two Greek words "heis Sabbaton." The literal translation to heis Sabbaton is "one Sabbath."

If you really want to understand the word "week," you have to dig a little. Could it be that the concept of a week, or seven days, actually used the Greek word for Sabbath to reference it? This is what is sold in Sunday keeping Churches. Why not look at Acts Chapter 28, verse 14 when the author of Acts (probably the same author as the Book of Luke) used the term "seven days" to designate a seven day period. If the word Sabbaton was synonymous with the English word "week," why didn't the text state that they stayed in Puteoli for a "Sabbaton?" This is simple, because they didn't stay from Friday sundown to Saturday sundown. They stayed for seven days!

Since the concept and translation of the words "seven days" is clearly found in Acts, I can't fathom how any reasonably intelligent person cannot understand that Sabbath worship is the only worship in the New Testament. A Sabbath isn't seven days, it is one day out of seven that was named by God as His day.

On "one Sabbath" Mary visits the tomb. It wasn't breaking any Jewish Law to walk to the tomb on Sabbath. It is only the stories of the authors of Mark and Luke that tries to tell you that Mary and others went to the tomb to anoint the body of Jesus. No other gospel account supports this account. In fact, John has told you that Joseph of Arimathea has already anointed the body with Nicodemus.

The author of Luke will tell you in the same chapter that Jesus was in the tomb for three days and three nights. Why would Mary try to anoint the body so late in the process? You have already learned from the death of Lazarus that the body would have already begun to decompose and stink. Besides, who would have been there to roll away the stone? What about the tomb being sealed by the Jewish leadership? What about the guard that was posted?

There are so many errors in this last chapter from the gospels that I am appalled that Christians have never questioned the "first day of the week" translation as well as many others. Are we so perverted by tradition that we cannot use our God given gifts of wisdom and discernment? Let's see what is in store in the close of the gospels.

Matthew Chapter 27, verse 61 through Chapter 28 verse 20 The following day the chief priests and Pharisees come to Pilate to ask him to make the tomb secure. Jesus had stated that He would rise from the dead on the third day. Pilate sends them away to put guards on the tomb and to seal it.

Chapter 28 opens at the close of the Sabbath as it was dawning on the first *day of the* week. Mary Magdalene and another Mary come to the sepulchre. There is an earthquake. The angel of the Lord came and rolled away the stone from the door and sat upon it. Those watching over the tomb are petrified. The Angel tells the women not to fear, for he understands that they are seeking Jesus. He explains that the Lord has risen and shows them the place where Jesus had laid.

The angel instructs the women to go and tell the disciples that Jesus has risen from the dead, and has gone to Galilee before them. They run from the sepulchre with joy and fear to the disciples, but on the way Jesus met them and they held Him by the feet and worshiped Him. He tells them not to be afraid, but to go tell the disciples to go to Galilee where He will meet them.

Those that were at watch at the sepulchre came into the city to give a report of what happened to the chief priests. The chief priests give them money to say that the disciples came and stole Him away while they slept. Then the eleven disciples went into Galilee to an appointed place where Jesus revealed that all power had been given to Him in heaven and earth. They worshiped Him, but some doubted. Jesus gave them the following charge: "Go ye therefore and teach all nations, baptizing them in the name of the Father, and of the Son, and of the Holy Ghost: Teaching them to observe all things whatsoever I have commanded you: and, lo, I am with you always, unto the end of the world. Amen."

Mark Chapter 16 After Sabbath had past, Mary Magdalene, Mary the Mother of James, and Salome brought spices to anoint Him. And, very early in the morning on the first *day of the* week they came to the sepulchre at sunrise. They said to each other, who shall roll away the stone? When they arrive, they find the tomb open with a young man sitting on the right side clothed in a long white garment. They are fearful, but the man tells them not to be fearful as they have come to seek Jesus. He explains that Jesus is risen and sends them to the disciples to tell them to go to Galilee as Jesus had previously instructed them to do. They left happy and amazed.

On the day that He had risen, Jesus first appeared to Mary Magdalene, and she went and told the disciples, but they did not believe. Then He appeared to two brethren in the country side, who, when they told the disciples, they didn't believe them either. After this, Jesus appears to the eleven while they are eating and was upset with them for having a hardened heart, and not believing that He had risen.

With this, He told them to go into the world and preach to every creature. He that believes and is baptized will be saved, but if they do not believe, they will be damned. Those that believe will be able to cast out devils in His name and shall be able to speak in new tongues. They shall handle serpents and drink deadly things with no harm. Finally, they shall lay their hands on the sick, and the sick shall recover. Directly after this speech, Jesus ascended up to heaven and sat at the right hand of God. The disciples did as He had asked.

Luke Chapter 24 On the first *day of the* week, very early in the morning, Mary Magdalene, Joanna, Mary the mother of James, and others with them came with spices and found the sepulchre empty with the stone rolled away. They went in and found it empty. As they were standing there, two men in shining garments appear by them. Those there bowed with their faces to the ground. The two men asked why they were looking for Jesus among the dead, and explain that He had risen from the dead as He had told them He would. They came back and told the disciples all that they had seen.

When the women tell them of what they saw, the disciples dismiss the account as if it was a tale. But then Peter runs to the sepulchre, seeing that it is empty, wonders to himself. Two followers of Jesus go into a nearby town and along the way a stranger joins them for the walk. They do not know that it is Jesus. He asks why they are sad. They explain that Jesus of Nazareth, who was a mighty prophet, had been put to death by the Jewish leadership. They had hoped that He was the Christ to deliver Israel, and today is the third day since He had been crucified. In fact, they told the stranger, that certain women and even men among them had visited the sepulchre in the morning and had found it empty.

Then Jesus explained to them all of the scriptures, and how they related to His suffering and the glory. As they drew near to the destination, they asked Him in for the evening. As He sat to eat with them, He took bread and blessed it and broke it for them, and then their eyes were open and they knew it was Jesus.

Then they arose up and quickly came to the disciples back in Jerusalem and told them all that they had witnessed. And as they were telling all, Jesus appeared to them and said: "Peace be unto you." They were terrified and thought that they were looking at a Spirit. Jesus asked them why were they afraid. He shows them His hands and asks them to handle Him, to show them that He is flesh and not a spirit. Then He asked them for something to eat, and ate before them.

He then explained that he had explained all these things while He was still with them, but these things had to be accomplished as they are written in the Old Testament. Then He gave them an understanding of the scriptures and taught them to preach about repentance and remission of sin to all nations. He told them that He would send the promise of the Father to them, but that they needed to stay in Jerusalem until they received it.

Jesus walked with them to Bethany and blessed them. As He was blessing them, He ascended up to heaven while they worshipped Him. Then they returned to Jerusalem in great joy.

John Chapter 20, verse 1 through Chapter 21, verse 25 On the first *day of the* week comes Mary, when it was still dark, unto the sepulchre, and discovers that the stone is rolled away. She leaves immediately and finds Peter, and the disciple whom Jesus loved, and told them that Jesus had been taken away and didn't know where they had moved Him. The other disciple out runs Peter to the sepulchre, and peered in at the linen on the ground. Peter arrives and goes directly in and observes the layout of the linen and napkin.

The other disciple then enters and they believe that Jesus must have risen, although up until now they had no instruction or knowledge of this miracle of the resurrection. Then the disciples left and went home, but Mary stays to weep. When she stooped down and looked in again, she sees two angels in white sitting where Jesus had laid. They asked her why she was weeping? She exclaimed that someone had taken her Lord, and she didn't know where to look for Him.

When she turned around she saw a person standing and thought it was a gardener. He asks her: "Woman, why weepest thou, whom seekest thou?" Mary asks the man, if you have moved Him, tell me where you have moved Him and I will take Him away. Then Jesus says: "Mary."
She then turns to Him and says: "Master."

Jesus warns her not to touch Him, as He has not yet ascended to the Father. He sends her to the disciples to tell them that He was going to His Father and their Father, His God, and their God. She immediately went to the disciples to tell them what has happened.

That evening, Jesus comes to the disciples in a locked room where they were staying in fear of the Jewish leadership. He showed them His hands and His side. This uplifted the disciples, and He told them "Peace be unto you" as the Father had sent me, so will I send you. With this, He breathed on them and said: "Receive ye the Holy Ghost. And He exclaimed that whose sins you remit, they are remitted and whose you do not remit, are not remitted.

But the disciple Thomas was not there. When he arrives the others tell Him what had happened, but He would not believe. He tells the others that unless he can touch the nail holes and the spear wound in His side, he would not believe. Eight days later, Jesus again appears to them in a locked room when Thomas is present. Jesus asks Thomas to touch His wounds. Thomas replies to Jesus: "My Lord and My God." Jesus states to Thomas: " because thou hast seen Me thou hast believed: blessed are they that have not seen and believe." Many other things were done by Jesus. Those that believe that Jesus is the Christ and the Son of God will be saved.

After this, in Chapter 21, Peter, Thomas, Nathaniel, James and John all went to the sea of Tiberias to fish. They fished all night and caught nothing. Jesus is on the shore, but they don't recognize Him. He asks them if they have any food, and they tell Him no. Then He instructs them to cast their nets in on the right side of the boat and they will catch some. They do, and they have so many fish that they cannot get them into the boat.

John recognizes that it must be Jesus and tells Peter, who immediately jumps in the water and swims to shore. The others followed with the ship, dragging the fish in the net. Jesus had laid a fire and has fish and bread waiting. He instructed them to bring in the fish and Peter went back and pulled in the net, which normally would not hold that many fish. Then Jesus told them to come dine with Him. For some reason Jesus does not look like Himself, but they all dine with Him as they know that it must be Him. This is the third time that Jesus had shown Himself to the disciples after He was risen.

After dinner, Jesus asks Peter: " Do you lovest thou me more than these?" Peter tells Him that He knows that he loves Him. Jesus tells him to feed His Lambs. Then Jesus asks Peter : " Do you lovest thou me?" Peter tells Him that He knows that he loves Him. Jesus tells him to feed His sheep. Jesus asks Peter a third question: " Do you lovest thou me?" Peter tells Him that He knows all things, and He knows that he loves Him. Jesus tells him to "Feed My sheep."

Jesus then predicts the life that Peter will have. Peter will live a full life, but at the end, Peter will be taken where he does not desire to go, which will glorify God. Jesus then takes Peter on a walk, and Peter turns and sees John following and asks what his fate will be. Jesus tells Peter to mind his own business.

The book ends with a testimony from the author of the Book of John that it is he that wrote this book, the same that was the Apostle that Jesus loved and the one that asked the Lord who would betray Him at the Last Supper.

What did we learn? Matthew tells the story of the Jewish leadership going to Pilate to ask to have the tomb secured. He tells any reader that really wants to know specifically that <u>it was the day after the day of preparation</u>. Better put, it is the day after the preparation day or "We are here on the day we are waiting for." Think, think, think! That would mean that the Jewish leadership would have had to come to Pilate on the day that the Jews were preparing for. It is some great celebration that they had to be preparing for! That is why it the day after the day of preparation. This is "the day," or the reason, why the Jews had to get the bodies off the cross. It was a celebration where no work could be performed. The author of Matthew has made it clear in the chapters preceding this chapter that this day was a day when no work could be done. This is why they had to break the legs of those on the cross. Those on the crosses had to die and be removed before <u>this day</u>, the day that this author is telling you that they are now WORKING on. It makes no sense.

On the day when Jesus is discovered missing, the Book of Matthew tells you that Mary of Magdalene and another Mary come to the tomb and there is an earthquake. This is the only record of the earthquake and The Angel of the Lord sitting on the stone. It is dawn on the first *day of the* week. The author of Mark tells you that after Sabbath has past, at sunrise, on the first *day of the* week, Mary Magdalene and two other women come to the tomb with spices to anoint the body and find the stone rolled away. The author of Luke tells you that it was Mary Magdalene, Joanna, Mary the mother of James, and others with them that came on the first *day of the* week with spices and found the stone rolled away. John tells you that it is only Mary that comes to the tomb and it is still dark on the first *day of the* week.

Can you establish what day Mary really comes to the tomb and who came with her? Only one story is correct. John already told you that Jesus' body was already anointed. In John's account it was one woman that discovered the tomb by herself without spices. In the Book of Matthew's account there are two women who came with no spices. The Book of Mark tells you it is three women who brought spices. Finally, the author of Luke tells you it is at least four women that discovered the tomb disturbed who also came with spices.

One account tells you that an earthquake moved the stone, but this one is more troubling if you look at it. In the Book of Matthew, you read that "The Angel of the Lord" sat on the stone that was rolled away from the tomb. Who is The Angel of the Lord? In the Book of Acts, the prophet Steven tells you that "The Angel of the Lord" is the voice of the burning bush. That is the bush that spoke to Moses in the wilderness. It is the I AM. Jesus tells you that He is the I AM.

This gets into who Jesus Christ is, or more specifically, who He was before He was Jesus. But that is another topic for my next book. But, only the author of Matthew makes the claim that The Angel of the Lord appeared on the stone.

The author of Mark tells you that the "first *day of the* week" falls after the Sabbath. How could this be if the first *day of the* week is literally translated into "one Sabbath." How can "one Sabbath" directly follow a Sabbath. It's all too simple.

Jesus is crucified on the day of preparation for the Passover, which is a High Sabbath, as John has already told you. You have the 14th and 15th days of Abib when Jesus is in the tomb. Both of these days are feasts and High Sabbaths. They are the Passover and the first day of the Feast of Unleavened Bread. The following morning Jesus is risen. This is a Saturday morning. It is also a Sabbath. This explains that Jesus was crucified on a Wednesday.

Jesus was buried and has been in the ground for Wednesday, Wednesday night, Thursday, Thursday night, Friday, and Friday night. He has been in the ground for three days and three nights and is visited at the tomb on "one Sabbath," by Mary. This happens to be the first Sabbath after the Passover.

I always find it humerus when anyone tries to say that the gospels are all correct and then tries to explain the three days and three nights in the tomb, with a Friday crucifixion and a Sunday morning before sunrise resurrection. Remember to look at when the gospels try to say that Mary came to the tomb. It's before the "day" begins. There is no "midnight start of a new day" in the Bible. It is the evening until morning until evening. That is what constitutes a day in the Bible.

So Jesus was buried before a Sabbath, which happened to be a High Sabbath, rests the next Sabbath (another High Sabbath) and is risen on the third Sabbath in a row. Do the math. That is why all the gospels say that Mary arrived on "one Sabbath."

Even though it is very clear from the Book of John, that the day Jesus was crucified was not prior to a weekly Sabbath, the other gospel tell you that it can't be a Friday crucifixion and a "before sunrise" on Sunday resurrection. According to the author of Matthew, Jesus would follow the sign of Jonah. Matthew Chapter 12, verse 40, states that as Jonah was in the belly of the whale for three days and three nights, so will the Son of Man be in the heart of the earth for three days and three nights. In the Book of Luke it states plainly in Luke Chapter 24, verse 21 that it was the third day after the crucifixion when the two followers of Jesus are walking with Jesus on the day of His resurrection. So how can you count out three days and three nights between Friday evening and before sunrise on Sunday? You can't. Let's get back to the circumstances surrounding the resurrection.

In the Book of Matthew, it was supposedly "The Angel of the Lord" that gives the Good News that Jesus Christ has risen and sends the women to tell the disciples. On the way, Jesus meets with the women and they hold Him by the feet as He instructs them to have the disciples go to Galilee for a meeting. Once the disciples arrive in Galilee, when Jesus arrives, some doubt. Here is a real problem. You may want to doubt, but don't you think that those doubts would be before you see Him? But the text states that once there, "They worship Him: but some doubt."

The author of Mark has a different take. Remember that the author of Mark has an additional woman with the two Marys when they arrived at the tomb. There has not been an earthquake and there isn't "The Angel of the Lord" sitting on the stone. These ladies are bringing spices and as they arrive and they find the tomb open. There is a young man sitting on the right side clothed in a long white garment. They are fearful, but the man tells them not to fear as they have come to seek Jesus. He explains that Jesus is risen and tells them to tell the disciples to go to Galilee as Jesus had previously instructed them to do.

In Matthew, when the disciples hear that they are to go to Galilee, they go and meet with Jesus. But here in Mark, the disciples are first told by Mary about Jesus' resurrection and they do not believe her. Then two believers from the country side come back and tell them, and they don't believe them either. Finally, Jesus has to meet with them while they are eating and He rebukes them for not believing. In Matthew, they do go to Galilee to meet Him, but here in Mark it is apparent that they do not go, let alone believe that He is risen.

The Book of Luke doesn't have anything about meeting in Galilee anywhere. In the Book of Luke the women come back, and even though they don't believe their story, Peter goes to the sepulchre to see for himself. Two followers are on the way to a neighboring city and Jesus joins them, even though they don't know that it is He. The author of Mark tells you of two followers in the country side that come back to say that they have seen Jesus, but the disciples don't believe their report. But in the author of Luke's version, when they come back to tell the disciples, Jesus appears with them. There is no rebuke of the disciples in the Book of Luke as there was for the disciples in the Book of Mark. Do you note how the disciples are afraid of Jesus when He appears in the Book of Luke? It is because they think that He is a Spirit. What ever happened to the power that Jesus had given them over devils and spirits? Just another little inconsistency.

One more thought about the two gentleman walking in the countryside with Jesus in the Book of Luke. Remember this is the day that Jesus is found risen. Did you note that they tell Jesus: "and besides all this, today is the third day since these things were done." If you are not bright enough to understand the significance of this statement, it is telling you that the author of the Book of Luke understood that Jesus was in the ground for three days and three nights. Even if it was a Sunday, then Jesus had to be in the grave by Thursday. This means that the Sabbath that the authors of Matthew, Mark and Luke are referring to, that was following the crucifixion, can't be a weekly Sabbath.

But then we have the Book of John. Mary came on "one Sabbath" in the morning while it was still dark and discovered the tomb was open. She leaves immediately and goes to find Peter and John. So there is no one at the tomb, no guards, no Angel of the Lord, No man in the tomb, not even two guys that appear while she is looking-on in the empty tomb. Just an empty tomb and she runs to find those that she knows will care about what has happened.

Before we go any farther. In the Book of John, there is no discussion of placing a guard at the tomb or placing a seal on it. Why would there be? What did the Jewish leadership need it for, according to the gospel as recorded by the Apostle John? They were wanting to put Jesus to death. Once dead, that was it. Now, if they really thought that He was the Son of God, I imagine that they would have wanted to secure it. But they didn't really believe that He was the Son of God, or they wouldn't have messed with Him. They didn't fear His followers, they were common people that scattered as soon as a multitude showed up. So, Jesus died, and Joseph of Arimathea is allowed to take the body from the cross and place it in the tomb after he and Nicodemus anoint it.

Now, Mary has shown up once before daylight, found the tomb empty, and then went to find Peter and John. Peter and John come to the tomb and enter, ponder and realize that He may have been raised from the dead. They leave, but Mary stays. This is her second time arriving at the tomb that morning. After Peter and John leave, when Mary looks in again, there are two angels. But they just ask her what she is looking for?

I have to ask you, is there any real correlation between any of these gospels to this point of the story? Other than the name Mary being stated many times, what two gospels have told the same story from the crucifixion until this point? Be truthful, none of them have. So you have to pick one and live by it, or throw them all out.

In the Book of John, it isn't until Mary thinks that she is talking to a gardener that she understands what has happened. Jesus reveals Himself to her. But you must note that He will not let her touch Him until He has ascended to the Father. This again places this story directly opposed to the story given by the Book of Matthew. Remember, in that account, when the women run from the tomb, Jesus meets them on their way to the disciples. It states, "they came and held Him by the feet and worshipped Him." Which one is it? John tells you that Jesus could not be touched until He had ascended to the Father.

In the Book of John, there is no mention that any of the disciples do not believe Mary when she comes back to tell them what has happened. As they are gathered that evening, Jesus appears in the midst of them, even though the building is locked. Jesus shows them who He is and then gives them the gift of the Holy Ghost.

This is opposed to the story told by the author of Luke when they are told to stay in Jerusalem until they receive the "promise" from the Father. This receiving of the Holy Ghost is supposedly completed in the second book of the author of the Book of Luke, the Acts of the Apostles. In it, the Holy Ghost is received by the disciples at Pentecost. So what was it that Jesus gave the disciples when the Apostle John is telling you that Jesus "Breathed on them?"

But only ten of the remaining disciples are present when Jesus appears to the disciples in the Book of John. Thomas is absent. This alone is a contradiction to the other gospels where it specifically states that Jesus appeared to the eleven that evening.

There is another weird difference in the doubting of Thomas. We are talking about doubting. Don't forget, in the gospel account recorded by John, Jesus has not prepared the disciples for His death, and resurrection. They have a real reason to fear and doubt when He is crucified.

That isn't so in the Book of Matthew, Mark and Luke. Jesus has told the disciples over and over that He will be killed and then in three days will rise again. According to the author of Matthew, Jesus does not appear to the disciples in Jerusalem. They are sent to Galilee where He meets them, but some doubt? Doubt what? They are meeting with Him.

What's there to doubt? This is a great example to show that the believers during the early years had heard John's account but didn't fully remember what had happened. Then it was put in writing and when compared to John's account. There are noticeable problems with the stories. So all the stories show that there is doubt, but in the Apostle John's account, Thomas had a reason to doubt. He had never been told by Jesus that there would be a death, and resurrection.

In John Chapter 21, John makes it perfectly clear that when Jesus appeared to them at the Sea of Tiberias, that Jesus was noticeably different in His outward appearance. The disciples know it is Him, but do not want to ask. John also tells you that this is the third time that Jesus has appeared since His resurrection. So the three times are: first to the ten disciples, second to all eleven, and last was here at the Sea of Tiberius.

Peter is asked by Jesus if he loves Him. Jesus asks three times. The first two times the word for love is "agapao" which is the love that someone would have for God. The last time it is "phileo" which is to have affection in very high regard. Oddly enough Peter always answers with the phileo form of love to Jesus. It seems to be odd when you read this in the Bible. It looks like Jesus is asking Peter the same question three times and Peter becomes frustrated. But if you look at the translated word it draws a different conclusion.

Jesus is asking Peter if He loves Him as a God over those that are with Peter. Peter tells Jesus that he holds Him in high regard. Jesus asks Him if He holds Him as a God. Peter again tells

Jesus that He holds Him in High regard. Jesus then asks Him if he really holds Him in high regard. Peter tells Jesus that He knows that he holds Him in high regard.

Is Jesus Christ God? Peter is telling you that he holds Him in high regard, but He is not God the Father, He is the Son!

The author of the Book of Mark has the most troubling closing to me if you want to believe that it is the inerrant word of God. It is even more troubling if you believe in the phrase once-saved-always-saved. Re-read Mark Chapter 16, verses 17 and 18.

"And these signs shall follow those that believe; In My name shall they cast out devils; they shall speak with new tongues; they shall take up serpents, and if they drink any deadly thing, it shall not hurt them..."

Think of what is specifically written here. If you are a follower that believes in Jesus, and I am, I can drink any deadly fluid or hold a diamond back rattle snake in my hand and it will not harm me or you. What a test. So if you ever professed Jesus, as is taught by once-saved-always-saved, you will not be harmed. I'm sorry, I really do not believe this teaching found in the Book of Mark. Neither does any other Christian or why wouldn't those selling the idea prove it!

Unfortunately, this same author probably gave you the Book of the Acts of the Apostles. Do you think that he did any better with that book? Let's see.

The Book of The Acts of the Apostles

We have covered the fact that there are some areas in the Bible that are written by men that were fallible. There are many errors in the New Testament, so we can conclude that it is not written by the hand of God. It is believed that the New Testament is a compilation of various letters from church leaders to various groups of people for many different reasons. Finally, the gospels are very different from each other in their recollection of the order and happenings of events in the ministry of Jesus Christ.

Focusing more closely on the works of the author of the Book of Luke, I have previously suggested that he wrote two books, the Book of Luke and the Book of The Acts of the Apostles. These were purposefully written books, but not to edify the church. As mentioned earlier, if they were written by an early Christian, they were probably written in defense of Paul when he was in Rome. This is theorized by the opening in Luke Chapter 1, verse 3 "It seemed good to me also, having had perfect understanding of all things from the very first, to write unto thee in order, most excellent Theophilus..." This is a very formal opening to a Roman, possibly a lawyer.

By the time The Book of Acts is written, the author is on a less formal note starting The Book of Acts like this: "The former treatise have I made, O Theophilus..." As you can see, both the Book of Luke and the Book of Acts were written solely for the information to get to a man called Theophilus. Acts concludes with Paul being at Caesar's Palace awaiting trial. This does bring the point home that they may have both been written for an event centered around Paul's first imprisonment.

So, the Books of Luke and Acts were not written for the Christian's edification at all. It appears that they were written as a persuasion to help explain why Paul believed as he believed. You can accept this argument or you can reject it, but you will have to conclude after reading this chapter that the events, as told by the author of The Acts of the Apostles, are overly dramatized.

For years the Book of Acts was my favorite book of the Bible. It had wonderful stories of faith and persecution. I would get emotional over the way that Paul was abused and yet, still had faith to carry on. After exhaustively studying the text I have found it very much at odds with other New Testament authors that I totally trust, such as Paul. You will have to decide where you will cross the line between fact and fiction as you read through this supposed historical recollection of the early church.

I originally had more doubts as to the accuracy of the Book of Luke than I did The Book of the Acts of the Apostles. This is because, if the author was the physician Luke, he is an associate to

The New Testament, the Facts and the Fiction

Paul, at least later on. The stories he writes down about Paul would have been first-hand hearsay or possibly even first-hand witness sometimes. But a major problem with this way of thinking is that he is still very error prone when compared to Paul's own epistles. In the Book of Luke, he is very much in disagreement with the other gospel writers, and that is why I find the areas that only he writes about to be in question.

I know, I know this is the beginning of another slippery slope. If we doubt here, where do we stop? It is simple, look at it for what it was: possibly a defense document written by a man that had no first-hand knowledge of the events he is writing about until later into the ministry of Paul. Luke is only mentioned two times in the New Testament. Paul writes of him in Colossians Chapter 4, verse 14 and in 2 Timothy, Chapter 4, verse 11.

In the Book of Colossians, Luke is mentioned at the close. This is common in most of Paul's letters to give credit to those that are working with him at the time of the letter. If you read Colossians Chapter 4 you will see that Luke is not mentioned with the group known as the circumcision. This is how you know that Luke was not a Jew. Even if he was a Jew he would not have been accepted by Jews being uncircumcised. Hence, he would not have been with or around Jesus in Israel, or the early church for that matter. You will also note that Paul tells you that he is a physician.

If this book was written by Luke, where did he get all of those stories of Jesus Christ's life and the early church? Most of it had to be from Paul, who was also not a first-hand witness to anything that Jesus did or said. Remember the first time you see Paul mentioned is at the stoning of Steven and in that action, he was working against the church!

So, the million dollar question is this: are these books accurate? If Luke was a Gentile, would he have the same understanding of Jewish custom, as say, one of the apostles? The Book of Acts doesn't have another book that it can be tested against accept at the beginning of the book. It covers some of the closing events around the time just after Jesus' crucifixion. All the gospels tell a different story, and so does the Book of Acts.

One more train of thought: Is Paul given the power of healing in the Book of Acts? Of course, along with many others believers. Then why doesn't Paul make mention of this power, his ability to heal, in his own writings? In Fact, why doesn't any other New Testament authors refer to this power other than in the Books of Matthew, Mark, Luke, or Acts.

Why does Luke accompany Paul? He is referred to as Luke the physician in Paul's own writings. Why would Paul need a physician with him if Paul has the power to heal? Does Luke have the power to heal? If the power to heal was a gift from God, why would you need a physician around? Why wouldn't Luke be Luke the Healer, not Luke the Physician?

The gift of healing is mentioned in 1 Corinthians Chapter 12. This is the only place in the New Testament other than the Books of Matthew, Mark, Luke and Acts it is mentioned. So Paul explains that there could be a gift of healing, but then never, ever displays its use. When Paul boasts of his ministries in 2 Corinthians Chapter 11, he tells of all the things he has done or has been done to him. Healing is never mentioned.

In Acts Chapter 1 you read that the disciples stay in Jerusalem as they have been directed by Jesus until they receive the Holy Ghost. Only, In Matthew Chapter 28 and Mark Chapter 16 the disciples are instructed to go to Galilee if they want to meet with Jesus again. Then in Matthew Chapter 28, verse 16 you see the eleven going to a mountain in Galilee where they meet Him.

In Acts Chapter 1, verse 12, there is a very curious statement that the Mount of Olives was a Sabbath's day journey from Jerusalem. Do you understand that the Jewish leadership had identified that you could only walk a certain distance on the Sabbath, or it was considered work? Remember that a Jew will not do work on any Sabbath. Why this is important is that Passover is a High Sabbath.

If Jesus had eaten the Passover with the disciples as told in the Books of Matthew, Mark, and Luke, that would make the evening of the arrest a High Sabbath. He then took them to the Mount of Olives, as noted in these same books. Think about it. That would mean that the armed Jewish mob would have walked much more than just the trek mentioned here in Acts, when they had to come from Jerusalem to the Mount of Olives and back, not to mention all of the other various locations that evening.

But, the Book of John doesn't state this. First, it isn't the Passover in the Book of John. Passover is the next day. Secondly, in John it doesn't specify what garden they go to, just that it is a garden on the other side of the Brook Cedron.

You will note in Acts Chapter 1, verse 13 that the 12 disciples, minus Judas Iscariot are once again named. This list is in agreement with the one provided in the Book of Luke, but is different to the lists provided in the Books of Matthew and Mark. Once again this adds to the credibility that this book was written by the same author as the Book of Luke. It doesn't take a rocket scientist to understand that it would have been better for those that would like to say that the Bible is the inerrant word of God, if all four areas in the New Testament that do give the list, were all the same.

The New Testament, the Facts and the Fiction

In Acts Chapter 1, verses 16–19 you read the story of how Judas died. It is explained to have been from a head-first fall, and he burst asunder. But in Matthew Chapter 27, verse 5 you find Matthew's understanding that Judas passed away by hanging himself. Think about it. If the author of the Book of Matthew was the Apostle Matthew, he and Judas "hung" around together for years. Don't you think that he would have known how one of his 11 closest associates had died? Either way, only one of the accounts can be correct. That would make the Book of Matthew or the Book of The Acts of the Apostles dead wrong, hence, not inerrant.

For those that want to twist intellectual thought processes and try to say that Judas hung himself and them the rope broke and he fell and hit his head, take a breath! One states that he died one way and the other tells a different story, it is just that simple, but it gets worse. Who owns the field that Judas died in? It is plain here in Acts Chapter 1, verse 18 that "this man purchased a field with the reward of iniquity." But in Matthew Chapter 27, starting in verse 5, it is clear that Judas returns the money and the Jewish leadership purchases the potters field with the money!

Continuing in the same story, we have Peter addressing the believers in verse 20: "For it is written in the Book of the Psalms, Let his habitation be desolate, and let no man dwell therein: and his bishopric let another take." These are constant in the gospels and continues here in the Book of Acts. A verse from the Old Testament is taken out of context, and altered to fit the purpose. Let's look at the Psalms to see what it actually states.

First, there is no word Bishop, Bishoprick or Bishops mentioned in any Old Testament passage. There is a verse that has much of what Peter is supposed to have said, and it is found in Psalm Chapter 69. Do you know what David is talking about in this Psalm? He is laminating about those that have persecuted him. Even if you want to say that it could be a vision and is a foretelling of thoughts that Jesus may have in the future, the verse still doesn't fit. Let's look at the verses surrounding this statement: Psalm Chapter 69, verses 21-28.

"They gave me also gall for my meat; and in my thirst they gave me vinegar to drink. Let their table become a snare before them: and for welfare, and a trap. Let their eyes be darkened, that they see not; and make their loins to continually shake. Pour out thy indignation upon them, and let thy wrathful anger take hold of them. Let their habitation be desolate; let none dwell in their tents. For they persecute whom thou hast smitten; and they talk to the grief of those whom thou hast wounded."

To make the case that this is about Jesus is a very big stretch. Just because it has the words gall and vinegar doesn't link this to the cross in any way. It is gall to eat and vinegar to drink. It is a punishment at the table in this Psalm. They didn't give Jesus gall to eat and vinegar to drink on the cross as an additional punishment, He just wouldn't have taken it. They were offering Jesus a sedative.

Second, in Acts, it states: "Let his habitation be desolate, and let no man dwell therein: and his bishopric let another take." It sounds like they are talking about his body or position that Judas was holding. In the Psalm it is clear that David wants to have these people that are persecuting him to be trashed. It is clear that the verse quoted is about taking away the housing that they are living in, leaving them with nothing. There is no mention of taking away their position, as in discipleship. And if you look closely at this verse in Acts, it is the singular "his" but the plural "their" in the Psalms. It isn't a single person that this Psalm was asking to have cursed, it was the multiple of people that were doing this to David that he desires to be cursed by God.

In Acts Chapter 2, we open with the disciples receiving the Holy Spirit that danced around on each of them like cloven tongues of fire at Pentecost. This is when most Christians believe that the Holy Spirit was given to the disciples. From this point on in the Book of Acts, they are able to do miraculous things. What was the power that was given to the disciples in the Books of Matthew, Mark, and Luke where they could cast out devils, heal the sick, and no harm could come to them?

More importantly, what is meant in John Chapter 20, verses 21 and 22: "Then said Jesus to them again, Peace be unto you: as My Father hath sent me, even so send I you. And when he had said this, he breathed on them, and saith unto them: Receive ye the Holy Ghost."

So which account of the receiving of the Holy Ghost is gospel? In just over a chapter you have witnessed several hard contradictions and an Old Testament scripture taken out of context. If there is this much error so far where you can test the Book of Acts to other scripture, why would you think that the parts that can't be compared to other New Testament passages will be any more accurate?

Remember what Moses told you about testing whether a "prophet" is speaking for God or just a great story teller. Deuteronomy Chapter 18, verses 21-22: "And if thou say in thine heart, How shall we know the word which the Lord hath not spoken? When a prophet speaketh in the name of the Lord, if the thing follow not, nor come to pass, that is the thing which the Lord hath not spoken, but the prophet hath spoken it presumptuously: thou shalt not be afraid of him."

So Moses makes it clear that if someone isn't 100% correct, that the story they are telling is spoken presumptuously. He doesn't say that if the story sounds similar, then it is from God. The "thing has to follow." That means that it must come to pass exactly.

After the disciples are given the Holy Ghost in the Book of Acts Chapter 2, the disciples all begin to speak in different languages of foreign visitors that happen to be in Jerusalem for Pentecost. Many in the city believe that the disciples have been drinking, but Peter again stands up and explains that this event that they're seeing is foretold by the Prophet Joel.

This is again another example of taking the Old Testament out of context. If you line up what Peter is quoting from Joel, it is close, but different. There isn't any mention of prophesying in Joel and it isn't the notable day of the Lord as told here in Acts, it is the terrible day of the Lord.

In Joel the foretold prophesy was to occur after the "Day of the Lord" had happened. This is after a large army has come to trounce His people. In Joel Chapter 2, verse 18: "Then will the Lord be jealous for His land and pity His people." It then explains that He will begin to take care of them. And after He does, we read that the verses quoted by Peter will happen. There is no mention of talking in foreign tongues, or tongues of angels for that matter.

In Joel, those statements are followed by: "For, behold, in those days, and in that time, when I shall bring again the captivity of Judah and Jerusalem..." Joel is talking about a time in the future when God brings His chosen people back to Jerusalem. Is any of this happening at this time in the Book of Acts? No, so where is the connection between the prophecy of Joel and what is happening here in the Book of Acts? There isn't one!

When the New Testament tells you that an event is fulfilling scripture, then test it. If it doesn't pass the 100% accuracy test that Moses has told you about, then reject it!

The Book of Acts goes on to tell a nice story that I enjoy, but I have a hard time trusting them too much because of the prior errors. In Acts Chapter 4, Peter and John are brought before the High Priest for preaching in the name of Jesus. What is the name of the High Priest? It is Annas. Then it mentions several of his relations, one of which is Caiaphas. Don't you find it odd that in the gospels, Caiaphas is the High Priest and Annas is his father-in-law (John Chapter 18, verse 13)? I love the Christian apologetics on this issue. I have heard it said that they shared it, or traded off the duties. Go back and read how a High Priest was replaced. There is only one High Priest at a time, that is why he is the High Priest. He is replaced when he dies!

Chapter 5 shows the healing powers and the ability to heal those vexed with unclean spirits as seen in the Books of Matthew, Mark, and Luke. It's unfortunate that the power over unclean spirits is one power of the Holy Spirit that is not recorded by Paul in any of his letters or the Apostles John, Peter, or Jude and James. In the same chapter you see people bringing the sick to lay in the street, hoping that Peter might walk by and the passing of his shadow able to heal them.

Isn't it odd when you see the power that is attributed to Peter, James and John here in Acts Chapter 5, that for some reason it does not seem to be present just a few years later in the books written by the other authors? Take the third epistle of John. It is about a man named Diotrephes who is resisting the author of this epistle attributed to John. How could a church member even think of resisting one of these powerful Church leaders? For that matter, you have just read in Acts how when Ananias and Sapphira lie, they immediately drop dead! But this type of power is not recorded in any New Testament book except the Books of Matthew, Mark, Luke and The Acts of the Apostles.

The disciples are taken before the Jewish Assembly for speaking, healing and teaching in the name of Jesus Christ. They are beaten, instructed not to talk about Jesus in the future and then let go.

At the beginning of Chapter 6 the disciples have 7 brothers selected to work on the administration of charitable giving. Stephen and Philip are two of these men. Stephen grows in the Spirit to perform wonders and miracles and debates about Jesus. Stephen is arrested, but there is a peculiar note about him in verse 15. It states that his face looked like the face of an angel. I'm not really sure why the author of the Book of Acts tells us this. More importantly, how would those there know what the face of an angel looks like?

Chapter 7 has Stephen defending himself before the council, as he gives the genealogy of Abraham's family. Chapter 7, verse 4 you read that Abraham lived with his father Tarah in Charran until his father dies, then he goes to Canaan. This is in direct disagreement with the Book of Genesis.

If you read Genesis Chapter 11, verse 26 you will see that Abraham was born to Tarah before Tarah was 70 years old. Genesis Chapter 11, verse 32 explains that Tarah, Abraham's father, lived 205 years. For the Book of Acts to be true, Abraham would have been at least 135 years old before he came to Canaan.

As Issac was born to Abraham when he was 100 years old, it would mean that Isaac was born in Charran, and we know that this was wrong. So either Steven was wrong, or the author of the Book of Acts wrote it down wrong!

Of particular note is the story Stephen tells of the voice from the burning bush found in Acts Chapter 7, verses 30-34. Stephen identifies the voice as an Angel of the Lord. Next, the voice identifies Himself as the God of the Fathers, Abraham, Issac and Jacob. This is almost too important to miss. The Angel of the Lord has come to talk with Moses, but then states that He is the God of the Fathers. This shows that it was believed that if the Angel came in God's name, the angel now spoke "as God." The angel wasn't God, but it was recorded as if it was God.

But the fact is still stated that the Angel of the Lord was the voice of the burning bush. He was the I AM that spoke. When Jesus declared in John Chapter 8, verse 58: "Before Abraham was, I AM," only shows that Jesus may have been the Angel of the Lord before He was Jesus. The Chapter ends with Stephen being stoned while a young Pharisee named Saul, later becoming the Apostle Paul, watched on.

Chapter 8 explains that Saul, who will become the Apostle Paul, begins to persecute the church. In the mean time, Philip leaves Jerusalem and begins to preach in Samaria. While there he performs miracles to include casting out of unclean spirits. Once again this power is only recorded in the Books of Matthew, Mark, Luke, and here in The Acts of the Apostles.

In this same town where Philip is working is a man named Simon, who is a sorcerer. He too believes and is baptized, and wants the buy the power of the Holy Ghost from Peter and John. Peter curses him for the thought. Remember that this is happening in Samaria, the lowest of scum according to a Jew. They are baptizing these people and even those that have no redemptive properties, like Simon the Sorcerer are being baptized. It emphasizes the fact that these were not Jews living in Samaria in verse 25, just that they preached in many Samaritan towns.

This is important, as later in this book it is a marvel that the Holy Spirit is given to the Gentiles. But who are the Samaritans? This is why the disciples marvel that Jesus would talk to the Samaritan woman that was at the well. Samaritans were unclean. Read John Chapter 4, focusing on verse 9. It is apparent that even talking to a Samaritan was considered unclean.

Next, Philip explains Jesus Christ to a very important eunuch from Ethiopia, who is baptized. Philip baptizes the eunuch and immediately Philip is transported away as the eunuch is brought up out of the water. Think of the significance of this verse found in Acts Chapter 8, verse 39. Philip is "caught up" and is transported through space and time to a town called Azotus. This power is shown only once in the New Testament. It is found in John when Jesus entered the boat after walking on water. Why would Philip have this supernatural gift? Why wouldn't he just bring the eunuch up out of the water and then walk to where God wants him to work next? Think of all the times in the Old and New Testament when a gift such as this could have been used by God to save righteous people from peril, but it is not. And then after this Philip falls into obscurity within the future text.

In Chapter 10, Saul requests and receives power from the High Priest to imprison Christians that are living in Damascus. On the way there he is struck down by the Lord with a great light, and left blind. Saul understands that he has been at war with God and Jesus Christ, in his zeal to keep Judaism pure. A man in the town named Ananias comes to Saul and restores his sight by the name of Jesus. But note that when the Lord comes to Ananias to tell him what to do, Ananias is not fearful of the command from God and actually disagrees with the Lord. Have you seen anyone in the Bible that isn't fearful of what God has told them to do in the Bible? Saul is filled with the Holy Spirit and is baptized.

Paul begins to preach that Jesus Christ is the Son of God, which amazes everyone. The Jews decide to kill him, but he is let over the wall at night and traveled to Jerusalem. The disciples don't trust him at first, but Barnabas forges the trust needed to build a bond between Saul (Paul) and the other disciples, "coming in and going out at Jerusalem."

It is clear from these passages in Chapter 9, that Paul was first converted, and then went to Jerusalem to meet with the disciples. Here is the problem. From Paul's own letters we find this to be untrue. Read Galatians Chapter 1, verses 14-19. Paul is telling you that after his conversion he did not go to Jerusalem, but went to Arabia for 3 years, then came back to Damascus. After that he does go to Jerusalem, but met only with Peter and James (the brother of Jesus), and expressly points out that he met with no others. Then he goes on another trip to Syria and Cilicia.

What ever happened to Barnabas taking Paul under his wing and bringing him to the other disciples? Paul is telling you in the Book to the Galatians that this story, found in The Acts of the Apostles is not true! This story of Paul's conversion is proof positive that you cannot take anything in this book to be accurate. So why make doctrine based on anything found in it?

Back to the story found in Acts, even if it isn't that accurate. After Paul is working with the disciples in Jerusalem, he begins to annoy Jews living there to the point that they want to kill him, so he is sent first to Caesarea and then to Tarsus. Acts Chapter 9 closes with Peter living in Joppa with a man called Simon the Tanner. Peter healed a man in Lydda and a woman in Joppa.

A centurion in Caesarea has a vision and is instructed to bring Peter to his home to teach them of Jesus Christ in Chapter 10. He sends three men to fetch Peter. About the time they arrive, Peter is on the roof top praying and thinking about eating. Peter enters into a vision where a sheet from heaven is lowered down to him with a voice that tells him to: " Rise Peter, kill and eat." The sheet is filled with Levitically unclean animals. Peter responds: "Not so, Lord, For I have never eaten anything that is common or unclean." The voice responds: "What God hath cleansed, call thou not common." This happens three times and Peter doubts what the vision meant.

This vision of Peter being told to eat Levitically unclean foods is the most common passage that so-called Christians quote more often than not to explain why they eat pork and shell fish. Is that what this vision teaches? It is a sure case of taking a passage out of context, for self serving reasons. Any fifth grader reading the next several sentences would tell you that Peter learns what the vision meant, and it wasn't to eat Levitically unclean foods.

While Peter is pondering the vision, the Spirit instructs him to go with the three men, doubting nothing as the Spirit had sent them to him. Peter asks them to stay the night and the following day Peter departs with them for Caesarea. When Peter enters the centurion's house, the centurion falls on his knees, but Peter picks him up and tells him that he too is just a man. Peter then explains the meaning of the vision of unclean beasts to those gathered at the centurions house, beginning in verse 28.

Even though it is unlawful for a Jew to enter into any other nationality's home, Peter explains that God had told him that he should not call any man common or unclean. That is why he, Peter, came when he was directed. After the centurion explained the vision that he had received to fetch Peter, Peter said: "Of a truth, I perceive that God is no respecter of persons." Peter explains to those gathered at the centurion's house who Jesus was, and how He died for our sins. While Peter was speaking, the Holy Spirit fell on all that heard the word, and Peter baptized them in the name of the Lord.

In Chapter 11, the circumcised brethren in Jerusalem are unhappy that Peter had stayed with and baptized Gentiles. He then explained to them about the vision of the sheet full of unclean animals that was to show him that God is not a respecter of persons and how the Holy Spirit had rested upon these Gentiles. With this, they praised God and now knew that repentance unto life had been given to the Gentiles.

A special note here. Was the vision to allow Christians to now eat unclean food such as snake or swine (pig)? No, of course not. This story tells you the meaning twice. It was to show that God doesn't consider only Jews worthy of eternal life. Do we see a giant pig roast held in celebration of this new found revelation?

The word had spread far and the brethren in Jerusalem sent Barnabas to Antioch, to strengthen the fledgling flock that was there. After he had exhorted them all, he left for Tarsus in search of Saul (Paul). He and Saul returned back to Antioch for a year to teach the people. At the year's end, they returned to Jerusalem with an offering from the church.

Chapter 12 opens with King Herod having James, the son of Zebedee, killed with the sword. He also captured Peter and put him in prison. Verse 3 tells you that it is the days of the Feast of

Unleavened bread. Verse 4 states: "And when he had apprehended him, he put him in prison, and delivered him to four quaternions of soldiers to keep him; intending after Easter to bring him forth to the people.

It's time to do a little homework again. Remember that this letter is not signed, but it is believed to be written by Luke, a Gentile that was not there. I don't agree that it was him, but I cannot tell you who wrote it either. This I do know, it was written by someone who did not understand Jewish Holy days and their feasts.

First, there is an intentional mistranslation in the King James version. It is in many translations, but I have quoted the King James. The celebration that they are talking about in verse 4 is translated into the English word "Easter." The Greek word in the text is "pascha." It is correctly translated into Passover, not Easter. Pascha was translated a total of 29 times in the New Testament with all other 28 translations into Passover. So why call it Easter here? I don't know why, or when this occurred, but it does lend itself to the Roman Catholic celebrations!

So the text states that Peter is in prison and it is during the days of the Feast of Unleavened Bread. After Passover, Herod plans to kill Peter to please the Jews. Only, the author of the Book of the Acts of the Apostles does not really understand the order of events surrounding these two different, yet linked celebrations.

If you don't recall from earlier explanations of theses celebrations, read Leviticus Chapter 23. Within the first 10 verses you will learn that Passover comes first, on the evening of the 14th day of Abib. The Feast of Unleavened bread follows beginning on the 15th day of Abib. So the Passover has already happened when we are in the days of Unleavened Bread. This is just one more excellent example to show that this New Testament history book is riddled with errors that no amount of Christian Apologetics can really explain.

Back to the text. The Christian brethren continue to pray for Peter. The evening before Peter is to be killed, the Angel of the Lord frees him. Peter makes his way to the house of the mother of John Mark, where he tells them to get word to James, then departed to another location.

Herod was displeased when he found that Peter had escaped and had the guards executed. Herod is smote by God, because the people proclaimed that he had the voice of a God. The chapter concludes with John Mark joining with Paul and Barnabas.

In Chapter 13 the church at Antioch sends Paul and Barnabas on their first ministry trip, after being directed to do so by the Holy Ghost. They journeyed through many cities and were accompanied by John Mark. On the Isle of Paphos they encounter a false prophet named Bar-

Jesus, that wanted to keep Paul and Barnabas from speaking to the deputy of the country. Paul rebukes Bar-Jesus and he is immediately blinded. The deputy was astonished and believed. Paul and Barnabas continue on with the mission trip, but John Mark returned to Jerusalem.

When they entered Antioch, they sat in the synagogue on the Sabbath, and were invited to speak. Paul explains the history of the nation of Israel and the promise of the seed of David, a Saviour, Jesus. He then showed how John the Baptist and the scriptures foretold of Jesus Christ's life and death, and now has been brought back to life by God. Understanding and believing on Him will provide justification to the believer.

Many Jews and proselytes followed Paul and Barnabas. Even the Gentiles ask to have them preach to them on the next Sabbath. On the next Sabbath, the entire city came to hear the word of God. But when the Jews saw that everyone was there to hear the word, they were filled with envy. Paul and Barnabas then told the Jews that they were to be given the first chance to hear the word, but now we will turn to the Gentiles.

The Gentiles were glad to hear this and those that were ordained to eternal life believed. The Jews stirred up many against the disciples and they were forced to leave their coasts.

Before I leave Chapter 13, what deep insights did you learn about the first encounter? Verse 48 explains that those that are ordained to eternal life, believed. That means that those that are not ordained to eternal life will not believe. Unfortunately this shows that the author of the Book of the Acts of the Apostles believed that you have to be preordained to be saved!

Secondly, what day did Paul enter the synagogue? It was on the Sabbath. What day did the Gentiles ask to be taught by Paul? Verse 42 shows that the Gentiles asked Paul to preach to them again on the next Sabbath. So what ever happened to the first day of the week? Where is the Lord's Day service? Remember, this is after Easter, if you believe in Easter. You will never see a Sunday worship service in the entire Bible. It is a Roman Catholic compromise between Christians and Pagans that has become a tradition of men taken over a Commandment of God.

In Chapter 14 they have arrived in Iconium and they went into the synagogue to teach. Many Jews and Gentiles believe, but those Jews that do not believe, stir up the city. Still, the brethren stay for a long time teaching and doing wonders. Finally, those opposing Paul and Barnabas appear to have the consent of the rulers to stone them, so they flee to the cities in Lycaonia.

At Lystra, Paul heals a man that had been lame from birth. The population of the city believe that Paul and Barnabas must be gods to be able to do such a feat. The people are about to perform sacrifices to them when Paul runs in among them trying to explain that they are just normal men, that have come to preach about God. Jews from Antioch and Iconium persuade the people to stone Paul and leave him outside the city, believing that he is dead.

Two things of note from the above paragraph. When Paul healed the lame man, Paul noted that the man "had faith to be healed." Whose power is it that is doing the healing? If God is working though Paul, does it really matter if the man that Paul has decided to heal has faith or not? What if the man didn't really have faith, would have Paul's words: "Stand upright on your feet" been powerless to heal the man?

Second, isn't it odd that at just the moment when Paul has walked into the crowd to stop the sacrifices, there would be Jews from Antioch and Iconium just standing around in Lystra, waiting for the perfect time to have the people riot to stone him? Do you think that the governments back then gave unemployed people welfare to hang out in other cities, waiting to cause trouble? Why would they have been there in the first place?

After the stoning, Paul stands up and brushes himself off and and re-enters the city. Why didn't the people stone him again? It is obvious that they want to kill him? Nevertheless, the next day he and Barnabas leave for Derby. Soon, they traveled back through the cities where they had taught and ordained elders in each of them. They traveled though several more cities and then returned to Antioch where they rehearsed all that had happened to them.

Chapter 15 is one of my biggest pet peeves with the Book of Acts. As you have witnessed, there are many contradictions between the message found in this book and the other New Testament epistles. This chapter teaches very bad doctrine that is claimed by most modern evangelical Christian Churches, only it cannot be backed up in any way by any other text.

It opens with men from Judea teaching that Gentile Christians need to be circumcised or they cannot be saved. After arguing with these men, they decided that Paul and Barnabas and others would go to Jerusalem to discuss this matter with the apostles and elders. When they arrive in Jerusalem they declare all that God had done with them.

Certain of the Pharisees among them declared that the Gentile Christians need to be circumcised and keep the Law of Moses. So the elders and apostles decide to consider the matter. After much disputing, Peter stands up and explains that there is no difference between a Jew and a Gentile, as God had purified their hearts with faith. He then asks why they want to put a yoke on the Gentiles that they could not keep either.

Paul and Barnabas then declare all that they had done among the Gentiles and how God had provided them with great wonders. With this, James stands up and declares the sentence that is ruled by him for the council.

Acts Chapter15, verses 19 through 21 "Wherefore my sentence is, that we trouble not them, which from among the Gentiles are turned to God: But that we write unto them that they abstain from pollutions from idols, and fornication, and from things strangled, and blood. For Moses of old time hath in every city them that preach him, being read in the synagogue every Sabbath day."

With this, they write letters to the churches of the Gentiles and inform them of this major decision. So what is my problem with this chapter? First, what was the original complaint? Those from Judea were teaching that Gentile Christians need to be circumcised. But the finding is that if you are a Gentile that has become a Christian, you do not have to consider the Law at all. You have to only concern yourself with abstaining from four things: pollutions from idols, fornication, from things strangled, and blood. This is all that most modern Christian churches say that you have to worry about. This is how they throw out the 10 Commandments, to include the Holy Sabbath.

This is so ludicrous that I have a hard time reading the chapter. Let's say that it is correct. What does this sentence allow a Christian to do? Fornication and adultery are two totally different things. That is why when you read those things that a Christian must not do in other passages in the Bible, adultery and fornication are both listed together. They are both a sexual sin, but they are different sinful acts. If they were the same thing, then only one would be listed, but they are always both listed. The best I can make out, fornication may be prostituting your body, but adultery is just having sex with another married person. So under this finding, a Christian is in his or her right to have sex with another married person if you don't charge for it.

You can eat anything that you like as long as it is not blood, or it was not strangled. What does strangled have to do with anything? Even a Jew could eat something that was strangled. Look up the word strangled in the concordance and you will see that it is only used here in Acts. There isn't a Hebrew requirement. So this passage is telling Gentiles that they are forbidden to eat something that a Jew was allowed to eat. This is how you know that this chapter and book was not written by a Jew. It is how you know that this "sentence/decision" never happened. But it gets worse.

What about theft, or covetousness? How about embezzlement? Can you now murder another? How about bearing false witness? It is preposterous to think that this conversation ever happened. This is supposed to be a meeting where Paul is present. Paul is the one that warns against all of these sinful ways. Read Romans Chapter 13.

For an even better set of verses, why not look up Galatians Chapter 5, verses 17 through 21. "For the flesh lusteth against the Spirit, and the Spirit against the flesh: and these are contrary the one to the other: so that ye cannot do the things that you would. But if ye be led of the Spirit, ye are not under the Law. Now the works of the flesh are manifest, which are: adultery, fornication, uncleanness, lasciviousness, idolatry, witchcraft, hatred, variance, emulations, wrath, strife, sedition, heresies, envying, murders, drunkenness, revellings, and such like: of the which I tell you before, as I also I told you in time past, that they which do such things shall not inherit the Kingdom of God."

It is clear from this passage in Galatians that there are a lot of actions that a Christian cannot do, if they want to enter the Kingdom of God. By the way, where is the strangled flesh? But there was more to the council's demand that is overlooked by modern churches.

Read Acts Chapter 15 verse 21 closely. Right after the four above mentioned requirements there is the statement: "**For Moses of Old time hath in every city them that preach him, being read in the synagogues every Sabbath day**." The following verse (Acts 15:22) states that this pleased the council and so they sent the word of their findings to the various Gentile churches. Do you understand what this means? I believe this means that the early church didn't believe in the extra rules that the Jews of the day were living, but they did expect them to live by the Law delivered by Moses **and four more things**. These were not precursors to salvation; they were simply identifying what sin is and what to avoid. This is called "obedience."

Too many modern churches hang their hat on this chapter. If the decision was "God-sent" and written by God's hand, you could make the case that a Gentile Christian is not under the Law at all. Obviously, you have to forget that Acts Chapter 15 verse 21 is located right in the middle of it, but let's say that you desire a more liberal read to this chapter, as most modern Christian churches follow. Was this a decision ordained by God?

Where is the prayer for the guidance to the council before they make the sentence? There is no reference of asking God for leadership in the decision. Even if this council happened, and I believe that it did not, like most of the events recorded in the Book of Acts, where is the righteous judgment before the sentencing. Do you remember what happens when God's people try to make a major decision without asking for God's guidance? Do you remember the story of the Gibeonites?

Read Joshua Chapter 9. You have the Gibeonitess that know that they are going to be wiped out by the Israelites as soon as they come to their city. So they trick the Israelites to make a mutual assistance pact with them. Do you believe that God knew what the Gibeonites were up to? Of course He did, but He allowed them to progress with their deception. God had commanded the Israelites to kill everyone that was in the land, which included the Gibeonites, but the elders gave their word not to harm those from Gibeon.

What did the Gibeonites have to do with Acts Chapter 15? Did the Israelites go to God in prayer and fasting before they made the deal with those from Gibeon? No, and according to Acts 15, the elders in the church did not either!

I have a hard time believing that the Books of Matthew, Mark, Luke and The Acts of the Apostles are given to us by God. That is because there are so many obvious errors in the text. This text, in the Book of Acts, is one more chapter that I have a hard time believing to be the will of God. After all, it will contradict the fruits of the Spirit and allows the lusts of the flesh if you do not add the Mosaic Law. Do you believe that you can have the lusts of the flesh, as pointed out in Galatians, and still be a saved Christian?

Back to the text. Paul, Barnabas and Silas return to Antioch. Once there, they decide to head out on another mission trip. Barnabas wants to take John Mark with them again, but Paul refuses. He is unhappy that Mark left them early on during the last mission trip. This division is so great that Paul takes Silas on the mission, and Barnabas takes Mark on a separate mission.

This is the last that we read of Barnabas in the Book of Acts. Paul does write about Barnabas in his letters, but they are of events at various cities. The last occasion you hear of Paul in his letters talking about Barnabas is at Antioch, when Peter is also there and Paul has to rebuke both of them over the same matter. This is not recorded in the Book of Acts.

Mark too is no longer recorded in the Book of Acts. He is mentioned in the Book of II Timothy when Paul is asking to have him brought to him while he is imprisoned at Rome. In this passage it is obvious that Mark is very helpful in the ministry. Why I bring this up is that in the Book of Acts, Mark has been disowned by Paul and there is no remorse or forgiveness. The Book of Acts ends with Paul imprisoned in Rome, but in Paul's own epistle to Timothy, while imprisoned in Rome, he is calling Mark "profitable to me in the ministry."

Which one is it? Is Mark disowned, or profitable? It kills me when Christians try to say that Paul was imprisoned twice in Rome. Where does the text show you this? It isn't anywhere in the New Testament. For that matter, Paul was probably executed the first time that he was in Rome. From Paul's own letters you cannot find mention of a trial that he had gone through that included being imprisoned in Rome. The sad truth is that he is asking Timothy to bring him some comfort in His Roman Imprisonment!

Early in Chapter 16, Paul meets Timothy, a young man whose father is a Greek. Paul circumcises him. Why? If Paul had fought the council to end this requirement, and the council had just made the ruling not to do it, why does he do it? Also in this and the next chapter we see Paul preaching and reasoning on the Sabbath. If the Sabbath is of no consequence, why not preach and reason on Sundays? The author of the Book of Acts affirms that Paul is also casting out a Spirit in Chapter 16, verse 18.

There isn't too much more in the book that you can collaborate on or test. But the early stuff is just as much off-target as the Book of Luke. I'm confident that the events surrounding Paul might have been a little more accurate if the author is Luke the Physician, who worked closely with him in the later years. There are a few more inconsistencies and facts that I will show, but I will not be covering the rest of the chapters so thoroughly.

In Chapter 18 we see the meeting of Aquila and Priscilla by Paul. They are in Corinth. They are there "Because that Claudius had commanded all Jews to depart from Rome." So, Aquila and Priscilla are in Corinth because all Jews have been ordered out of Rome. Don't you find this fact odd? If all the Jews have been ordered out of Rome, who openly meets with Paul in Caesar's Palace in Acts Chapter 28, verse 17? "And it came to pass, that after three days Paul called the chief of the Jews together: and when they were come together, he said unto them..." This becomes even more bizarre when you realize that in Paul's letter to the Romans, Chapter 16, verses 3-5 you read that Paul knows of Priscilla and Aquila who have a church in their home in Rome.

While in Corinth we again see Paul reasoning in the synagogue on the Sabbath. This fact about Sabbath reasoning and preaching would not be such a big deal if the text shows him meeting with the Gentiles on a separate day, but it doesn't. Jews, Greeks and Gentiles hear him on the Sabbath.

In Chapter 19, starting at verse 12 we see the author of the Book of Acts affirming that Paul has the power to take a handkerchief and send it to someone that is devil possessed or sick and they are immediately healed. What an awesome power, unfortunately Paul never writes of this power in his epistles anywhere. He does tell others by what great ways and authority God has appointed him as an Apostle, but supernatural powers are not listed as any proof that he is sent from God. Remember, the Book of Acts is not written by Paul.

Directly following these powers is a story where some Jews try to displace devils from someone in the name of Jesus. The devils tell them that they know Paul, and they know Jesus, but they don't know those that are trying to use this great power to evict them from their host. So the devils overcome them and prevail against them. This kind of makes sense if you believe in devil's possessing someone, but it is in direct conflict with Mark Chapter 9, starting at verse 38. This is where John is supposed to have stated that there was one that was casting out devils in Jesus' name, but John had stopped him as he did not follow them. Jesus rebukes John and tells him to let the man continue.

At the beginning of Chapter 20, verse 7, we see the "first *day* of the week" reference again. If you don't remember how the translators came to this bad translation from the two Greek words "one Sabbath," go back and review the last chapter. But note when this Sabbath occurs. It happens to be right after the Feast of Unleavened Bread. When was the last time that you saw this reference? In all the Gospel accounts the "first *day* of the week" reference is after the Feast of Unleavened Bread had begun. And, it is the same here.

By the way, in this same verse it has the word "morrow." It means the next day. To reference Sunday, as everything is referenced in relationship to Sabbath, it would have been the morrow of the Sabbath. But if you look at the Greek, it tells you literally, one Sabbaths, not first day of the week!

What great happening occurs in this chapter? A young man named Eutychus falls out of a window to his death. Paul brings him back to life. Once again, as when Paul supposedly cast out a demon from the damsel in Acts Chapter 16, this is one supernatural power or gift of the Holy Spirit that Paul never references in any of His letters.

In Chapter 21 Paul has returned to Jerusalem, and is with the disciples. James tells him starting in verse 21 "And they are informed of thee, that thou teachest all the Jews which are among the Gentiles to forsake Moses, saying they ought not to circumcise their children, neither walk after the customs...Do therefore this that we say to thee...and all may know that those things, whereof they were informed concerning thee, are nothing; but that thou thyself also walkest orderly, and keepest the Law."

This is a major problem with the Book of Acts. It is telling you that God has two different standards. One for a "born" Jew that has faith in Christ, such as Paul, and one for a Gentile that has faith in Christ. In verses 21 through 25 it is apparent that a Jewish Christian kept the Law, but a Gentile Christian is only required to stay away from idolatry, fornication, strangled animals and blood. Once again, I can't fathom how anyone who has the slightest understanding of God's righteous judgment can accept this double standard, let alone believe that a Gentile can still commit murder, adultery, be covetous and so on, and still be saved under Grace. But it is very clear here that the author of the Book of Acts feels that Paul has always kept the Law, and the disciples want to help him prove it.

To make this point even more bold, in Chapter 25, Paul has been arrested and is at Caesarea for over two years. Festus becomes the new governor and has asked the Jews to come and accuse Paul, if they have a case. After they have spoken, Paul begins to make his defense. Acts Chapter 25, verse 8: "Neither against the Law of the Jews, neither against the Temple, nor yet against Caesar, have I offended anything at all." This is as bold of a statement as you can make. Paul is telling you that he has never broken the Law, or civil law. So if Paul hasn't broken the Law, what makes you believe that it is OK for you to ignore it?

The last chapter in the Book of Acts is Chapter 28. It opens with Paul shipwrecked on Melita in the winter. As Paul is gathering sticks for a fire, a viper fastened on his hand. Remember, we are talking winter and they need a fire to get dry and warm. A viper is a cold blooded snake. What do vipers do when the weather begins to turn cooler. They hibernate in a hole in the ground until the temperature begins to climb again. Have you ever seen a snake in the winter? If you did, it couldn't move because it is cold blooded. I lived on Crete for two years. It snows at sea level in the winter time!

But the author needs to add more dramatics and states that the viper fastened itself to Paul, and he shook it off in the fire. Then Paul is said to heal all there that are diseased.

After they leave the island and are on the mainland they come to Puteoli. Here Paul meets some brethren and stays with them for seven days. I'm not saying that this didn't happen, but did you forget that we have a centurion and his men? Centurions have 100 men. There were 276 persons on the ship, mostly prisoners. So Paul meets some friends and the centurion decides to hold all 276 persons at this town for a week while Paul spends time talking with his friends in Puteoli.

Did you notice that the Biblical text stated that Paul stayed with them for "seven days?" Whatever happened to the word week? Week wasn't a Greek word. If they wanted to stay for a week, they stayed for seven days, just like it states in this text. So each time you saw the phrase"first day of the week," this text in the Book of Acts re-enforces the fact that it is a bad translation. This proves that Jesus rose on "one Sabbath."

How did I get to "fact" that the mistranslation of the "first day of the week" passages should state "one Sabbath?" Right here you will note that they used the term "seven days" to designate a seven day period. If this isn't true, why didn't the text state that they stayed in Puteoli for a "Sabbaton?" This is simple, because they didn't stay from Friday sundown to Saturday sundown. They stayed for seven days!.

Since the concept and translation of the words "seven days" is found in Acts I can't fathom how any reasonably intelligent person cannot understand that Sabbath worship is the only worship in the New Testament. A Sabbath isn't seven days (the poor translation for the English word week), it is one day out of seven that was named by God as His day.

The book closes with Paul in Rome under house arrest. He is met openly by the Jews living there. But, do you recall back in Chapter 18 where Aquila and Priscilla and all other Jews were forced to leave Rome under order of Claudius Caesar? Where do these Jews come from if they are all ordered out of the city? Paul is not alone in Rome without friends. Paul knew many Jews in Rome Go back and read the closing chapter in the Book of Romans. He sent salutations to no fewer than 22 persons all residing in Rome. This Book is very confusing as to whether it is teaching that Jews lived in Roam or not at this time. It teaches both ways.

As a young believer I enjoyed the Book of The Acts of the Apostles. I would feel sorrowful for Paul and the other early Christians. I felt indebted to them for their faith and long suffering. But, as I matured and began to read the stories for what they are, I began to understand that this cannot be the Word of God. Not that there isn't some truth to the stories, but since a large majority of it is focused on Paul, it can be tested. When tested to his own words, it doesn't pass the "prophesy test" given to us by Moses. If some of it is wrong, then it isn't from God.

Remember to look for two witnesses for any truth, especially in the history books. I say this because of the damage that Christians do by leaning so heavily on the areas found in the Book of Acts, like the council's decision found in Acts 15. It is a story that is used by Christians, wanting a little more sin in their lives, to justify almost anything. Under the new found freedom that Christians claim by using this chapter, you could commit murder or a number of other sins and still be saved.

I tell you this because I want you to look for a second witness to claim this freedom. There isn't one found anywhere in the New Testament. It is only found in the Acts of the Apostles, and this appears to be a legal document written for a purpose other than the edification of the church.

Yes, I do like the Book of Luke and the Book of Acts, but it is very easy to see that they are not too accurate. Read the books a few times and compare "like" events with the other New Testament books and you will have to agree that these are probably the least accurate of the New Testament accounts of events.

Are the History Books Trustworthy?

This is the slippery slope that most Christians do not want to contemplate. Is the posed question about the trustworthiness of the history books actually questioning the validity of Christianity? No, it is questioning the accuracy of the history books. So much of what we call Christian doctrine comes from the gospels and the Book of Acts. Can you honestly say that after reading this book, you believe that the Bible is the inerrant Word of God? Did you note errors while you were reading these books? Of course you did. That tells you that at least some of the books that you read have errors, demonstrating that they are not the inerrant Word of God. But the Word of God is found in the Bible.

There are many outside sources other than the Bible that can be referenced to show many of the events that are recorded in the Bible actually happened. It is the details that the Bible gives that must be tested from time to time. Should this challenge your Christian walk? No, it should strengthen it. By knowing that the history books have errors, then you can investigate what these errors are, and how they may have been recorded.

Jesus walked on this earth. Jesus was my Passover. He is the reason I have been given eternal life. He lovingly gave His life for mine and the Father has allowed it. Paul is the author that a Christian should use to form doctrine as a Christian. But what you should have learned, is that not all of the New Testament is accurate.

This is a very hard truth for most so-called Christians to face. Are you really trying to live your life as God the Father wants you to live? Are you really using wisdom and discernment when you read your Bible? Or, are you following along like sheep, behind a pastor that is following years and years of tradition. Let's look closely at these books. You should be able to draw your own conclusion to the trustworthiness of the history books by now. I will take the next couple of pages to share how I feel about them.

As you have read, there are two very distinct stories of Jesus' life on earth. There is the one that is found in the Book of John, and there is the one that the other three gospel authors have written. John's account is totally in line with what the Messiah was to be, as documented in the Old Testament.

A close look at the the authors of Matthew, Mark and Luke's account show that they disagree with each other continually, but they do follow the same path. What is that path? They show a Jesus that was born of a virgin, visited by wise men from the East and the babe spends time in

Egypt. All this is supposedly to fulfill scripture. But when you look at the scripture that it was to fulfill, it doesn't apply. Besides, all three tell something that makes the other's account impossible, such as visiting Jerusalem for Passover each year although they stayed in Egypt until the death of Herod.

They have a Jesus that has manifested Himself to His disciples as Christ, the Son of God, early on in His ministry and has been preforming all types of miracles to include bringing back the dead, casting out devils, creating food on multiple occasions (feeding of 5000, and 4000), and even producing money at will (coin in the fish's mouth).

He has even given this power to His followers in the sending forth of the 12 and the 70. What more could a disciple or follower want? In this rendition of Jesus' life, He is obviously the Son of God and has given His power to the 12 closest disciples that are following Him, to include James and John believing that they even have the power to call down fire from heaven on a city that they dislike (Luke 9:54). But, don't forget, John does not make any claim that he or any other apostle was given any such powers by God or Jesus in his gospel account.

In the authors of Matthew, Mark and Luke's rendition, one of the 12 disciples decides to exchange all of this power for 30 pieces of silver. Judas, through selfish greed, who has seen Jesus do all these things including walking on water, believes that he has something to gain by selling Jesus out to the Jews. Does this really make sense?

In contrast you have the Book of John. He doesn't make any of these ridiculous claims. John shows Jesus as the Son of God in Spirit, not literally. He <u>doesn't</u> try to squeeze Jesus into scripture and make claims like, He was the son of a virgin. It wasn't a requirement for the Messiah. For that matter, no other New Testament author states that Jesus was the son of a virgin either.

He doesn't show God speaking from heaven, except at the end of His ministry, and these events aren't recorded by the other three gospel writers. As you look at Jesus' ministry in the Book of John, it is more about teaching than supernatural powers. Yes, He does perform miraculous events from time to time, but look closely at how it went. He is recognized by John the Baptist as the being that would baptize with the Holy Ghost. He changes water into wine and then spends some time teaching the Samaritans. The Samaritans are unclean people!

Do you remember when the water was changed into wine. John Chapter 2, verse 1 tells you it is three days after the "John the Baptist event." That would be 37 days before He was to be coming out of the wilderness according to the other authors!

According to John, Jesus heals a few people, but this is only said to be healing. So, if you are sick, He can make you well again. We see Him arguing with the Pharisees about His ability to heal, even on the Sabbath. His argument is that if it wasn't from God, how could He do it? So if God the Father wanted to allow Him to heal on the Sabbath, it was God working through Him.

With the feeding of the 5000 we see His ability to change matter, and to make matter from nothing. It can't be from nothing, so He had to be able to harness energy to make the food that fed the people. Right after this event, He defies gravity by walking on the water. This is quickly followed by <u>teleporting the ship</u> that He climbed into, through space and time, to the distant shore (John 2:21). This ability was not recorded by the other authors.

Then, nearing the end of His ministry he restores the sight to a man that is born blind. This is a new power shown by Jesus. Have you noted that Jesus has only healed the sick to this point, and only a few times in the Book of John. This is very different from the version told by the other gospel authors. Restoring sight isn't a healing. The man didn't need to be healed, he wasn't sick. In the Book of John, it states plainly that this had never been done before in Israel. Once again, if you look at the other gospels, he has restored sight to the blind many, many times by now.

In the Book of John, when He restores the sight to the blind man, this was supernatural to them. It is an increasingly more powerful display of miraculous powers that culminated in the raising of Lazarus just before His crucifixion. It is only the Book of John that brings you the raising of Lazarus. He is the brother to Mary and Martha. Jesus loved Lazarus, but the Books of Matthew, Mark and Luke do not even mention him, yet he is the only man that Jesus raised from the dead according to John! The Jews understand the significance of this miracle and want to put Lazarus to death along with Jesus (John 12:10). Do you see this concern by the Jewish leadership when Jesus raises Jairus' daughter or the man from Nain in the other gospels?

Jesus hasn't been healing here and healing there and raising the dead all over the place. It is a steady increase of power shown in the Book of John. Do you see one miraculous power that Jesus doesn't have that the other gospels says that He does? Where is the power to cast out devils or evil spirits from a man? This is critical. It is only found in the Books of Matthew, Mark, Luke and the Acts of the Apostles (thought to be written by the author of the Book of Luke). This power is found nowhere else in the entire Bible. Not even in any other book in the New Testament!

Which brings up the point: can demons, or evil spirits actually occupy a human body? If mankind didn't have the Books of Matthew, Mark, Luke, and Acts, Christians wouldn't have any reason to believe in the concept. But, then there were the pagan beliefs of the day. Pagans believed that it was possible. This is where you have to start looking at the "whys," for why the other gospels were written. Why was this concept of devil or spirit possession written in these books? We will get to that shortly.

The Book of John doesn't show Jesus giving His powers to the 12 closest disciples, let alone to an additional 70 guys later (Luke 10:1). No, in John's account, it is a Jesus that increasingly shows the power that is given to Him by God the Father, and only Jesus.

Did you notice that John doesn't show a greedy Judas plotting to get a little money by betraying Jesus? John makes it clear that Satan entered into Judas (John 13:27). Judas' body isn't entered into by just any old evil spirit, it is the Devil, Satan. Judas is a pawn that is required for this specific task. Someone has to betray Jesus. Do you really think that if you had been given the power to cast out devils or heal the sick, that you would exchange that power for 30 pieces of silver? Give me a break! This is key to understanding the trustworthiness of the other history books.

Read the events after Judas is indwelt by Satan in the Book of John. You never read any criticism of him from this point on, let alone about his betrayal of Jesus. How could there be? If he is being controlled by Satan, how is he responsible for his actions? If Judas had betrayed Jesus for the money and had not been indwelt by Satan, then it was his sin. But according to the Book of John, that wasn't so. Judas had not made a deal with the Jews, he was indwelt by Satan. More importantly, do you see Satan being cast out of Judas by Jesus or one of the disciples? Once again, the power to cast out spirits is not found anywhere in the Bible except in Matthew, Mark, Luke, and the Acts of the Apostles.

This fixation of having the power to perform exorcism is key. Do you really feel a man in the power of the name of Jesus will force fear and trembling into a spirit? Read Jude Chapter 1. In this short chapter you learn that we are not to even speak ill of dignities and explains in verse 9: "Yet Michael the Archangel, when contending with the devil, he disputed about the body of Moses, durst not bring against him a railing accusation, but said, The Lord rebuke thee."

Do you really feel that mankind has the authority to speak controllingly to those that walk before God? Even Michael the Archangel did not feel that he was authorized, and he is doing the work of God the Father. If you didn't have what I believe are the false stories in Matthew, Mark, Luke and the Acts of the Apostles to lead you astray, Christians wouldn't be so foolish.

There is no mention in the entire Bible of someone being possessed by an evil spirit, as in from Satan, except in the history books. Literally, it is not mentioned anywhere else. But, in the Books of Matthew, Mark, Luke and Acts, and it is everywhere! In the Book of Acts, Paul casts out a spirit that is in a young woman that is following after him. The story starts in Acts Chapter

16, verse 16. Don't you find it odd that Paul, in his own books, never mentions this great power? Remember, Paul didn't write the Book of Acts, it was probably the same author that wrote the Book of Luke. Paul lists the fruits or gifts of the Spirit several times in his letters. You have prophesy, healing, teaching, languages, helps, but not casting out of spirits. So Paul never makes mention of it in his books, and doesn't list it as a power given by the Holy Spirit, and yet, all the history books but the Book of John affirms to you that it is a common power. Doesn't that set off an alarm in your head? What is worse, if Judas had the power over evil spirits, how can he be possessed by one? Use some discernment.

There was one more power attributed to Paul that was slyly woven into the Book of Acts. In Chapter 20 you see Paul bring back the dead. Did Paul ever mention this power as a Fruit of the Spirit? No, and he never mentions this great power as one that he has used in any of his letters. Why? Because Paul did not have this power over the dead! It is fiction to bolster the story.

The Passover or Last Supper is huge. Here is one area where you can't say that the Apostle John just forgot to write about the event. It isn't like the raising of Jairus's daughter and the man from Nain, or the Mountain of Transfiguration, or the destruction of Israel. In those events although John may have been recorded to be there, he has not written about them. In the Last Supper, John completely contradicts the notion that it is the Passover. He expressly points out that the Passover has not occurred as yet. This can be referenced in John Chapter 13, verse 1; Chapter 18, verse 28; and Chapter 19, verse 14. It is clear that Jesus has not and will not eat the Passover with the disciples, and yet the other three gospel accounts are adamant that the Last Supper was the Passover. One of these two stories is <u>wrong</u>. I side with the Apostle John. Jesus was my Passover Lamb! That was the purpose of the cross.

When I began to write this book I was under the impression that the Apostle Matthew may have written the Book of Matthew, John Mark might have written the Book of Mark, and Luke the Physician probably wrote the Books of Luke and the Acts of the Apostles. I put their errors down to the fact that Luke was a Gentile, Mark was too young and Matthew was not there all the time. After writing this and studying the texts I am sure that I was wrong. I see no evidence that any of these characters had anything to do with the texts that are credited to them.

Take the Book of Matthew. I was sure that he would line up with the stories that he and the Apostle John would tell during the same time period. I was sadly mistaken. Matthew and John almost never line up. So, who wrote the correct gospel? The author of Matthew is one of the three authors that tells an orchestrated story of the life of Jesus, but as you have read, he is in constant disagreement with the Books of Mark and Luke. The author of the Book of Matthew references the Old Testament to show why his gospel is correct, only, the Old Testament references almost never apply.

This is why after I had written the rough draft of this book, I painstakingly went back and added each of his references for your review. Did it really look like his references passed even the most basic of discernment tests? I counted two references to John the Baptist. One was good and the other was not. There were several references to circumstances and most did not apply. But the most noteworthy were the references that he made to Jesus from the Old Testament. Out of the dozens of references that he tells his readers were to fulfill scripture, only one was sort of close, and then one was dead-on at the cross.

The two that he got right are coincidentally found in the Book of John. Why is this so important? Because I believe it shows that the Book of John was previously written and the author of Matthew knew the story. But this author had to show a more powerful Jesus.

But, I think that the most telling of all, is again, the casting out of the demons, devils, or evil spirits theme found in the Books of Matthew, Mark, Luke and Acts. This is why I have begun to believe that they were probably written many years later, maybe as much as 200 years or more, possibly at the formation of the Roman Catholic Church to appease or scare the pagans of the day.

Do you remember who put the Bible together? Who gathered the letters together and decided what to put in the New Testament? It was the Roman Catholic Church. Did the early members of the Roman Catholic Church believe in demon or devil possession? Of course they did, as it was commonly accepted by the pagan religions of that day. It is still believed today by pagans. Unfortunately, because of the Books of Matthew, Mark, Luke and Acts, it is believed by most Christians today. Christian stories and pagan rituals were the beliefs that made up the foundation of the Roman Catholic Church. All Christianity has it's roots set in Catholicism and the traditions created by them.

Catholicism was a melding of the early Christian's God and pagan beliefs. We have no documented manuscripts from the New Testament authors older than the third century, and those are only bits and pieces. They are also not original letters, just supposed handwritten copies. Who copied these letters? Unfortunately most Christians want to show a separation between Protestantism and Catholicism. But the founding documents that we hold dear are those given to us by the Roman Catholic Church. Where else could have they come from? The Jews did not save them for us. Islam was not formed for at least another three hundred years. Face it, we only had the Roman Catholic Church!

Could the Books of Matthew, Mark, Luke and Acts be as fake as the Books of Mary and Judas? Remember, just because these books might not be inspired, doesn't mean that the remainder of the

Bible isn't? It is 66 separate books put together by the Roman Catholic Church. I find this thought process too tempting to resist. How else do you explain the devil possession? It isn't one of the fruits or gifts of the Spirit that are spoken of by Paul! This ability to control a person's actions would not give man a free spirit to choose right from wrong. Once you understand that this was a pagan belief, it begins to explain why other odd beliefs are in these books.

Look hard at devil possession once more before we dismiss the concept. It isn't anywhere in the Old Testament. In fact, you will see people with evil spirits that are placed in them, but who does it? We know that God hardens hearts, but who places evil spirits in man if it is done at all? Why not read I Samuel Chapter, 16 verses 14 and 15. "But the Spirit of the Lord departed from Saul, and an evil spirit from God troubled him. And Saul's servants said unto him, Behold now, an evil spirit from God troubleth him." So where do evil spirits come from? They come from God. Do you see any mention of Satan bringing an evil Spirit upon anyone anywhere else in the entire Bible? It is spoken of all through Matthew, Mark, Luke and the Acts. According to these books, all of the early church members cast out evil spirits. Remember, according to Acts Chapter 16, verses 16 through 18, Paul casts out a spirit that is in a damsel.

Yet in Paul's own writings, he lists the fruits of the Spirit many times. As stated earlier, you see prophesy, teaching, healing and several others. What is strangely missing is the gift of casting out of evil spirits or devils. It is plainly not there in any of his or any other New Testament author's writings. He never references himself doing such an act. Even when he lists the things he has done for the Lord or events that have happened in his life, demonic possession is not listed. Doesn't this one fact about devil or spirit possession scream at you? It should "haunt" you if you believe in demon or devil possession!

Christians are fearful of the thought that someone could be devil possessed, and yet it wasn't found in Old Testament times, not recorded by any signed New Testament letter, not referenced by Paul, and isn't seen today by anyone. But, because it is found in the Books of Matthew, Mark, Luke and Acts, all unsigned works, it is believed today.

But then you have those you may know that truly believe that they have either done this feat or witnessed it being accomplished. I affirm that I believe it not to be true. First, there are those that are just plain crooks. They will do anything, or stage anything, for money. You find this all over Christian television or radio. Secondly, I believe that there are people that believe in their heart that they have actually performed exorcism.

I put this down to a willing participant that wants to perform such an act and a person craving attention enough to fake that they have a spirit dwelling within them. Both are joyfully satisfied when the experience is over. The exorcist believes that he or she has removed the spirit, and the participant who stated that they had one dwelling within them, has received the attention that they so desperately desire.

What do I base my belief in? Go back and look at persons that have been indwelt by spirits and been credited for powerful acts. In the Old Testament you had Samson. It wasn't an evil spirit, it was the Spirit of God. This is the only indwelling of a Spirit in the entire Bible besides those found in the New Testament history books where an indwelt person has incredible strength. When he was indwelt, could anything stop him? No!

Now, take the story of the men or man at the tombs that had a legion of Spirits indwelling in him or them, found in the Books of Matthew, Mark and Luke. Why do I say him or them? Because the story is told as either one or two men that were indwelt, depending on which book you read it in. Could anyone stop him or them? No. The authors of the history books knew the stories of the Old Testament, so the power looks to be the same.

What does this have to do with modern exorcism? How does the power attributed to indwelt persons of the Bible compare to the power that we attribute to those that are indwelt by spirits today? What we see today is a joke. I have worked in the medical field for over 30 years. You can sedate anyone, anytime, anywhere with medication. Do I believe that Samson could be sedated? Not possible, because it wasn't his body doing those great things, it was the spirit within him doing those great things.

One more thought: Who does, or could, perform exorcism according to the the authors of Matthew, Mark, Luke and Acts? It wasn't just Jesus and those that He gave the power to, it was also those that stated "In Jesus' name" without Jesus' blessing or permission (Mark 9: 38-41). You might sell that idea as it was in Jesus' name, but what about those that had no affiliation to Him at all? Whose power is used in Luke Chapter 11, verse 19? In this verse Jesus is stating that those claiming His powers are from Beelzebub also have children that are casting out devils. So, it appears that according to the authors of Matthew, Mark, Luke and the Acts, just about anyone can perform exorcism! Do we see this today? Basically, these books teach that almost any mortal could cast out a supernatural being. This flies in the face of Jude Chapter 1, where it teaches not to even speak ill of the devil.

Think about it, why did or do pagans sacrifice to their gods/demons? They wanted to appease the devils or receive power from them. Man is obsessed with power. This "gift of the spirit," the receiving of power over devils, was better than appeasing the evil spirits, it was a shield where no harm can come to you from them. The power to cast out devils is a power greater than a devil. Once again, this is not located in the gifts or fruits of the spirit as recorded by Paul. It is a power only told of in the Books of Matthew, Mark, Luke and Acts. I believe that it has to have been an added power that would make Catholic worship more powerful than pagan worship of that day. You have to decide for yourself from the facts given.

How about the virgin birth? Think about how the Roman Catholic Church had to sell the idea that Jesus and God the Father were greater than the pagan's belief in demons and devils or other gods of the day. First, recall that the virgin birth of Jesus was not actually foretold in Isaiah (Isaiah 7-9). In that prophesy it was a different child that had a different purpose. So why the virgin birth in Matthew and Luke if it is not prophesy? It could have been used to explain why Christian worship was greater than the pagan worship that was being followed in pre-Catholosizm. The great God in Heaven, gave a Son to worship, through a virgin birth. This is an impossible feat that could not be duplicated by pagans. Is there any reference to the Messiah being born of a virgin in the Old Testament? No!

And look what they did with this virgin birth. It is worshiped. Mary is worshiped. They pray to Mary. That is idolatry. But, why would that be a shock? The Roman Catholic Church was a blending of pagan idolatry and early Christianity.

Besides the aforementioned pagan powers that were presented in the Books of Matthew, Mark, Luke and Acts, the pagans got something else out of Catholicism. They got their worship day, Sunday. They replaced the sun god with the Christian God, but replaced the Christian Sabbath with the lord's day worship on the pagan's chosen day. Do you ever see Sunday worship in the New Testament? No, there is only the purposefully mistranslated Greek word "Sabbaton," which means Sabbath, into the English word "week." But, they only did it in a few choice locations in the New Testament.

But we already noted in Acts Chapter 28, verse 14 that they used the term "seven days" to designate a seven day period or "week". If this isn't true, why didn't the text state that they stayed in Puteoli for a "Sabbaton?" This is simple, because they didn't stay from Friday sundown to Saturday sundown. They stayed for seven days!

Since the concept and translation of the words "seven days" is found in Acts, I can't fathom how any reasonably intelligent person cannot understand that Sabbath worship is the only worship in the New Testament. A Sabbaton isn't seven days, it is one day out of seven that was named by God as <u>His</u> day.

One more twist should be recalled when you look at the beginning of the Books of Luke and the Acts of the Apostles. Who do they appear that they were written to? It was a man named Theophilus. It is a series of two books that starts with the supposed birth of Jesus and ends with Paul in Rome, awaiting trial. If this is true, then the Book of Luke could have been the first of the three written gospels of Matthew, Mark, and Luke. They may have been written just before Paul's trial before Caesar, but then, they may have been written many years later.

It would explain why it has more stories than the others. The Books of Matthew and Mark could have been rewrites to the original of what we call the Book of Luke. But does it make the Book of Luke correct? Is it more accurate than the Book of John? First, remember what appears to be the purpose of this book. It was written to persuade a man named Theophilus, possibly a Roman. How persuasive would the Book of John have been to a pagan educated Roman?

I used to love reading Matthew, Mark, and Luke. I enjoyed them much more than the Book of John. They have wonderful stories that at first glance seem original. But if you look at the building blocks for many of these stories you will find that they are retold stories from the Old Testament. I'm certain that the authors of Matthew, Mark and Luke had a good understanding of the Jewish scriptures. This is why they tried to weave the Old Testament into their rendition of the life of Jesus. They needed the Old Testament to solidify their stories.

The stories found in the Books of Matthew, Mark, Luke and Acts give Christians false faith and power. If you want "it", you can have it, if you have faith. The "it" is just about anything that you want, as long as you have faith that you will receive it.. Take the woman with the issue of blood found in all three of these gospels. Read Luke Chapter 8, verses 43 through 48. She walks up behind Jesus and touches Him and "immediately her issue of blood stanched."

In this rendition of the story, Jesus states: " I perceive that virtue has gone out from me." Think of what is stated. Christians feel so good about this story, but if you look critically at it, what does it teach? If you want something bad enough you can take it without permission. You can even "take" virtue from Jesus without His permission, if you believe!

What about the story of those casting out demons in Jesus name, without even being a follower. This is found in Mark Chapter 9, verse 38, and Luke Chapter 9, verse 39. This story implies that if you believe that you can cast out a demon in Jesus' name it will work! So, why not heal in Jesus' name if this is so? We don't need any doctors, just walk up to a sick person and say, "In the name of Jesus, you are healed." But we don't see this. Even so-called Christian healing rooms are nothing but a fraud. If they really worked we wouldn't have hospitals. That isn't how God works. You don't have power because you want it. God will give power to whom He will give power, yet Christians believe these false stories.

If you want to believe the stories found in the Books of Matthew, Mark, Luke and the Acts you should reflect back on the story of Jesus casting out a devil starting in Matthew Chapter 12, verse 22. What was Jesus' defense as to why He was not casting out in the name of Beelzebub? It was that their children too were casting out devils. So not only can someone cast out a devil in Jesus' name according to the authors of Mark and Luke, but a Jew could do it without His name according to the author of Matthew. Think about what the story has taught.

How about the power to move mountains, if you believe. Do you believe that this is so? It is found in the Books of Matthew, Mark and Luke. But, where is the glory in this? How would your ability to move mountains bring glory to God? It won't, so why would He give this power? Why would Jesus tell you it is possible if it isn't a realistic power? John never talks about it or other ridiculous powers you may get by just believing or having enough faith.

The Books of Matthew, Mark, Luke and the Acts teach that Jesus taught that you must leave all things and then you can have everlasting life. The quickest reference is the rich young ruler who would not follow Jesus as he was to leave all that he had to the poor. Is that what was taught in the Book of John or the rest of the Bible? If you are to leave all things, who are you to leave them to? Who is asking for money each week? Does the church have a role in this redistribution?

I'm not implying that you should not share your wealth, but does wealth signify a lost soul? What about Nicodemus? He was wealthy, but do you really believe that he is lost? Only John tells the reader of him. The other three authors don't know who he is, and that is the point. John talks of him in three different settings. He buries Jesus in John Chapter 19.

Contrast the context of Nicodemus in the Book of John with the parable of the rich man and Lazarus found in Luke Chapter 16. The only thing noted that was wrong with the rich man in the story is that he is rich. But where is Lazarus in the end of this parable, found in the Book of Luke? He was in Abraham's bosom.

So let's look at wealth and the righteous men found in the real scriptures. If you forgot, the scriptures are the Old Testament. Abraham is in the Old Testament. The same Abraham of whose bosom Lazarus is supposed to be in. He was wealthy. So was Issac, Jacob, David, and Job. There were many others, but lets look at these names. When you want to claim the promises of the Old Testament they are the promises made by God to Abraham, Issac and Jacob.

Abraham had his own army and took down three kings in one day. He had huge herds and many servants. So did his son Issac, along with his son Jacob. They were wealthy and blessed at the same time. Jacob is later renamed Israel and had the 12 sons we call the Children of Israel. One of these sons was Joseph who became second only to Pharaoh in Egypt, the world superpower of the day!

Jesus is/was to be a Son of David. The statement that David had God's heart is found throughout the Bible. If you have a lack of knowledge of the Old Testament, God gave all of the Kingdom of Israel to David.

If you read the Book of Job you will see that God gave Job a good life, then allowed it to be taken away to prove a point to Satan. When it was all over, God gave Job two-fold of all that he had before He had allowed Satan to take it away. So were God's righteous men-of-old, poor? Most times not, at least not for long.

Luke Chapter 10 has the rich man whose "ground brought forth plentifully." What is his sin in this story? It is that he built barns to store the abundance for years to come. It doesn't say that he refused in his heart to share it with those in need. This notion that it is sinful to be productive and save is found throughout the Books of Matthew, Mark and Luke. Take the time and read the Book of Ruth. Does Boaz seem to be a rich man that is blessed with storehouses? Is he righteous?

My point is that it is not sinful to have wealth. God had many righteous men for you to read about that were very wealthy, and I know that they will be with me in everlasting life. The books of Matthew, Mark, Luke and Acts will lead you to believe that you cannot enter into eternal life if you have wealth. We all know the supposed line from Jesus found in Matthew Chapter 6 and Luke Chapter 16, "You can't serve God and mammon." Or, how about the proverb that teaches that it is easier for a camel to get through the eye of a needle than a rich man to enter into eternal life? Where are these passages found? The Books of Matthew, Mark and Luke!

For those that listen to Christian apologetics, there was no gate in Jerusalem named the "eye of a needle!" This is confirmed when the disciples then ask Jesus, "Well, then who can get in?" They understand in this story that it is an impossible mission for a wealthy person to enter into eternal life.

The entire point of this book was to show that the entire Bible is not the inerrant Word of God. It can't be if there are any errors. You have to agree that there have been plenty of errors. From the history books you have to pick one of two stories of the life of Jesus. They both can't be correct. One is wrong. You either get all of John's account or you get all that is told by the authors of Matthew, Mark and Luke's account. It is an all or nothing. You can't take a little here and a little there and glide over those passages that are inconvenient. If you choose to pick the one taught by the authors of Matthew, Mark, Luke and the Acts then you get all those stories that are cherished by so many Christians. But then, what do you do when they disagree with each other?

Take the Legion possessed man or men at the tombs. Matthew Chapter 8 teaches that it is two men. Mark Chapter 5 and Luke Chapter 8 tell you it is one man that is devil possessed. So is Matthew correct or Mark and Luke? How about Jairus' daughter? Matthew tells you that she is dead when Jairus comes to ask Jesus to save her in Chapter 9. But in Mark Chapter 5 and Luke Chapter 8 she is very much alive when Jesus is requested, but then she dies while He is on the way. Once again, Mark has agreed with Luke over Matthew's account. You have the man that was stricken with palsy where Jesus states "Man, thy sins are forgiven thee." Was he found by Jesus as He left a boat recorded in Matthew Chapter 9, or was he lowered through the roof as found in Mark Chapter 2, and Luke Chapter 5? As you can see, Matthew is the odd man out in these stories.

The author of Luke isn't much better. Luke tells you that John the Baptist is already in Herod's jail very early on in Jesus' ministry found in Chapter 3, yet all three other authors testify of John's imprisonment much later in their stories. Luke is at odds with Mark and Matthew on most time sequenced events. If I was to mention all the discrepancies between Matthew, Mark and Luke I might as well re-write the conclusion of each chapter. What I am trying to point out is that if you choose to discount the Book of John, then you have to explain why the story line found in the Books of Matthew, Mark and Luke do not line up either. With that said, and it is obvious that they do not reenforce each other, why would you trust a story where only one of them tells the story? After all, if all three told the story, at least one story would contradict the others!

Finally, when you are contemplating the accuracy of the history books ask yourself this: Who was there to record what was written in each book? The Book of John is easy, he is there or someone else that is a follower is there to record the event. But in the Books of Matthew, Mark and Luke you have stories told that had to be from vision if they were real.

How did anyone know what was happening in Herod's court for the events that are recorded? How about when the wise men are talking with Herod? How about the beheading of John the Baptist? Moses has told you that if the story isn't 100% correct then it can't be a vision from God. You have already learned that all three accounts by Matthew, Mark and Luke disagree with each other much of the time, so according to Moses it is presumed.

What about the conversations recorded at the cross? Only John records that they were there at the foot of the cross, so you can understand why he has recorded what he wrote. The other authors tell you that it is women at best, and they are off at a distance. So, why would you believe what those authors record when John, the guy that was there, tells you that something totally different was said and happened?

The New Testament, the Facts and the Fiction

How about the assention? Do any of the four accounts agree? They are not even close. Just to drag the Book of Acts into the mix, how did Judas die and who owned the field that he died in? It really depends on whether you trust the author of Matthew or the author of the Book of Acts. In the Book of Matthew, Judas hangs himself and the church bought the potter's field. In the Book of Acts, Judas buys the field and then falls in it and bursts asunder. Which one is it? They both can't be right.

If the Books of Matthew, Mark, Luke and Acts were not written by the authors that modern theologians and most Christians want to attribute them to, then who or why were they written? Focus back on the Book of John. Do you see any comparisons between the Jews and gentiles in this book? Not at all. There isn't anywhere in the Book of John where Jesus pulls a comparison about faith or chances for everlasting life between Jews and Gentiles. But the Books of Matthew, Mark, Luke and Acts do.

The greatest acts of faith appear to be of those that are outsiders. Take the centurion in Matthew Chapter 8, and Luke Chapter 7. According to these passages there is no one in all Israel that has his faith, and he is a Roman. Or, the ten healed lepers, where the only one that came back to thank Jesus was the Samaritan leper found in Luke Chapter 17. Samaritans were the lowest of lows to the Jewish people. How about the parables comparing the Jewish leadership to the wicked vineyardmen in Mark Chapter 11. Who is the vineyard to be given to? It will be given to others. Christians believe that they are the "others." Compare these wholesome Gentiles to the disdain that Jesus has for the Jewish leadership in these same books. The word "faith" isn't even mentioned once in the Book of John!

Matthew Chapter 27, and Luke Chapter 23 show that Pilate could find no fault in Jesus, yet the crowd called for His death. When stating that he, Pilate, was to wash his hands of this matter the Jewish crowd exclaimed that His, Jesus', blood would be on them and their children (Matthew 27:25). This verse is a death sentence to all Jewish people and could only insight riot against them if it was true. Why have the Jewish people been persecuted over the years? It is from this and many more similar passages.

What ever happened to the blessing of Israel that goes: "I will bless those that bless you and curse those that curse you (Genesis 12:3). This is talking about the Children of Abraham, the Israelites. In the Book of John you have many Jewish leaders that are obviously righteous. Who was Nicodemus? Do God's blessings have a time limit?

In the Book of John, Jesus isn't talking against the whole Jewish leadership, He is arguing against the fact that they have replaced the commandments of God with traditions of men that have been handed down over the generations. There is no condemnation of the Jewish people. He has compassion on them, and yet the Books of Matthew, Mark, Luke and Acts are drumming up anger against the nation.

Paul tells you that the nation is blinded but will soon see the error of not recognizing Jesus in Romans Chapter 11 and II Corinthians Chapter 3. All New Testament writers other than the authors of Matthew, Mark, and Luke look upon themselves as Jews that are enlightened. Contrast this to the loveless feelings towards the Jews that is found in the Books of Matthew, Mark, Luke and the Acts.

If you haven't come to the conclusion that the Books of Matthew, Mark, Luke and Acts are not inspired by now, then I guess that you never will. If you want to believe them then you have to discount the Book of John. After all, according to the authors of Matthew, Mark and Luke, the Apostle John was only one of three apostles that was with Jesus when He Raised Jairus' daughter back to life, was at the Mountain of Transfiguration, and prayed with Jesus in the garden. But, John does not record these most critical events.

What's worse is that the other three gospel authors do not record what John tells you is Jesus' first miracle or the most powerful miracle, the raising of Lazarus. In fact, these two stories of the life of Jesus have only a couple of things in common.

So, what do I think that you should do with the gospels and the Book of Acts? I believe that you should study them, line them up, and then use discernment to decide what is righteous knowledge and use it, but allow the rest to land by the way side. After writing this book I can't possibly believe that they were written by Spirit filled men or the hand of God for that matter. I will study them just for the purpose of helping others to understand that they are clearly filled with errors which lead astray those that want the truth.

The gospels and the Book of Acts are the best proof that the Bible, the one you hold in your hand today, is not the inerrant Word of God. Much of what God has told us He expects from us, is found in it's pages, but then, there are obvious errors that were both inadvertently and or purposefully polluted in these same pages.

One of my most favorite questions is, "What is the best type of lie?" The answer is: a 99% truth. Simply put, if you teach something that sounds mostly correct, then it is simple to squeeze in something additional to those correct facts that is actually incorrect.

Think about the word compromise. Does it sound heinous? Don't we think of it as part of everyday life. We compromise on everything. But is compromise wrong? If we know that something is incorrect, and yet we allow it because it is providing a path for us to get something else that we believe to be needed, are we doing something wrong? We have lowered our standards in one area to get the standard we want in another, but is it wrong?

If we are allowing something in our lives that is forbidden by God to obtain something else, even if it is a righteous item or area of life, we have just compromised against God. This is how Christianity was led astray.

Go back and read Revelation Chapters 2 and 3. It is the seven letters to seven churches. These are seven churches that believe that they are following "Christianity of the day." This is within one generation of Jesus on earth. It is written by the Apostle John. How did these churches fair? Not very well. They had compromised the very values that they were supposedly following.

It is over 200 years later when the first New Testament is compiled. Do you really believe that only the copies-to-the-copies of the letters written by the early church leaders made it into this compilation? What about the letter to Laodicea that Paul references at the close to his letter to the Colossians? Why isn't it in the New Testament? Either the letter didn't survive, or there was something in the letter that offended those that were putting the New Testament together!

We know that there were many forgeries. Remember the Gnostic gospels? Why isn't the Gospel of Mary or the Gospel of Judas in the New Testament? Because they were obviously against, and not supported by, any other book. Which leads me to ask, "Just because the Books of Matthew, Mark, Luke and the Acts of the Apostles have some good news and loving kindness in them, aren't you concerned about the obvious compromise that they pose to the Real Church of God?"

We know that they have some falseness, so where do you draw the line? How truthful do they have to be before you believe that you should begin to live your life by them? Moses told you that the prophet had to be 100% correct or you should not fear them. They are not from God because they are not 100% correct! These books teach lessons that are not a truthful recollection of God, so why do Christians take anything that they teach as "Godly Lessons," or worse, the record of the Life of Jesus Christ? They totally disagree with those areas where the Apostle John and they tell the same story, so why would you believe anything that only they record?

Most Christians believe that the Old Testament happened, and they should. But the recording of the Old Testament is more simple to verify than the New Testament. The Old Testament was translated by the Greek government hundreds of years before Christ in a document called the Septuagint. I believe that it was delivered to mankind by God and recorded in just this way. But just because the Bible has the Old Testament in it's content, does that make the entire Bible a correct document delivered by God?

Do you believe that the Koran is a document delivered by God? Most Muslims do. Its been around for about 1400 years. Do you know that even the Muslims believe in the Old Testament? It is part of the Koran. Does this make the Koran a document from God? No, it just shows the power that God has delivered in the Old Testament is appreciated by the Muslims too. So what does this have to do with the Books of Matthew, Mark, Luke, and The Acts of the Apostles?

All these books have perverted texts from the Old Testament as proof that their account to the life of Jesus, as they have portrayed, is prophetic. This perversion is only found in these books. John, Paul, Peter, James, and Jude do not make any of these false references to the Old Testament.

Should any of this new knowledge shake your faith in the Bible? It should make you question the validity of these books, but how should that change your faith? It is still Jesus that has paid the price for your sins, but as you will learn if you read the rest of your Bible, and more importantly the other New Testament authors, we are not under Grace as a license to allow a little sin in our lives.

Most modern Christian movements warn against a "works trip." What's a works trip? They will tell you it is trying to "work" your way to heaven by trying to follow the Law. Only, if you really read the New Testament, or better yet pull out your concordance, you will see that you will be judged by your works! Read Revelation. Grace is not mentioned, but the fact that you will be judged by your works is mentioned over and over. Their softer, gentler God is supposedly found in the Books in Matthew, Mark, Luke, and the Acts.

But the coming judgment of your "works" is even found in the gospels if you look for it. Read Matthew Chapter 16, verse 27, "For the Son of Man shall come in the glory of His Father with His angels; and then He shall reward every man according to his works." In the rest of the Bible, God is expecting those that are His to treat Him as a Father and to <u>obey</u> Him.

But obedience out of Love is the obedience that God is looking for. I lovingly follow those statutes, ordinances and Laws that He has set out before me. This is not portrayed in the Books of Matthew, Mark, Luke, Acts or the modern Christian church. As a closing thought, why was Abraham given the promises that we Christians try to claim today?

God told Issac the answer in Genesis Chapter 26, verses 1 through 5. Why not read it for yourself. It had nothing to do with faith or grace, it was that Abraham was obedient. But obedient to what? Why not read it for yourself?

www.ingramcontent.com/pod-product-compliance
Lightning Source LLC
LaVergne TN
LVHW061213060426
835507LV00016B/1908